Competitiveness through Technology

Competitiveness through Technology

What Business Needs from Government

Edited by
Jerry Dermer
York University

Lexington Books
D.C. Heath and Company/Lexington, Massachusetts/Toronto

Chapter 2 © copyright 1986 by Robert U. Ayres

Library of Congress Cataloging-in-Publication Data

Main entry under title:

Competitiveness through technology.

Includes index.
Contents: Government policy and the competitive effects of innovation / Alan Kantrow—Computer-integrated manufacturing (CIM) and the next industrial revolution / Robert U. Ayres—Competing through technology / Bruce Rubinger—[etc.]
1. Technology—Addresses, essays, lectures.
2. Technology and state—Addresses, essays, lectures.
3. Competition—Addresses, essays, lectures.   I. Dermer, Jerry.
T185.C67   1986   338.97306   85-45379
ISBN 0-669-11604-1 (alk. paper)

Published simultaneously in Canada
Printed in the United States of America
International Standard Book Number: 0-669-11604-1
Library of Congress Catalog Card Number: 85-45379

The paper used in this publication meets the minimum requirements of American National Standard for Information Sciences—Permanence of Paper for Printed Library Materials, ANSI Z39.48-1984.
∞ TM

The last numbers on the right below indicate the number and date of printing.

10 9 8 7 6 5 4 3 2 1

95 94 93 92 91 90 89 88 87 86

Contents

Figures

Tables

Acknowledgments

T he chapters in this book were originally presented at the symposium "Competitiveness through Technology: What Business Needs from Government," held on April 24 and 25, 1985, at the Faculty of Administrative Studies, York University, Toronto, Canada. Arranging the symposium with those who presented papers and working through the revisions culminating in this book was, throughout, my great pleasure.

Much of the credit for the symposium and this book is due to the sponsors: the Department of Regional Industrial Expansion, government of Canada; the Ministry of Industry and Trade, government of Ontario; and the Max Bell Program for Business-Government Relations, York University; with additional support provided by the Social Sciences and Humanities Research Council. Michael St. Amant and John Male were especially helpful. Patrick Luciani played a major role in designing the symposium and arranging for the speakers. Support and encouragement were provided by Dean Alan Hockin, Faculty of Administrative Studies, York University. My secretary, Franca Dotto, devoted many hours to arrangements and is as responsible as anyone else for the success of the symposium. An enormous amount of gratitude is due to Elaine Gutmacher, administrative officer, Division of Executive Development, Faculty of Administrative Studies, who orchestrated the symposium and secured the financial support. Much of the work in assembling this book was conducted at the Faculty of Administrative Studies. Lee Brown contributed considerable editorial work, and secretarial staff members Franca Dotto, Barbara Davies, and JoAnne Stein carried the responsibility of preparing the book. My appreciation and thanks are extended to all these individuals.

The idea and initial financial commitment for both the symposium and this book originated with my colleague Professor James Gillies. The results are yet another example of his inspiration and leadership.

Introduction

T his book brings together twelve powerful chapters that juxtapose and explore the two concerns of its title: the role of technology in developing, sustaining, and defending competitive advantage and the changing nature of business–government relations as it relates to technology-based issues. Together the chapters transport readers across a landscape of the most relevant problems, solutions, and implementation barriers facing business strategists and formulators of technology-based industrial policy. The journey is far too demanding to be passive. Some areas are traversed only once, making it necessary for readers not to lose concentration lest an important topic pass unnoticed. Other areas are criss-crossed repeatedly but in different directions, with different objectives in mind, and reaching different conclusions. The result of the voyage is a landscape well explored, leaving readers with a better understanding of the current situation and the changes required, as well as a more realistic view of the role government can and should play in realizing them.

The route by which this understanding is best accumulated is far too complex to be explicated in a simple map. The heterogeneity of the authors' backgrounds and interests leads them to vary significantly across at least three dimensions: the unit of analysis considered, its life-cycle stage, and the point of view assumed. In the majority of chapters, multiple units of analysis are considered, ranging in levels of aggregation from intrafirm concerns with functional and/or project units, to those at the firm level, the industry level, the sectoral level, specific geographical locations, the nation, and multinational interactions. Different issues and concerns arise in each of these, dictated in part by what stage of the life-cycle model the unit of analysis is in: embryonic, startup, growth, maturity, or decline. In addition, the authors assume two different points of view: the managerial perspective of those inside the particular unit of analysis looking outward differs significantly from the more public policy–oriented perspective of outsiders attempting to influence the behavior of a particular unit of analysis.

Perhaps the best purpose this introduction can serve is to draw attention to two of the most pervasive topics that tie these chapters together and group them according to each chapter's relative emphasis on one of the two. These topics are (1) the relationship of technology to economic change and (2) the role of government in leading and/or facilitating change. A brief introduction to each chapter is then presented. Finally, six of the most prevalent themes running through the book are identified and discussed. This introductory overview is intended to assist readers in understanding how each chapter fits into the landscape and to keep them aware of what terraine has been covered and which areas still remain to be explored.

Part I: The Relationship of Technology to Economic Change

The five chapters in part I establish the importance of technology to economic growth and its pervasiveness in considerations of competitive advantage, firm–industry evolution, and changing national competitiveness. The need to consider technology as a strategic resource and to conceptualize and manage it integrally with strategy is inescapable.

Alan Kantrow in chapter 1, "Government Policy and the Competitive Effects of Innovation," focuses on firms and industries in the mature phase of their life cycle and questions whether their evolution to the decline phase is inevitable. He challenges a number of generally accepted assumptions by developing the relationship between technology and competitive advantage and illustrating the ability of technology to revitalize and rejuvenate apparently moribund industries. Using the automobile industry as an example, he presents the challenging possibility of dematurity, capitalizing on the potential for further growth by creating competitive advantage through the powers of technological change. Given the proportion of sunset firms and industries in Western economies and the undesirable consequences of their decline, Kantrow's examples of situations in which the innovative potential of technology was believed to be exhausted but later proved not to be so raise the disquieting possibility that opportunities are being overlooked.

One way that technology is changing markets and competitive relationships is through the use of flexible manufacturing systems. Robert Ayres believes that increases in organizational productivity depend on continual innovativeness, which in turn depend on an organization's flexibility, defined here as the ability to react creatively to market or technological changes. He traces the decline in many North American and European industries to the adverse effects of rigidities in their manufacturing systems that inhibit change. New technology, however, holds the potential for change through increased flexibility. A shift from hard automation to flexible automation using the new information-intensive technologies holds the potential for revitalization as the next industrial revolution gets underway. Ayres's chapter, "Computer-Integrated Manufacturing and the Next Industrial Revolution," exemplifies the challenges that changing technology is imposing on managers and formulators of industrial policy.

Based on his work at the Global Competitiveness Council, a Boston think tank with a significant interest in Japanese strategy–technology relationships, Bruce Rubinger presents a four-stage model linking the fundamental processes of technological knowledge creation to its ultimate utilization in individual firms and industries. The model drives home the tremendous leverage potential of certain basic technologies due to the breadth of products and processes they can potentially affect. In "Competing through Technology: The Success Factors," Rubinger makes the point that while politicians and policymakers are fighting over the location of assembly plants for their job content, the far more significant issue of the control of technological driving forces is ignored. Rubinger's approach is double barreled, reporting also on the lack of awareness of U.S. managers of technological developments in Japan. To Rubinger unemployment and trade deficits are the price paid for the lack of vision, the lack of appreciation of the power held by those controlling technological change, and the lack of awareness of what technological changes are occurring.

Mel Horwitch, in "The Blending of Two Paradigms for Private-Sector Technology Strategy," traces the evolution of four technology-based industries and uses them to show how firm roles and interfirm relationships have contributed to structural change and have themselves changed as these industries evolved. In addition to documenting the changing roles of business strategy and technology in the postwar period, Horwitch's analysis suggests which contexts encourage productive industry evolution and how the absence of these conditions leads to significantly less innovation.

Clive Simmonds, in "Frameworks to Increase Trade," links the strategic management of technology at the national level to the potential for internation cooperation to increase international trade. The theory of progress in trade and technology, developed by Masanori Moritani to trace the development of Japanese technological progress, is applied to central Canada to show the potential for trade increase. Simmonds argues that looking at trade from viewpoints other than those customarily assumed brings to the light opportunities yet to be explored. Methods that can increase trade without modifying the complex web of rules governing such relationships hold tremendous possibilities as low-cost ways to encourage international competitiveness and lessen unemployment. Simmonds includes a list of speculations about what the firm of the future will look like.

Part II: The Role of Government in Leading and/or Facilitating Change

We begin consideration of the role that government can play from the perspective of the individuals who must make it happen: the politicians. Michael Cassidy is a social democratic politician with both federal and provincial experience who possesses a unique mix of qualifications to address the issue posed in his chapter, "The Role of Government Action in Formulating Competitive Strategies." Cassidy reviews the well-worn reasons for ineffectual industrial policy: the lack of consensus as to the role of government, the dilemma of democracy (in which it is easier to retard change than to initiate it), the negative political consequences of unpopular government action, and the economic straightjacket in which most governments find themselves. He reviews the alternatives open to a democratic government and then makes a number of recommendations. Cassidy's basis for these recommendations is his extensive field experience with two political task forces exploring work, people, and technological change over the 1983–1985 period. This experience and his social democratic leanings appear to contribute to his conclusion: coping with today's changes requires a much greater sense of partnership among all stakeholders than is the norm in most Canadian enterprises. Changed relationships based on mutual obligations and shared responsibilities lead to his belief in the need for new models of work organizations suited to the world of the future. Cassidy believes the role of government is to create the framework for a new kind of partnership that must arise between all stakeholders in economic change. Activities such as local initiatives, cooperatives, joint ventures, and regional institutions can harness the potential of a well-educated and technologically adept population. Also needed are political structures by which government can recognize and encourage the adaption to change.

Two of the themes Cassidy emphasizes—the need for reindustrialization and the need for a policy framework by which it can be accomplished—are the topics of Roy Rothwell's chapter, "Technological Change and Reindustrialization: In Search of a Policy Framework." Rothwell assists policymakers by posing an extensive list of questions whose answers lead to the choice of appropriate technological initiatives and by presenting five criteria to which any policy initiative should aspire and by which it can be evaluated. These conclusions are based on a review of past attempts at innovation policies and tools and a discussion of three possible approaches toward establishing an appropriate innovation policy framework, as well as a discussion of the problems and the constraints encountered in working toward this end.

In "Strengthening the Technological Competitiveness of Industries: Potential Contributions of Government," Bela Gold responds to the challenges posed by the intricate complexities and pitfalls involved in the formulation and execution of technology-based industrial policy presented by Cassidy and Rothwell by calling for more precise analytical methods. Gold begins by analyzing the major sources of competitive advantages, differentiating between those that are potentially affected by technology and those that are not. He then proposes a number of specific actions that governments could undertake to increase industrial competitiveness. He lists the potential contributions of other groups, such as management, unions, and universities. While Gold argues persuasively that many productive actions could be undertaken, he also adds that realism requires the recognition that even if these efforts were undertaken immediately, benefits will emerge only gradually over a period of years. Given these requirements and potentials, he concludes by indicating his view of what constitutes realistic expectations of government.

Jack Baranson, in "Government Policies in Support of Automated Manufacturing: Japan, the United States, and Western Europe," compares economic environments in terms of being market driven versus centrally planned. He analyzes the impact of government policies on investments in automated manufacturing systems at both ends of this spectrum using Japan, the United States, France, Sweden, and West Germany as examples. Baranson concludes that the essential ingredient for innovational dynamics is the management of risk, which is dependent on the interrelationships of public policy, private-sector initiatives, and the role of financial institutions. Baranson draws attention to the need to balance innovative stimulations with the task of effecting economic and social adjustments to technological change within an economy.

This same trade-off is one of several considered by economic geographers John Britton and Meric Gertler in "Locational Perspectives on Policies for Innovation." Their insightful analysis of recent Canadian industrial policy reveals the dilemma of governments short of funds attempting simultaneously to satisfy the conflicting objectives of alleviating regional disparities and stimulating economic development. While urban areas such as the city of Toronto hold the potential for economic growth because of the desirability and strength of the existing infrastructure, political realities necessitate financial allocations elsewhere. Prescriptions flowing from agglomeration theory thus conflict with the political needs of the Canadian context. The resulting opportunity loss due to such factors as international leakage do not auger well for the country.

To date, the field of technology-based program implementation has drawn little from actual experience. The last two chapters in this book contribute to filling this void. They are distinguished by the high degree of importance of the particular types of initiatives undertaken, the high caliber of management involved, their concern with evaluation and learning, and the utility of their findings to others attempting similar thrusts. In a field filled with assumptions and unsubstantiated assertions, these presentations of empirical evidence are a welcome contribution.

Bill Hetzner and J.D. Eveland, in "Cooperative Research and Development Centers: Government, University, and Industry Roles, Responsibilities, and Results," relate their experience in planning and administering this frequently advocated partnership initiative. They trace the history of the National Science Foundation Centers program, which has led to the establishment of a number of university-based, industry-supported, and government-funded research and development initiatives. They report on the strategy taken to evaluate these initiatives and on what has been revealed by the evaluations completed thus far.

Louis Tornatzky's chapter, "State-Level Manufacturing Technology Initiatives: Design Issues," looks at the process of transferring manufacturing technology as essentially a social rather than technological problem. Tornatzky, a distinguished social scientist with considerable conceptual and research skills, takes a microlevel approach, which is in decided contrast to the macrolevel considerations usually discussed and considerably more useful to those designing their own programs. Using data gleaned from other countries, other state-level programs, and his own research, Tornatzky presents a set of principles for program design. His conclusion echoes the argument made by Bela Gold that such initiatives can be undertaken without straying into industrial policy.

Recurring Themes

At least six themes recur throughout this book. The first and most common is that technology is pervasive and important. The contribution of technology to economic growth highlighted by Ayres, the relationship of technology to developing and sustaining competitive advantage highlighted by Kantrow and Gold, and the linkage of technology to economic evolution described at the industry level by Horwitch and at the national level by Simmonds attest to the economic importance of technology.

A second theme is the belief that today there is an insufficient appreciation of the complex set of interrelationships requiring significant investments with highly uncertain outcomes demanded by technological evolution and growth. The following are typical symptoms: a lack of awareness of what is going on in technology (Kantrow and Rubinger), a lack of sufficient change in management and organization (Gold and Baranson), and a lack of action confronting technologically induced societal problems (Cassidy, Britton, and Gertler).

The discussions of what has and what should go on contribute to a greater appreciation of the changes needed and what is required to realize them. There is the need to reconceptualize issues in competitive business terms, clarifying especially the distinction among the various units of analysis and among differing perspectives. There is the need to accept a broader stakeholder framework to emphasize the shared responsibilities and joint benefits to be attained through increased competitiveness. There is also the need to establish realistic expectations of what is possible. There are no short-term solutions. Regardless of the short-term actions undertaken by the stakeholders concerned, the eventual outcome will be the result of slow, incremental change.

Collectively the chapters in this book highlight the conceptual, ideological, political, and managerial factors inhibiting change. Inappropriate conceptualization leads to inappropriate prescriptions. These difficulties are augmented by ideological biases pushing in diametrically opposite ways, such as immediate intervention versus reliance on market mechanisms. The need constantly arises to balance the political concerns of government survival in democratic societies against the harsh measures apparently required. The apparent reluctance of management to undertake these changes is also noted. In short, this book points to the need to have vision, to shoulder the uncertainty, and to make the necessary investments, all within an appropriately long-term strategy.

If these four themes serve to paint a precise picture of the challenge faced by policymakers, they also present an outline of a framework capable of encompassing them. Identification of variables and relationships of such a framework is the fifth theme of this book. Within the perspective provided by the framework, the difficulty of making prescriptions is illustrated by the historical descriptions of past developments and attempts at policy frameworks and by the cross-cultural comparisons of what has gone on in other geographical jurisdictions under varied government circumtances and political ideologies. Britton and Gertler, Gold, Rothwell, and Rubinger speak to these difficulties.

Finally, this book presents a realistic view of what government can and cannot accomplish. The role of government versus the role of other stakeholders such as management and labor is delineated and put into perspective. The problems of adapting to change, managing growth, and investing under uncertain situations in an environment lacking in consensus impose formidable barriers. Although several of the authors make specific recommendations for short-term government actions that appear sensible and undoubtedly should be undertaken, they also assert that government's primary role should be to establish a climate within which the other stakeholders can play their appropriate roles.

Desirable outcomes will be forthcoming only to those with an appropriate vision who undertake a long-term incremental development strategy, of which many steps are highly radical compared to traditional practices. Balancing many complex trade-offs while bearing that vision in mind is the task to be accomplished.

Part I
The Relationship of Technology to Economic Change

1
Government Policy and the Competitive Effects of Innovation

Alan M. Kantrow

Is Industry Maturity Inevitable and Permanent?

When she heard that Governor Thomas E. Dewey of New York was running for president yet again, Clare Boothe Luce was heard to dismiss his chances by saying that a soufflé never rises twice. We may speculate whether this is an accurate and appropriate sentiment in U.S. political life. But when it gets applied—as it has been applied both by policymakers in government, who perhaps have some excuse, and by managers in the private sector, who really do not—to the evolution of industry, then we have real problems. I sense a concern about not only the newer, smaller, startup growth industries, which are now just beginning to coalesce, but, as well, a much larger and broader question having to do with all the established industries now in place. Any modern industrial economy, simply by reason of political realities, let alone economic realities, has to be concerned about the range of its established manufacturing-based industry, industry that has been in place for a while and has served as the vehicle of its past industrial success. If the notion of "souffléism" applies there, then the pain must be incredibly great because the life-cycle model we have heard talked about so much, which is drawn from a biological analogy, argues that there is no escape from its one-directional progression toward decline. There is no return.

I find that analogy dangerous. It is convincing and plausible certainly, but there is no reason to assume that it holds as well in the industrial world as in the biological. We have just assumed it does. But now that assumption needs to be examined closely.

Need to Reconceptualize

If we take as gospel that a company's or industry's life cycle is irreversible, we fall into a lot of mistakes with real and practical consequences. We are increasingly tempted to make a handy set of distinctions between high-tech and low-tech industries: between the growth industries and those old dinosaurs, such as steel and automobiles. In the United States not long ago, there was a kind of corporate living will movement for those groups, a kind of plea for death with dignity. It is unseemly to watch U.S. Steel suffer; why doesn't someone put it out of its misery? Let us launch in its place a lot of bio-tech companies, which will employ people in the future. This is a caricature but not by too much.

First, this apparently simple distinction between high tech and low tech is a very slippery one, which on careful examination begins to fall apart. Who buys the products these high-tech operations are supposed to make? Who buys the capital goods? For years the major conduit into U.S. industry for all of the most modern advances in process technology has been the automobile industry. Automated transfer lines, robots, and industrial lasers made their entry this way. If the automobile companies did not buy these high-tech products, the folks who make them would be operating in a vacuum.

Second, these so-called low-tech, old-fashioned, and mature operations—steel plants and automobile plants, for example—are filled with high-tech equipment. In contrast, plants that make computers look like 1870 era rather than high-tech manufacturing: a lot of metal bending and assembly wiring and soldering. Let us get away, then, from any assumption that the difference between mature and so-called growth industries has to do with level of technology. It does not. That is a red herring.

Another red herring has to do with the belief in some quarters that growth industries are necessarily associated with technical novelty; they are doing sophisticated technical work, while the dinosaurs are trying to take five cents out of the way they install a bumper on an automobile. That is not so. Again there is no reason why the degree of technical novelty bears any necessary relation to the degree of competitive significance of any particular technical change. It may—or it may not. If some genius developed a nuclear-powered toothbrush, would it change the competitive dynamics of the toothbrush industry? Probably not. It would be a huge technical leap, to be sure, but competitively insignificant.

We must get the high tech–low tech distinction and the technical novelty issue out of the way and think straightforwardly about the notion that technical change, broadly construed, has some set of competitive effects that we need to understand. We need to understand what relevance those effects have and what they mean in terms of possibly reversing the assumed drift of industries toward maturity. Is it possible? How does it happen? What is involved at the level of government policy? What is involved by way of managerial responsibilities within a company?

An Example of Dematurity

The chocolate chip cookie industry provides a good example. For years, the problem with store-bought cookies was that they were as hard as rock. If you bit into them, they would crumble. This was not satisfactory. The chocolate chip cookie business has been a mature industry for years and, like many other food businesses, had low margins and relatively stagnant growth. What would change that industry? What would give it some new vitality? If the cookies could only be like mother used to make: crispy on the outside, chewy on the inside. The problem with making them that way was that cookies dry out and get hard. So if you want to get them to the customer right on the plate with a glass of milk before they get hard, you cannot have one huge central bakery where you can enjoy economies of scale in production because that bakery will be sufficiently far from the ultimate consumer outlets that no trucking system can get the cookies there before they get hard. Furthermore, even after you build a universe of satellite plants near markets, you will not be able to use the system typically used to distribute groceries. That will take too long. You need a separate fleet of delivery trucks, and even if you set up that fleet, you could not win because the cookies would get hard. They would still dry out, as everybody well knew.

It turns out that everybody was wrong: cookies do not get hard because they dry out; they get hard because their sugars crystallize. Also different sugars crystallize at different rates. So if you build a composite chocolate chip cookie with different sugars outside and in and assemble the two parts with a robot (process technology that has been around for years), you have a cookie that is crisp on the outside and chewy on the inside and will stay that way. It will not dry out. You can have the one central bakery, and you do not need a separate fleet of delivery trucks. All of a sudden, you have overturned the establisihed economics of a mature, slow-growth business.

This is a competitively significant change and an instance of dematury. I like this example because I eagerly consume the product, but I think the point stands in general terms: reversal is possible. The issue now has to be whether it is happening in any particular case. There are no general rules that hold across the board. We can no longer dismiss the possibility.

Competitive Significance of Innovation

A list of the sleepiest, most mature, utterly neanderthalic industries prepared in 1970 would have included banking, telecommunications, textiles, shoes, steel, automobiles, and railroads. Think of what has happened to the structure of those industries—the kinds of actions that have upset their apple carts and thrown things open again in the past quarter-century. Dematurity can happen. The question remains whether, in any particular instance, it is happening and what the managerial responsibilities are.

One of the things we are seeing in this range of instances is that industries that had been relatively mature and stable have experienced tremendous change. Where this is taking place, the same forces are not doing precisely the same things in the same degree in each instance. The mix is different. In some cases the engine is government regulations; in some differences in exchange rates and costs of production; and in some radical changes in the availability of key raw materials. But in most cases, the one dominant force in this dematuring process is technology.

Technology has become a kind of lever to unsettle the established terms of competition in a whole range of industries. It is not the only lever that can change it and in some cases may not be a relevant lever at all; but in a wide range of instances it is significant. The visibility of technology in products available for sale in the market is consistently greater now than it has ever been. Look at the kinds of product attributes that get advertised to consumers and the degree to which technology figures in them. Not only is technology more visible, it is more valued by consumers than it used to be. People are now willing to pay for newer technology.

What Bill Abernathy used to talk about as thin markets have long operated. For many product lines, often a small segment of the market is willing to pay a premium for high performance based on new technology long before that technology has been debugged and the cost has come down. The biggest thin market in the world is the U.S. military. Today, however, there is a spreading out of that kind of thin market; a broader range of the market is willing to pay for technology-based performance.

In addition, the variety of technology that is available in products for sale in the market is consistently greater now than in the past. In 1960 virtually no piece of technology available for sale on any car had not been available for sale on production model cars thirty years before. That is not true today. It is also the case that in 1960, an automobile purchaser would not have had much choice about what it was he or she bought. The main choices would have been color, the trim, and the interior. That was the way the industry competed: bend sheet metal a little bit differently from year to year and vary the trim, color, and leather. That was what sold the car. In technical terms, the car would have had a V8 engine in the front, with rear-wheel drive. On the other hand, the choices in about 1915 would have been stunning. Not only could a consumer have had a car with three wheels or four, a steering wheel or tiller, he or she could even have had a car that ran on gasoline or diesel or electricity or steam.

Maturity–Dematurity Process

In the early years of an industry's development, there is a certain amount of technical variety that tends to factor out as time goes on and the dominant design of the product locks into place. In fact, that process of weeding out tends to be what we think of as the process by which industries become mature. Early, there is a lot of ferment in the product. Who knows what a car is supposed to be like? What do we mean when we say *car?* How many wheels should it have? What should it run on? How should we brake it? How should we make it? What kind of transmission should it have? What is a transmission anyway? Over time these questions are answered, and the design of the product locks in. This process of weeding out variety and technical ferment is what we imply by the notion of maturity. Variety sifts out and narrows down; the dominant design locks in. In 1970 available for sale on U.S.-produced cars were six engine/drive-train packages. In 1980, there were twenty-one; in 1983, thirty-five. The variety of technology available generally for sale in products in the market is increasing, and the automobile industry is symbolic of the kind of change that is taking place in a range of industries: the return of variety. This is part of the unlocking process in the movement toward dematurity.

Migration to Maturity

Think about the competitive significance of innovative change. We have found it useful to think of innovation as having effects that can be measured along two axes. One, market linkages, includes the whole set of organizational competences and infrastructure, management training, control systems, and the like that support the way in which products filter into the markets. Any given technical change can work at one extreme to disrupt these established linkages, or it can work to entrench them further. The other axis has to do with the effects of an innovation on production systems. Here I mean not only the capital equipment on the floor and all the organizational competences that support it but also the managerial systems, the infrastructure, on which those competences rest. Innovation can work to unsettle or further entrench what is already there.

It is typically the case, early in an industry's or a new product's life, that the technical changes that are going on are very disruptive. They destabilize, throw open, and make obsolete products and processes. Over time there tends to be a migration toward a situation of established markets, established production competences, hardware in place, dealer systems in place, distribution networks in place, and a great reluctance to change. The name of the game in this kind of competition is high volume and low margins on each unit sold and standardization of product and process. Innovation of the incremental and perfecting type is where it takes place. Taking five cents out of the installation of a bumper or a headlight is where money is made.

During this migration, a search and learning process takes place on both sides of the market. The producer is figuring out what the product is supposed to be, how to make it, and what people want from it; consumers are figuring out what their expectations are, how much they are willing to pay, what product attributes are attractive, what the trade-offs are, and what trade-offs they are willing to accept. A kind of iterative learning process accompanies that kind of migration. No one side of the learning process drives the other; they happen together. Manufacturers are gaining experience, and so are customers. The people in the high-tech ceramics industry in Japan say very clearly they do not know what the dominant applications will be for structured ceramics. They also say that if they sit around in their offices and ask themselves, they will never find out. The only way they will find out is to put the applications out in the market and see. They will get responses back, going through those iterative cycles of experimentation and learning.

Managing Dematurity

In some industries during the last decade or so, there has been a reversal of this migration. Because manufacturers have customers, they cannot do what Henry Ford did when he came to the end of the life of the Model T: shut down the entire operation for nine months while engineers redesigned and retooled to build the Model A. That kind of luxury is not available today. In fact, manufacturers today have customers who have relatively clear expectations about what they want from a product, what they are willing to pay for it, what it should be like, and what attributes it should have. The real management question to focus on is what is involved in managing effectively during this reverse migration. We know a lot about how to manage the initial migration and what to do in organizational terms. Uncertainty is limited, or at least grows less. And since the name of the game is efficiency, what we have done—and with great ingenuity—is to insulate organizational units. We have packed buffers around those individual units in order to cushion them from exogenous shocks. We do not want anything to disrupt manufacturing.

A product like an automobile is composed of a number of systems—a propulsion system, a braking system, and so on. We can think of each of those systems in technical terms as representing a kind of pyramid of design problems. During the development of that product, there is a lot of experimentation early on with different ways to address the different pieces of each system. At some point in this process there locks into place a core idea that settles on the kind of braking system to use. The core concept, which then sits on top of this design pyramid, locks it into shape and by doing so defines the technical agenda of the remaining work to be done. When this core concept begins to lock in, perfecting innovations are made within the context of it. During the process of reverse migration, the top of the pyramid does not blow off first. Instead various forces start to eat away at the base, and the pyramid begins to unravel, almost like a double helix coming apart. At some point the whole structure becomes sufficiently unstable, and the top does fall off, which effectively reopens design problems whose solutions had been locked in.

In these kinds of changes, the managerial task is not like having an established puzzle from which you take one piece out and put another one in its place so that the puzzle is exactly the way it was before, except with one small substitution. Rather there is a change in the type of puzzle itself, a kind of system change. This migration is a system change in the products and processes that had been established. This kind of change poses real management challenges, which are not only difficult in themselves but also very different from the agenda of management work that has long been the bread and butter of established companies. If that is the case, what does business need from government?

What's Needed for Change?

If we are talking about organizations that are capable of learning, then by necessity we have to talk about people who are capable of learning as well. We must never forget the importance of the human capital in industrial organizations. Government must concern itself with the education and training of its people and retraining where necessary.

Beyond that when government sees the need to regulate product or process development and must choose an approach, it should take seriously into account the differential effects of various approaches on the learning potential of organizations. When the Clean Air Act went into effect, steel plants had to reduce every point source of polution to a specific acceptable level. More technologically elegant solutions were irrelevant. With the adoption of the bubble policy, a plant can be treated as a single source of pollution, and management has the choice of what kind of trade-offs to make within the bubble. That is a regulatory approach that does not specify, limit, or constrain the form of technological development. When the standards for fuel economy in automobiles were put into place, the way in which they were promulgated essentially made it impossible for the automobile companies to attempt longer-term, technically elegant solutions. They had to opt for a quick and dirty solution because there was no other way that they were going to be able to get within bounds in the time allowed. That requirement paralyzed or aborted any number of promising development efforts because all that they could really do in the available time was to take weight out of the car.

There are, then, ways to draw up regulations that foster and encourage technical experimentation rather than lock in the way things are done now and force people to try and do what they are already doing a little better. By definition, this is the course of diminishing returns, because each increment of progress becomes geometrically more extensive. Government must examine the long-term effects of the way it regulates industry. Another point is that both in terms of government procurement and in terms of the kind of incentives government can provide for the ways that companies do their own procurement, there is much to be said for not going to a procedure of sole sourcing. Certainly the way in which many U.S. producers have traditionally dealt with their vendors has not been smart. Long-term relationships make a lot more sense, as the Japanese have shown. But interpreting the Japanese experience to mean going to a kind of sole-sourcing arrangement means restricting the number of organizations that will be involved in the learning process and therefore aborting a lot of important iterative learning. I would argue strongly that we ought to consider carefully government policies that encourage sole sourcing. I am not arguing that it is government's job to go ahead and destabilize, but I think government's responsibility is not to retard the possibility of that kind of change. It can stabilize, nurture or support, or encourage the operation of thin markets.

When government protects industry, it usually exacts little, if anything, in return. There is no assurance that management will use the breathing space to face up to the deeper, wrenching, structural changes that must be made. This is the key. I do not believe in setting out to destabilize just to achieve that end, but I do believe in holding management's feet to the fire when the fire is already out there. As a research manager at Exxon once said to me, "Sometimes people can't read the handwriting on the wall until their backs are up against it."

2
Computer-Integrated Manufacturing and the Next Industrial Revolution

Robert U. Ayres

T here are four main topics that I will examine in this chapter. The first is something that many people involved in the field of technology take for granted, although it is surprisingly new to economics: innovation plays a critical role as a driver of economic growth. There is a theoretical justification for this idea, going back to Joseph Schumpeter's work in the early part of this century (Schumpeter 1935). Nevertheless, most economic growth models have emphasized capital investment and labor only. Yet econometric evidence compiled by the National Bureau of Economic Research in the early 1950s, plus voluminous anecdotal evidence from many other sources, have shown that output growth in the United States cannot be explained simply or even mainly in terms of increases in capital or labor. Recently I undertook a survey of some 800 major industrial innovations since the beginning of the eighteenth century, by decade and country of origin, to see when and where the innovations were coming from (Ayres 1984a). I found that about 50 percent of all the significant innovations occurred in the United States. Not surprisingly, the other two important centers were Germany and its immediate neighbors (especially Switzerland) and the United Kingdom. Those three small regions have accounted for close to 90 percent of all the world's key innovations in the past 250 years. They are also the richest countries in general. Clearly there is a strong causal relationship between innovation and long-term economic growth, though short-term linkages are apparently not strong (Bailey 1984).

The second major point is that the world is now in a period of slow economic growth—if not crisis—notwithstanding some recent good news. This slump is attributable to a general slowdown in productivity growth, especially in Europe and North America (tables 2–1 and 2–2 and figure 2–1). Economists differ somewhat with regard to the magnitude of the slowdown

The work reported here was supported in part by the National Science Foundation under grant R11-810-7019. Parts of this chapter are taken largely from a paper presentd by the author and printed in the proceedings of an NSD grantees meeting (Ayres 1985). It will be published in full in a forthcoming issue of *Prometheus*.

Table 2–1
U.S. Productivity Growth Rates
(percentage per year)

	1950–1965	*1965–1973*	*1973–1981*
Labor productivity			
Nonfarm business	3.00	2.14	0.64
Manufacturing	2.74	2.77	1.55
Multifactor productivity			
Nonfarm business	1.79	1.16	0.06
Manufacturing	2.16	1.95	0.56

Source: Computed by the author from annual data provided by the U.S. Department of Labor, Bureau of Labor Statistics.

and with regard to its supposed causes (Congressional Budget Office 1981b, Committee on Economic Development 1983). There is some consensus that flaws in the methodology of measuring productivity growth may have exaggerated the observed decline (by omitting some countervailing factors) and that a real slowdown has occurred nonetheless regarding earlier periods and other countries. The problem is most severe in manufacturing. It is no surprise that professional economists have tended to seek explanations in the realm of macroeconomic policy: money supply, credit, budget, taxes, regulation, incentives to save and invest, and others. To date there is little consensus within the economics community as to the efficacy and completeness of such explanations (see, however, Bailey 1984).

For a number of reasons, I believe that macroeconomic policy can account for no more than a fraction of the overall productivity slowdown (see Ayres 1984a). Just as productivity growth is fundamentally driven by technological

Table 2–2
Average Annual Rates of Productivity Growth in Leading Industrialized Countries, 1960–1973 versus 1973–1979
(percentage)

Country	*1960–1973*	*1973–1979*	*Change*
Italy	7.8	1.6	– 6.2
Japan	9.9	3.8	– 6.1
Sweden	5.8	2.5	– 3.3
Canada	4.2	1.0	– 3.2
United States	3.1	1.1	– 2.0
United Kingdom	3.8	1.9	– 1.9
France	5.9	4.2	– 1.7
West Germany	5.8	4.3	– 1.5

Source: New York Stock Exchange, *U.S. Economic Performance in a Global Perspective* (New York: New York Stock Exchange, 1981), p. 19.

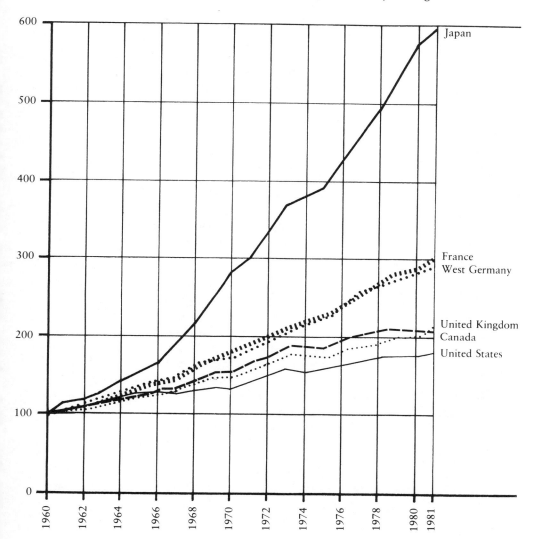

Source: Unpublished data provided by the U.S. Department of Labor, Bureau of Labor Statistics.

Note: In order to compare productivity growth rates, each country's growth rate for 1960 is assigned a value of 100. If this figure were to compare levels of productivity (instead of growth rates), it would show each country starting at a different level. While the United States began at a higher level than did the other countries shown, by the end of the 1970s the more rapid growth rates in other countries resulted in a convergence of productivity levels in much of the manufacturing sector.

Figure 2–1. Trends of Productivity Growth Rates: Indexed Labor Productivity-Growth Rates for Manufacturing Industries, 1960–1981

change, the causes of the slowdown must have at least some of their roots in technological factors. In the manufacturing sector, productivity increases in the past century can be largely attributed to such technological changes as the increased scale of production and increased power and speed of machines, increased product standardization, increased precision in cutting and grinding machines, and increased rationalization of the manufacturing process, including process optimization, job classification, and time and motion studies. All of these technological developments made it possible to replace many labor-intensive batch processes using general-purpose machines with capital-intensive mechanized processes using specialized automatic machines and, in some cases, to link such machines together by automatic transfer lines. This manufacturing technology, which evolved roughly from 1820 to 1950, encompassed the U.S. system of manufacturing and later mass production. (For an overall review, see Hounshell 1984; applications in the automobile industry are discussed by Abernathy 1978 and Abernathy, Clark, and Kantrow 1983).

Lester Thurow (1981) has said that "productivity is like a gold mine. Every vein of ore, no matter how rich initially, eventually peters out. If the same amount of gold is to be withdrawn from the mine, new veins of ore must be perpetually found." The important point is that the flow of productivity gains from mechanization and standardization began to show signs of exhaustion by the 1950s. Undoubtedly there were continued gains for some time as capital equipment embodying the most advanced forms of mechanization continued to replace older plants. This resulted in continued significant labor productivity improvements throughout the 1950s and 1960s as world markets expanded rapidly and much new capacity (employing the latest mechanical technology) was put in place. Gains in the 1970s came at a much slower pace because of saturation of demand in many sectors, which in turn cut back on new factory construction.[1]

From 1950 on, the areas of new technological opportunity in manufacturing shifted dramatically away from the mechanical to the electronic realm, with special applications to process controls. Technologically, manufacturing reached a period of very slow change and relative maturity in the 1950s and 1960s. The pace of change of manufacturing technology has increased since then, with increasing emphasis on applications of computers and electronics.

A third major theme I will explore is a partial explanation for the slowdown in productivity, growth, and, probably, innovation that we have experienced over the past twenty years or so. In short, there is a strong relationship between the innovativeness of an organization and its flexibility. By flexibility I mean the ability to adjust to changes in the market or the technological environment and react creatively to the changed circumstances. In many cases, the ability of large manufacturing organizations to bring new products to market—to innovate—has been adversely affected by rigidities in the manufacturing system as it evolved prior to the 1970s. Much of this rigidity arises from its mechanical origin.

Currently mass production technology is heavily dependent on highly specialized—in fact, dedicated—machinery and equipment that must be amortized over enormous production volumes and many years. Thus it has become prohibitively costly to introduce new products as the scale and capital intensiveness of production have increased. A further factor that contributes to the problem is the growing complexity of products, which has created pressures toward simplification of the production process and minimization of decision-making opportunities for workers so as to minimize problems associated with human error.

From the diagnosis of the problem of inflexibility, it is a short step to my fourth and final theme: there is a technological fix on the horizon. It is not available today, except in fragments and concepts, but by the end of the century something called flexible automation or computer-integrated manufacturing (CIM) will be available. Although CIM has many implications, notably for improved productivity, the most important by a considerable margin is that it offers a potential for breaking the gridlock in innovation that has resulted from nearly two centuries of increasing product complexity and increasing mechanization.

Manufacturing Trends since 1950

Manufacturing can be characterized as the combined activities of making, shaping, and finishing parts and assembling them into useful objects. Materials used in manufacturing include wood, paper, textiles, plastics, ceramics, glass, metals, and composites. Most products incorporate at least some parts that are rigid; hence metals play a major (though gradually declining) role. There is substantial overlap between manufacturing and metalworking. The following characterization applies to manufacturing in general but more to the manufacture of metal products.

Parts-shaping operations can be broadly classified as follows:

Casting or melt freezing of liquids in desired shapes (such as glass molding, injection molding, die casting, sand casting, or investment casting).

Compaction of powders or slurries into desired shapes, followed by baking or sintering (such as ceramics, thermosetting resins, or metal powders).

Deformation of plastic solids (such as rolling, pressing, stamping, drawing, extrusion, forging, bending, and glassblowing).

Cutting or machining of metals (or wood) or other solids.

Surface operations include washing, bleaching, grinding and polishing, vacuum deposition, electrodeposition, electroplating, anodizing, dipcoating or dyeing, and spraypainting. Assembly operations can be subdivided essentially into mating (insertion, engagement, forcefitting), stocking, winding or weaving (of fibers or wire), and joining (soldering, brazing, welding, cementing, sewing, stapling, riveting, bolting).

With a few exceptions, such as forcefitting and engagement of a nut and bolt (operations that are particularly dependent on tactile sensory feedback), the operations listed are virtually all mechanizable. That is, specialized machines are available that can perform most manufacturing operations accurately and fairly reliably at high repetition rates. Specialized machines are also available for parts feeding, loading, palletizing, and other materials-handling operations where the scale is large enough and parts are standardized.

For products that are standardized in design and manufactured in unlimited numbers, it is possible to organize the manufacturing process in metalworking to avoid almost all direct use of human labor except for a small number of operations, such as the insertion and joining of nuts and bolts or nonrigid parts. In high-volume manufacturing plants human workers are present mainly as machine supervisors to monitor the mechanized operations and to intervene when something nonroutine happens, such as when a tool wears out and needs changing or a workpiece breaks.

In a low-volume or multiproduct manufacturing plant, the situation is different because the machines are less specialized, and the monitoring, coordination, and control problem is correspondingly much more demanding. In a conventional job shop producing custom prototypes or small batches, the coordination of workflows has twin objectives: to maximize machine utilization and to minimize turnaround time (work-in-progress). This problem is so complex in practice that there is little attempt to do more than avoid bottlenecks. Usually each machine is independently set up to carry out one or more operations on a certain number of workpieces based on the number of items in the batch. The shop foreman is likely to order extras of each part to accommodate mistakes or faults. The partially completed good workpieces go into intermediate storage—most likely a bin—and the machine is set up again for something else. As the overall workload permits, the foreman eventually assigns another machinist on another machine to set up and run the next operation or operations in the sequence.

Fairly high machine and worker utilization can be achieved by completely separating each operation from the next in sequence but only by stretching out in-plant transit time for each batch and carrying a large inventory of unfinished parts. In fact, in most job shops, workpieces are being worked on during a very small fraction of the turnaround time between receipt of order and delivery to the customer. Shops producing larger and more predictable batches can increase output rates by utilizing specialized jigs and fixtures (which must be custom made for each job), bigger and faster machines with numerical controls, and more elaborate parts-handling systems for transfer loading and unloading the high-speed machines. But these aspects of mechanization leave the coordination and control problem untouched. Indeed as the investment in high-performance machines and parts-handling equipment rises, the economic importance of maximizing the joint output of the group of machines operating in sequence on a given part increases also.

The general-purpose manually controlled machine tool in a typical job shop can be idle much of the time because the machine is comparatively cheap; the major operating cost is the control function, provided by the skilled worker. To utilize high-cost, skilled machinists efficiently, it is important that no machinist should ever have to wait for a machine to become available. However, as individual machines have increased in power, degrees of freedom, and precision, they have also risen sharply in cost. In a plant using expensive high-precision, multiaxis equipment, the machines must be utilized efficiently to pay for themselves. One of the major ways to achieve high levels of machine usage is to reduce setup time by adopting numerical control (NC or CNC).

The role of the skilled machinist is thus shifted gradually from that of machine operator to that of general supervision and setup. Once the program is prepared and calibrated, an NC machine tool can machine complex three-dimensional shapes at a much higher rate than its manual-controlled predecessor.[2] In fact, NC can increase output per machine by up to a factor of five, although the average improvement is probably closer to half that much.

Since 1954 the trend in discrete parts manufacturing has been toward increasing individual machine capability and internalizing more and more machine-control functions. This further reduces the operational role of the human operator. The machine tool controller (now a microprocessor) has taken over more and more decisions, beginning with automatic actuation and stop conditions. An obvious extension is automatic tool changing. Whereas in a dedicated machining cell or hard-automated synchronous transfer line, tool change can be scheduled in advance by the designer, this is not the case with a group of multipurpose machines producing a wide variety of different products. In the latter situation, records of each tool's use (material being cut, speed, cutting time) must be kept and stored in memory. Moreover, the information must be available at the scheduling level of a hierarchical control system—a level higher than the machine-control level—so that individual machines are not shut down for tool changing in the middle of production runs.

One strategy to minimize such difficulties in multiproduct shops is to incorporate into a single machine tool all the machining operations needed for a given part (such as milling, drilling, boring, facing, threading, and tapping). Extremely general-purpose machines called machining centers have been developed in recent years explicitly to exploit the capabilities of NC. Such machines may have as many as ninety different tools and programmable tool-changing capability. But the strategy of increasing the flexibility of individual machines is limited by the fact that only one of the ninety tools can be utilized at a time. Moreover, the more tools and degrees of freedom the machine has because they might be needed, the more its maximum capability is likely to be underutilized during any particular operation.[3]

Thus, another major trend in multiproduct shops since the 1950s is computerized integration of individual multipurpose machines into linked sets— called manufacturing cells or flexible manufacturing systems (FMS)—to produce families of parts. Such families are based on classification by geometry and size (known as group technology, or GT). These classification systems, together with computers, are an important tool for deciding how each part type can best be produced (on what machine). To exploit GT and integrated systems of machines, a hierarchical top-down control system—as opposed, for instance, to distributed control—is strongly indicated. The reason is that detailed instructions for the actions to be performed by each particular machine must be converted into machine language specialized to that machine interface. For efficiency, however, it is virtually necessary for production engineers to be able to program design, coordination, and scheduling functions in a single higher-level language. Thus a supervisory computer must be able to translate from the high-level language used by the human engineers to the detailed machine-level languages understood by each machine.

Hence a third and related trend in factory automation is toward permitting instructions to be given in truly functional terms. Ideally it should be possible for a machine or a machining cell to be instructed in natural language, for example, "Make ten copies of model XYZ/123." The supervisory computer would then consult an on-line data base to determine what parts are required and how many of each. It then consults a stored file of existing programs, decides (based on a scheduling algorithm) which machine (or cell) is to make the part, calls for the needed bar stock or other material requirements from inventory, downloads the instruction program for each desired part number to the microprocessor controlling the designated machine (or machining cell), and activates it. When the part is finished and inspected, it is sent to a storage depot, to shipping, or to the next process stage.

A very long-term trend is worthy of notice here. In brief, the complexity of products manufactured has increased dramatically since the beginning of the industrial revolution. Apart from woven textiles or carpets, very few products manufactured in 1800 involved more than one hundred parts. An elaborate clock, a church organ, or a piano would be among the very few exceptions. A musket had about a dozen parts. A simple wood or brass clock of the early nineteenth century would have had around fifty parts, including about a dozen gear wheels. A sewing machine of the 1850s would have had around two hundred parts. An 1895 bicycle had over five hundred parts (mainly spokes and chain). An early automobile (c. 1900) might have had around two thousand parts. The number of parts in a car increased rapidly as capabilities were added to the vehicle and each subsystem was refined and elaborated. By the 1960s, a typical carburetor alone had about forty different mechanical parts, with three adjustable controls, and modern electronic fuel injection systems are even more complex. Altogether a modern automobile has about twenty thousand parts (roughly 70 percent mechanical and 30 percent electrical), and a small commercial airliner or diesel electric locomotive has at least ten times that number. A manufacturer of capital goods must keep track of enormous numbers of design variants. GE or Westinghouse must be prepared to manufacture any one of over fifty thousand steam turbine blade designs; the flame-cutting shop of a capital goods manufacturer will have to keep track of one hundred thousand possible similar two-dimensional

Table 2–3
Breakdown of Decisions by Type

Synchronization decisions
Load:	When to load next part in sequence
Weld:	When to move weld gun to next position in sequence
	When to squeeze gun
	When to fire gun
	When to quit squeezing gun
Pierce/drill:	When to move to next position in sequence
	When to pierce/drill
Transfer:	When to move shuttle to get new job
	When to lower shuttle onto job
	When to close shuttle
	When to pick up job
	When to move job to destination
	When to lower job
	When to open shuttle arms
	When to get shuttle out of the way

Flexibility decisions
Load:	Whether to add parts
	Which sequence to parts to add
Weld:	Whether to execute weld
	Which sequence to weld
Pierce/drill:	Whether to execute pierce/drill
	Which sequence to pierce/drill

Quality decisions
Load:	When to move conveyor
	Whether to adjust part
Weld:	When to move conveyor
	Which schedule to run at particular weld spot
Pierce/drill:	When to move conveyor

shapes. A major worldwide manufacturer like Caterpillar Tractor Company may have as many as twenty-five thousand suppliers around the world.

The inescapable implication is that the central problems in manufacturing today lie less in the process realm than in the sphere of organization and coordination. In short, manufacturing today is information processing. Obviously information is to some extent embodied in the design of products. The creation of any useful object from inert (nonuseful) materials can thus be regarded as a localized accumulation of negentropy, balanced by an entropy increase in the environment from the available work used up in the manufacturing process, as the Second Law of Thermodynamics requires. Information is also needed, in the sense of control decisions, at every stage of materials processing and fabrication. These are microdecisions, made on the shop floor, as opposed to the macrodecisions made in the executive suite.

The increasing complexity of products suggests, on the one hand, that the number of microdecisions in manufacturing is increasing continuously. On the other hand, the inherent error proneness of human workers, combined with declining costs of electronic sensors and information processors capable of performing similar functions, implies that the percentage of such decisions being made by machines must be increasing. Data from a case study currently being carried out by Bereiter (1985) at a General Motors truck plant confirms this conjecture. Table 2–3 lists a number of categories of decisions related to vehicle body welding operations. Table 2–4 compares the actual number of decisions involved in old and new (more automated) versions of the process. The most startling result is that the total number of decisions more than doubled, while the number of machine decisions increased almost tenfold (from 1,622 to 15,907) and the number of human decisions declined by two-thirds (from 4,553 to 1,511).

Table 2–4
Comparison of Decison Makers and Purposes

Decision maker	Synchronization	Flexibility	Quality	Total
Old process				
Machine	1,615	7	0	1,622
Human	4,023	293	237	4,553
Total	5,638	300	237	6,175
New process				
Machine	12,626	125	3,156	15,907
Human	1,147	111	253	1,511
Total	13,773	236	3,409	17,418

Manufacturing Technology and Innovation

The link between inflexibility and the use of hard automation arises from the fundamental fact that flexibility implies options and decisions among them. Decisions, in turn, require information. Thus flexibility is inextricably dependent on information processing capability. In fact, when the matter is analyzed further, it can be seen that the amount of information that must be processed to arrive at an optimal (or even approximately optimal) choice among a number of alternatives is an increasing function of that number.

Let me expand on this point. Imagine a product consisting of N different parts, each produced by a specialist firm. With a very few and minor exceptions, each part must physically link to at least two others.[4] In practice, there are many parts that link to more than two and some parts that link to many. In an automobile engine, the block, camshaft, crankshaft, and piston are examples. Each such link requires a distinct design and manufacturing coordination process—an information exchange. For instance, to change the dimensions of one part (perhaps to strengthen it) would often require that other parts be altered to fit. At the very least, the possibility would have to be considered, and in some cases a cascade of successive compensations would be required. For instance, any weight added to the engine of a car requires that all elements of the suspension be strengthened.

In the manufacturing and assembly process, the number of coordinations required is proportional to the number of part interfaces in the product. Each interface implies dimensional tolerances that are either acceptable or not. The key point is that if there are N parts, the number of decisions is more than N (but probably somewhat less than N^2). Thus the amount of information that must be processed in manufacturing is at least proportional to product complexity (N). Realistically it can be assumed to increase as N raised to some power P such that $1 < P < 2$. The general form of this relationship will have to be determined by mathematicians.

Until the advent of microprocessors and artificial intelligence, the only way to acquire information needed for decision making was by the eyes, ears, and hands of human workers. This was just as true for microdecisions (such as starting or stopping a machine or picking a part from a bin) as for macrodecisions (such as purchasing, scheduling, and shipping). Moreover, many of the macrodecisions require messages from the microlevel (such as the location and condition of tools), which traditionally have to be communicated from one human worker to another. In short the information acquisition, interpretation, decision-making, and communication skills of the workers have been an essential ingredient and limiting factor in flexible manufacturing. The cost of increased flexibility is thus traditionally tied to the cost of labor.

Moreover, the inborn limitations of human senses, together with natural human tendencies to be emotionally distracted, bored, irritable, or inattentive for other reasons, results in an unavoidable and irreducible minimum number of errors and defects.

Until recently the only feasible strategy open to management to maximize output per unit of capital and minimize defects (and quality problems) was to simplify and standardize the product, employ specialized tools, and link the machine tools mechanically by means of a sophisticated automatic transfer line. But this is tantamount to minimizing the number of possible options for each machine and workpiece. In an extreme case (exemplified by an automobile engine plant) there is no flexibility at all; machines are designed at the beginning of the life of the plant to perform one and only one task. The transfer line has only two possible states: on or off. Thus, for large enough production volumes, human workers can be largely eliminated from roles involving direct interface with machines or with workpieces, except to intervene when problems occur.

Unfortunately the mechanical integration that has been introduced to increase the output of capital equipment also sharply raises the cost of major product design change (Abernathy 1978). This kind of inflexibility makes it difficult for U.S.-based firms to compete in a dynamic fashion on the basis of introducing continued improvements in product equality or performance. The problem is most acute in established mass production industries where U.S.-based firms once were, but are no longer, the low-cost international producers. A more flexible manufacturing technology that would permit an accelerated rate of product innovation without making the production facility obsolete is becoming highly desirable in principle.

In the recent past, new manufacturing strategies have begun to emerge. Artificial senses such as machine vision and computers now offer the potential for making process control decision in more complex situations where there are many possible options. Thus, achieving flexibility without depending on humans as eyes and ears for machines will be increasingly practical over the coming decade or two. This is the essence of CIM.

Conclusion

The declining international competitiveness of the United States in manufacturing is the basic driving force leading to the adoption of CIM. For many U.S. manufacturers, the only feasible path to ensure immediate competitive survival against Japanese and other competition from East Asia appears to be to move their most labor-intensive operations (especially assembly) offshore to places like Malaysia, the Philippines, and Hong Kong where labor costs are much lower. On the other hand, national security concerns and increasing worry about unemployment raise the pressure on Congress to protect the jobs of U.S. workers by imposing import quotas, domestic content rules, and other nontariff trade barriers. Further, the geographical separation of design and engineering functions from manufacturing exacerbates difficulties of quality control, inventory control, and responsiveness to the market. Hence a strategy focused on raising productivity by exploiting more advanced manufacturing technologies is beginning to appear attractive. Indeed even the most militant labor unions would much rather see remaining U.S.-based manufacturing facilities modernized and rationalized than closed and moved abroad.

The emphasis on flexibility neglects a number of potential short-term benefits, including direct labor cost savings, materials savings, and downstream savings to intermediate or final consumers. What is in the offing is a quantum change in manufacturing technology that will, by the second or third decade of the next century, reduce the number of people employed directly in factories to a few percentage of the working population. These few people—with the help of smart machines—will be able to provide all the manufactured products need. (The few people who still work directly in manufacturing by 2020 will be mainly building machines that produce consumer goods, not the goods themselves.)

Still, the productivity improvements offered by CIM may be less important in the long run than the increased flexibility. The extreme inflexibility of conventional mass production technology has severely inhibited technological innovation in mature mass production industries. This internal conflict of interest, dubbed the "productivity dilemma" by Abernathy (1978), has kept the United States from using its historical strength in innovation as a competitive advantage in the mass production sectors. CIM potentially offers a kind of technical fix for the problems created by excessively inflexible hard automation.

Notes

1. There is significant worldwide overcapacity today in metals, electric power, chemicals, petroleum refining, automobile manufacturing, and even semiconductors.

2. NC machine programs are not in general interchangeable among machines, mainly because of variations in the amount of flex or looseness in the joints of each machine. These characteristics depend on the age and history of the machine, as well as its initial characteristics. When a program developed for one machine is to be used on another, some recalibration is normally required.

3. *Degrees of freedom* refers to an axis or vector of motion, such as up and down or from side to side.

4. In a "stock," each part must mate at least with one below and one above.

References

Abernathy, William. 1978. *The Productivity Dilemma*. Baltimore: Johns Hopkins University Press.

Abernathy, William; Clark, Kim; and Kantrow, Alan. 1983. *Industrial Renaissance: Producing a Competitive Future for America*. New York: Basic Books.

Ayres, Robert. 1984a. *The Next Industrial Revolution*. Cambridge, Mass.: Ballinger Publishing Company.

———. 1984b. "The Man-Machine Interface." Robotics Institute Report CMU-RI-TR-84-26. Pittsburgh: Carnegie-Mellon University.

———. 1985. "Vision/Tactile Sensing Key to Flexible CIM." Paper prepared for National Science Foundation Grantees Conference, March.

Bailey, Martin Neil. 1984. "Productivity Outlook I. Capital, Innovation and Productivity Growth." *Economic Impact* (Fall).

Bereiter, Susan R. 1985. "Modeling Process Control for Computer-Integrated Manufacturing of Discrete Parts." Working paper. Pittsburgh: Department of Engineering and Public Policy, Carnegie-Mellon University, May.

Committee on Economic Development. 1983. *Productivity Policy: Key to the Nations Economic Future*. New York: CED, April.

Congressional Budget Office. 1981a. "The Productivity Problem: Alternatives for Action." Washington, D.C.: January.

———. 1981b. "The Productivity Slowdown: Business and Policy Responses." Staff memo. Washington, D.C.: June.

Hounshell, David A. 1984. *From the American System to Mass Production, 1800–1932*. Baltimore: Johns Hopkins University Press.

Kendrick, John W. 1984. Productivity Outlook II, "Factors That Point to Improvement." *Economic Impact* (Fall).

Schumpeter, Joseph. 1935. *The Theory of Economic Development*. English translation of 1912 German ed., 1935. Cambridge, Mass.: Harvard University Press, 1961.

Thurow, Lester B. 1981. "Solving the Productivity Problem." In *Alternatives for the 1980's, No. 2, Strengthening the Economy: Studies in Productivity*. Washington, D.C.: Center for National Policy, November.

3

Competing through Technology: The Success Factors

Bruce Rubinger

W e have crossed the boundary of the familiar. The pace of change is accelerating, technology plays a new and critical role, and advanced research is flourishing around the globe. This new operating environment is turbulent and unforgiving of ignorance. Nations that can harness technology under these conditions will prosper. These are what we call the foresight nations, following the maxim, "To be prepared, one has to foresee." But despite the high stakes, many nations are woefully unprepared for the new industrial competition. They have fallen prey to obsolete assumptions and outmoded institutions. As a result, their policies are increasingly reactive and crisis oriented. They muddle through and pay a high price in terms of unemployment and large trade deficits.

Foresight Nations versus Muddlers

A few nations have emerged as the masters, rather than the victims, of technological change. These foresight nations are universally recognized as the leaders in technology-based competition. They perceive technological innovation as a multilevel synergistic process and scan the globe to identify emerging technologies and new ideas. Consequently their policies are anticipatory and forward looking.

To facilitate adaptation from domestic to international competition, the foresight nations have created a decision-making infrastructure geared to the new operating environment. They gain an early awareness of the powerful forces restructuring the international economy, a realistic sense of their evolving competitive position in the global marketplace, highly focused research programs, and an efficient balance between internal research and development (R&D) and assimilation of foreign technology. With such institutional

Susan Weiner, manager of the Japan Desk, Global Competitiveness Council, assisted in preparing this chapter.

insight, the foresight nations are positioned to identify swiftly and exploit new opportunities. This adaptation of the decision-making process to the global environment holds the key to the foresight nations' success.

Nations with foresight recognize that competition is continually evolving and that the only certainty is change. Their leadership places a premium on information and stresses group decision making. The management styles of the foresight nations and muddlers are summarized in table 3–1. Foresight nations monitor the global chessboard and widely disseminate and discuss

Table 3–1
Comparative Management Styles

	Mechanistic Adaptation, or Muddlers (U.S. Mode)	Organic Adaptation, or Foresight Nations (Japanese Mode)
Objectives	Return on investment; stockholders' gains.	Market share; new product ratio Multiple objectives with emphasis on growth.
Strategy	Orientation towards wider domain. Agility resources development; effective use of management resources. High "stars" ratio. Meeting competition head-on. R&D emphasizing product improvement.	Long-term accumulation of management resources. High "dogs" ratio. Niche strategy. R&D emphasizing basic research and new product development.
Technology	Routine	Non-routine
Organizational structure	Mechanistic (highly formalized, highly concentrated, highly standardized). Systematization of horizontal relations; strong power of control finance division. High degree of divisionalization. Sophisticated performance appraisal and clear linkage between performance and remuneration. Self-contained divisions with vertical control.	Organic (lowly formalized, lowly concentrated, lowly standardized). Strong power of production division. Low degree of divisionalization. Simple performance appraisal and weak linkage between performance appraisal and remuneration. Incompletely self-contained divisions with horizontal coordination network.
Organizational process	Decision-making emphasizing individual initiatives. Conflict resolution by confrontation. Output control.	Information-oriented leadership. Group-oriented consensual decision-making. Orientation to change, job rotation, and promotion from within.
Personal predisposition of managers	Specialist. High value commitment. Initiative; innovative. Track-record-oriented.	Generalist. Interpersonal relations skills.
Organizational improvement	Related to change in top management. Top down. Gradual improvement emphasizing primary functions.	High change. Reform emphasizing secondary functions.

Source: I. Nonaka and A. Okumura, "A Comparison of Management in American, Japanese and European Firms," *Management Japan* 17, no. 1 (Spring 1984):40.
Note: I have added *Muddlers* and *Foresight Nations* to this table.

the resultant information. This promotes consensual decision making and a collective sense of purpose.[1] As a result, their policy debates focus on tactical issues: the policy choices for achieving important national goals.

The foresight nations perceive technology in a dynamic, strategic sense. They recognize that technological change alters the rules of competition and serves as the foundation for sustainable competitive strategies. Since these opportunities are multidimensional, they cannot be addressed successfully in a piecemeal fashion; therefore foresight nations have developed the necessary diagnostic tools.

Foresight nations do not subscribe to the "stars" and "dogs" portfolio management theory popular in the United States. They understand the key synergies among sectors and skillfully exploit these links. Mature industries are not viewed as cash cows but as the technology drivers for the industries of the future. Guided by such insight, the foresight nations focus their resources on nurturing those sunrise industries where a sustainable competitive advantage is feasible.

In contrast, the muddlers perceive technology in a narrow, static sense. To them, technology policy implies investing in high-tech industries and liquidating mature industries. The muddlers are led by professional managers who perceive information as power. They routinely withhold information from subordinates and share little information even within their organization. Decision making emphasizes individual initiatives and control of output. Power is highly concentrated, and conflicts are resolved through confrontation.

Operating within these two behavior modes results in a major divergence between the policy agendas and response patterns of the two groups (table 3–2). The muddlers focus on what, and the foresight nations focus on how. While the former seek to identify and interpret emerging developments, the latter are molding and implementing public-sector initiatives that will yield a commanding share of the technology-based industries of the 1990s.

Thus the United States is still trying to ascertain whether it has a problem, while Japan is focusing on higher-level issues. For instance, the big debate in the United States is over whether the massive trade balance deterioration means the economy is being deindustrialized. While many accept deindustrialization as a given, others believe "deindustrialization is more nearly a matter of myth than of substance."[2]

Japan, in contrast, avoids meaningless debates over terminology. Instead its government and think tanks prepare thoughtful plans for the future. There is an order-of-magnitude difference in the quality of the data and analysis that supports decision making in the United States and Japan. It is this understanding of global trends and international competitive dynamics, rather than some bureaucratic planning mechanism, that gives credibility to government's actions in Japan.[3] The effectiveness of Japanese policies is a

Table 3–2
Adaptation Modes and Response Patterns

Foresight Nations	*Muddlers*
Decision making is guided by knowledge of international competitive, dynamics and awareness of global, opportunities.	Decision making emphasizes the fine-tuning of old remedies within the constraints of traditional economic theory and a flawed information base on global developments.
Leadership is information oriented. Information is broadly disseminated to promote group-oriented consensual decision making.	Leadership emphasizes individual initiatives and output control. Managers perceive information as power and withhold same from their subordinates.
Technology is perceived in a global, strategic sense. The synergies among sectors are nourished.	Technology is viewed in a narrow, static sense. Mature industries are considered liabilities and marked for harvesting.
Public policies are forward looking and anticipatory, focused and integrated, strategic rather than ad hoc.	Public policies are reactive and crisis oriented, ad hoc instead of strategic.
Impact: These nations are the masters of technological change.	Impact: These nations are the victims of technological change.

matter of public record. This central role of information in Japan's industrial policy has been described by the Japan External Trade Organization:

> The accumulation of policy information within the government and its presentation are probably the most fundamental tools to compensate for the limitations of the market mechanism and to guide industry in the right direction from a dynamic viewpoint in the present, fast changing and complicated times. An old saying claims, "To have foresight, one has to see, but perhaps that ought now be rendered, 'To be prepared, one has to foresee.' "[4]

A New Perspective Is Needed

The challenges of the 1980s cut across managerial and public policy lines. They are complicated by the significant interrelations between sectors—such as the technological links between semiconductors and computers or the managerial and financial links inherent in the Japanese industrial group (*keiretsu*) structure. The synergies between corporate policy and public policy add a further level of complexity. Moreover, these issues are markedly interdisciplinary and cannot be addressed in a piecemeal fashion. Competitive advantage is multifaceted, spanning technical innovation, manufacturing cost, quality, strategic flexibility, and a number of other dimensions. A strategic advantage along any dimension can be converted into a competitive advantage along other dimensions. For instance, a cost advantage creates a profit stream, which provides the innovative products and processes of the future through its investment in R&D. Similarly market share creates jobs and provides the experience necessary for further movement down the manufacturing cost curve.

Because of its multifaceted nature, an accurate assessment of a nation's competitive position or the likely impact of alternative policies cannot be obtained using a narrow analytic framework. As a result, these complex, subtle, and interdisciplinary issues are inadequately addressed by both economists and public policy analysts. Their approaches lack the high level of interdisciplinary focus and an appropriate analytic framework. For instance, econometric models, although they provide adequate projections during periods of continuity, are unsuited for an era of rapid change. These trend extrapolation techniques are the staples of U.S. number mills, yet they ignore many critical factors that drive competition in the 1980s, including the critical role of technology, the links among sectors, and the dynamic union between government policy and corporate strategy.

Reliance on outmoded shibboleths can have disastrous national consequences. In the early 1950s, before Japan evolved into a foresight nation, it considered promoting the automotive sector by designating it a basic industry eligible for special government aid. The proposal ran into stiff resistance from the economic establishment. The economists argued that consumer welfare would be maximized by importing less expensive cars from Europe and the United States. They also claimed that "since Japan should develop its foreign trade on the basis of international division of labor, efforts to develop the automobile industry will be futile."[5] Had such orthodoxy prevailed, Japan would have remained a second-rate economic power. However, the technocrats from the Ministry of International Trade and Industry realized that the growth of Japan's automotive industry would promote the modernization of a host of allied industries. They had an instinctive sense of the shortcomings of economic theory and won over key allies to their position. The pragmatic Japanese went on to create a new competitive era. They rendered obsolete many established industries and also discredited much of the conventional wisdom regarding international competition.

While the Japanese were able to make the transition from incrementalism to a radically new perspective, most other nations are still shackled by the intellectual baggage of the past. Nowhere is this more apparent than in the massive erosion of U.S. economic competitiveness.

Despite the competitive edge conferred by its large, affluent markets and the spillover benefits from Defense Department and National Aeronautics and Space Administration procurement policies, U.S. firms have been supplanted in global markets in industry after industry. It is ironic that the decline of U.S. competitiveness has been accompanied by the explosive growth within the United States of management consulting. (As Herman Melville noted, the death of the whaling industry created a new industry:

Table 3-3
Summary of Recommendations on Innovation by Government Commissions and Task Forces

Proposed Actions	Bowen (1966)	Charpie (1967)	Williams (1971)	Ancker-Johnson (1977)	Baruch (1979)
Federal R&D					
Demonstration grants	X			X[a]	X
Federal support of interdisciplinary university institutes	X			X[a]	X
Direct support for R&D where it can influence innovation rate	X		X		
Trade policy					
Priority to export promotion			X	X	X
Intensify efforts to insure U.S. technological lead			X	X	X
DOC, Treasury, & SEC cooperation on trade				X	
Technology assistance to less-developed countries				X	
Venture capital					
Government should provide availability information				X[a]	X
Modify barriers to institutional purchases of venture capital		X			
Government policy					
Study of innovation by DOC with universities		X		X	
Review policies to assess impact of federal actions on innovation		X		X	X
Interagency group should aid & advise regulatory agencies & others regarding their impact on innovation		X		X	
Facilitate adjustment to change	X		X		X
Economic incentives					
Tax credits					
Lengthen time allowed for deduction of losses		X		X[a]	X
Increase depreciation allowances		X		X[a]	X
Accelerate depreciation allowances				X[a]	X
Increase investment credit for R&D plant				X[a]	X
Increase tax depreciation allowances for R&D plant				X[a]	X
More generous capital gains tax rate for new firms				X[a]	X
New tax credit for R&D expenditures			X		X
Permit tax credits for contributions to nonprofit R&D institutions					X

Permit R&D expenditures in U.S. to be allocated solely to U.S. income				X
New tax credits for industrial R&D performers		X	X[a]	
Capital gains treatment same for casual inventor as businessperson inventor	X			
Liberalized stock options	X			X
Regulations				
Agencies must issue long-range statement of intent				X
Performance rather than design standards				X
Reevaluate antitrust policy		X	X	X
Provide economic incentives to offset regulatory costs				X
Strengthen data base for rule making	X		X	X
Account for impact on innovation	X		X	X

Source: Reprinted from "Industrial Innovation: Implementing the Policy Agenda," by B. Rubinger, *Sloan Management Review*, Spring 1983, p. 45, by permission of the publisher.

Note: Procurement actions, manpower development policies, and patent revisions have been omitted from this table.

[a]Study proposed that the government investigate the use of these policies.

writing about whaling. Similarly the decline of U.S. competitiveness has coincided with the growth of management consulting.)

Awareness of the decline in U.S. industrial competitiveness has led to calls for new federal policies to stimulate industrial innovation. A review of the literature reveals scores of studies and recommendations by presidential commissions, government task forces, congressional committees, and industrial associations. These efforts span more than twenty years; selective recommendations are summarized in table 3–3.[6] Despite the time devoted to these issues by business and government leaders, today the United States is no closer to their resolution than it was a decade ago. Good intentions will not suffice to meet the challenge of international competition. The policy debate lacks an adequate understanding of the success factors associated with competitiveness through technology and the means by which government policies can reinforce these factors.

Monitoring International Technical Progress

The process of monitoring international technical progress is a key element in adapting to the internationalization of technology and approaching technology management in a long-term strategic sense. It sets up the contextual framework within which technical planning can proceed logically. Specifically monitoring of international technical trends creates the knowledge base required to address a host of strategic issues facing senior managers.[7] These key issues include the following:

How competitive are we in technology?

What is the global status of pacing technologies with the potential to change the basis of competition?

Which are the sunrise industries where the United States should focus its resources?

How effective are government-funded R&D programs?

Should we innovate or pursue a fast follower strategy with technology acquired from external sources?

The process of technology monitoring also benefits research managers, senior policy analysts, and individual researchers. It increases R&D productivity by providing the information needed to determine when to shift to new technologies with greater potential. It yields insight into alternative approaches, enables public-sector managers to avoid duplicating existing work, and results in an efficient balance between technology assimilation and original research.

A firm can manage only technologists, not technology, if it does not acquire the required knowledge base through technology monitoring. This knowledge base is also critical at the national level to support the formulation of coherent science and technology policies.

To assess the technology management process and how it might be aided, the Global Competitiveness Council (GCC) carried out a study on U.S. knowledge of global technology. It focused on how Americans follow Japanese R&D efforts. The study analyzed for seven technical areas the methods used by managers and researchers to follow Japanese R&D, the timeliness and quality of R&D information, and the perceptions of gaps in the available knowledge base. Next, the quality of the information channels and data bases U.S. decision makers rely upon was assessed. GCC used its in-depth knowledge of Japanese data bases and research dissemination practices, augmented by information from its Japanese affiliate. Finally, a literature search identified important information overlooked by managers and researchers.

GCC interviewed more than one hundred managers and researchers considered by their peers to be particularly knowledgeable about Japanese efforts. They included a cross-section of government, industry, and university-based professionals. The first round of interviews was detailed, providing extensive information, including a comprehensive list of experts on Japanese activities. When this second list of experts was interviewed, names of other experts were solicited. This process concluded when interviewees were unable to add names to the list of those already contacted.

The study revealed that managers followed developments in an unsystematic manner through reliance on a variety of information sources. Their first choice was through visits to Japanese laboratories, which allowed them to see the technology and supporting facilities and to engage in dialogue with the researchers. Other primary information sources included feedback from overseas marketing representatives, scanning of technical literature available in English, international conferences, analysis of patents, and consulting arrangements with technological gatekeepers who allegedly had close ties to Japan's research establishment. These sources were augmented through briefings by Japanese marketing organizations based in the United States, meetings with Japanese professionals touring U.S. facilities, computerized literature searches, subscription to multiclient studies, use of Chemical Abstracts or similar services, contacts with colleagues who had recently visited Japan, and links to Japanese firms.

The experts agreed that the open literature is two to three years old. They also felt that its coverage is spotty. For instance, little is published in English on R&D conducted by Japan's industrial sector or government laboratories. This gap is most pronounced in areas with commercial applications. The general consensus was that the United States lacks details about Japanese R&D.

GCC then carried out an independent assessment of the information channels and data bases managers rely on to keep abreast of Japanese activities. It included a search carried out in Tokyo on a technical area where few Japanese patents were revealed by the major U.S. data bases. The search utilized Japanese-language materials not available in the United States. These findings were then compared against information supplied by the CLAIMS data base and the World Patent data bases.

Only 20 percent of the patents identified by the Japanese search showed up in the U.S. data bases. This shortfall is characteristic of most U.S. computer-based information services. A common problem is the omission of documents published in Japanese, reflecting the substantial cost of large-scale translation. Typically the only Japanese materials included in the data bases are those with an English summary.

Many respondents complained of information overload. They have difficulty assimilating even the limited data that are readily available, and they are not ready to cope with additional data. Inundated by hundreds of technical reports, managers will scan only those articles flagged as important.

Only 19 percent of Japanese scientific and technical periodicals are covered by the Western abstracting services. Since Western researchers gain most of their knowledge of foreign publications through abstracting services such as Chemical Abstracts and Engineering Index, they are largely unaware of many articles not covered by these services. As one writer has concluded, "U.S. researchers may well be in for some surprises from Japanese researchers, by virtue of the fact that they are not aware of the majority of research conducted in Japan."[8]

Exploiting the Synergies between Sectors

A nation's industrial infrastructure is a fabric of highly integrated and synergistic elements. Each product segment represents a source of capital, technology, and market demand for a variety of other segments. In a technology-based economy, the competitiveness of any industrial group is linked to the fortunes of other sectors, which provide a continual stream of technical advances for the development of new products and manufacturing processes. Without a significant demand for such technologies, it is highly unlikely that the more glamorous high-technology segments of an economy could flourish. GCC developed a conceptual model of technology linkages to show the significance of these synergistic relationships (figure 3–1). The model disaggregates the economy into four technical layers, with each component contributing to the technology flow and value-added chain.

Technical advance of the most fundamental type occurs within the outermost layer of the model. It is subsequently modified, transformed, and

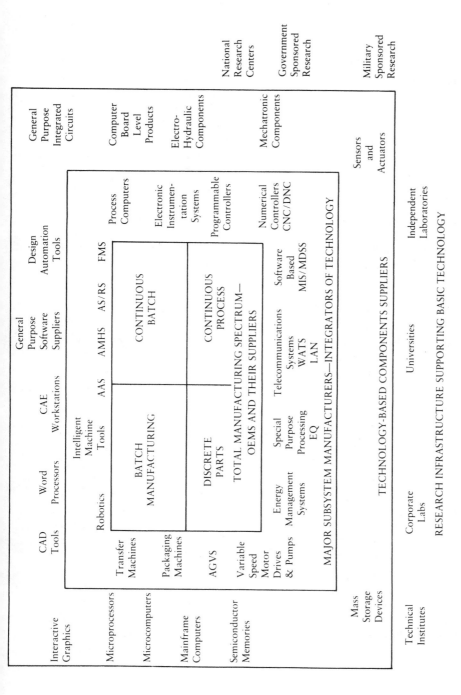

Source: Global Competitiveness Council, Boston. 1984.

Figure 3–1. Conceptual Model of the Critical Technology and Manufacturing Links among Sectors

integrated into diverse products and systems as it flows toward the ultimate consumer, located at the center of the diagram.

As an example of technology flows, consider the transportation sector (automobiles, trucks, and agricultural equipment). It is often considered to be a mature, slow-growth segment of the economy. Nonetheless it represents a significant portion of the demand for the products of systems and component manufacturers, a glamorous high-growth, high-technology group. Transportation is the major customer for intelligent machine tools, computer-aided design and manufacturing tools, automatic material-handling systems, programmable controllers (microprocessor based), flexible machining systems, and robots.

Let us now consider the case of textiles, another mature industry, which the West considers a low-technology business. Figure 3–1 shows that from a manufacturing perspective, the spinning of thread is quite similar to the creation of carbon fiber, a lightweight, high-strength material critical in such areas as aircraft manufacturing. From our analytic perspective, the textile and carbon fiber sectors overlap. Not surprisingly, the boundary between high-technology and mature industries is blurred since this dichotomy is an artificial contrivance. In fact, Toray, an old-line Japanese textile firm, has emerged as one of the world's leading carbon-fiber producers. The Japanese have exploited the inherent links between sectors to preserve jobs and ease the transition from low- to high-technology sectors. In contrast, the West tends to denigrate mature industries such as textiles in its pursuit of more glamorous sunrise industries. Since high-tech and mature sectors reinforce one another, this strategy is likely to hurt the West in both sectors in the long term.

Conclusions and Policy Recommendations

The knowledge base and the analytic tools that support industrial planning in the United States are seriously deficient. We must question the viability of government policies based on a flawed foundation. In fact, government's actions are reactive rather than anticipatory and ad hoc instead of strategic, and they undermine the competitiveness of U.S. industry in international markets.

Survival requires adaptation. If it is to break this pattern of reactive policies, the United States must take a fundamentally different approach to decision making rather than merely fine-tune traditional remedies. It must pursue forward-looking policies that reflect a global perspective and the dynamic manner by which technical advance is integrated into products and processes throughout the national economy. The government must also take into account the synergies among sectors and their implications for competitive advantage in global markets. Then it can identify and focus its resources on those sectors where it can sustain a competitive edge.

The foresight needed to meet international competition cannot be legislated into existence, nor can it be gained through an emphasis on policy formulation. Instead foresight will be achieved only through the creation of an institutional infrastructure geared to facilitate decision making in the new competitive era.

There are several mutually reinforcing actions that the government can take to develop such an infrastructure. First, it should provide financial support for the creation and broad dissemination of a strategic data base on global market and technology trends. Second, it should introduce into the public policy process the advanced management tools that are now standard with many of the nation's leading corporations. For instance, strategic planning models enable descriptions of both the direct and ripple effects of alternative policies. These tools provide a quantitative means for projecting the impact of potential policy scenerios and evaluating their effectiveness. Through such screening, the most attractive policy solutions could be identified and become the focus of the public debate.

Government should tap the broad expertise available at universities. It could provide funding to business schools for the collection and analysis of corporate performance data. This would provide government decision makers with timely information on competitive trends at the microlevel while enabling business schools to generate relevant case studies to enrich their curricula on international business.

When the U.S. government creates such an infrastructure and develops the advanced management tools needed to mold powerful new initiatives, it will be following the path taken by the foresight nations. The Japanese began in the 1950s by creating institutions, such as the Japan Information Center for Science and Technology, to follow global R&D activity systematically. Only those nations that accurately diagnose changes and respond in a realistic fashion will prosper in the late twentieth century. The stakes are high. A reliance on old nostrums will not suffice.

Notes

1. Ikujiro Nonaka, and Akihiro Okumura, "A Comparison of Management in American, Japanese and European Firms," *Management Japan* 17, no. 1 (Spring 1984):23–40.

2. David Warsh, "Doomsayers May Be Wrong about American Industry," *Boston Globe,* July 4, 1985, p. 19.

3. Dezso Horvath and Charles McMillan, "Industrial Planning in Japan," *California Management Review* (Fall 1980):11–21.

4. "Japan's Industrial Structure: A Long Range Vision." JETRO, (Japan External Trade Organization) 1975.

5. See Hiroya Uneo and Hiromichi Muto, "The Automobile Industry of Japan," *Japanese Economic Studies* 3 (Fall 1974):3–9.

6. Bruce Rubinger, "Industrial Innovation: Implementing the Policy Agenda," *Sloan Management Review* (Spring 1983):43–57.

7. This section is based on Bruce Rubinger, "Japan-U.S. Technical Information Exchange: A One-way Street?" *Automotive Engineering* (March 1985):68–72.

8. See testimony of Robert Gibson, "The Availability of Japanese Scientific and Technical Information in the United States," Hearings before the Committee on Science and Technology, U.S. House of Representatives, Washington, D.C., March 6–7, 1984.

4

The Blending of Two Paradigms for Private-Sector Technology Strategy

Mel Horwitch

This chapter deals with the nature of postwar, private-sector technology strategy in the United States. Two major themes are emphasized. First, the vitality and remarkable performance of U.S. technology during much of the postwar period in the commercial sector can be at least partially explained by the eclectic interrelationships and complex coexistence of two distinctly separate types of technology strategy patterns: small-firm, high-technology entrepreneurship and large-scale, corporate R&D and technological diffusion. The second major theme is that these two major patterns of technology strategy behavior have been undergoing a significant transformation since at least the mid-1970s. The salient characteristics of each pattern have been diminishing as institutions from each side are attempting to capture some of the benefits of the other. This overall current trend, the blending on an ad hoc or permanent basis of small, high-technology entrepreneurship and large-scale, corporate R&D and technology diffusion is one of the most important developments in modern technology strategy.

Before discussing in some depth these two major types of private-sector technology strategy patterns, the term *technology strategy* itself requires elaboration and explanation. In a sense, technology strategy must first be distinguished from other overlapping technology-related aspects of business practices. For example, although such acitivities as R&D management, new product development, process improvement, or even overall technological innovation obviously form part of technology strategy, they do not usually encompass such key aspects of corporate strategy as top management involvement, high-level planning, and strategic resource allocation.

Technology itself is an ambiguous concept. It can be viewed as the ability to create a reproducible way for generating new or improved products, processes, or services. This capacity is both a formal and an informal activity. Its result can be radical or incremental in nature. But whatever the process or impact, technology has increasingly become recognized as a strategic variable in its own right as opposed to a more specialized and more purely technology-related matter of concern.[1]

Strategy is an even more ambiguous term than *technology*. Definitions of *strategy* abound, but there is general agreement that strategy encompasses the interplay of three sets of dimensions: present and future, internal and external, and explicit and implicit managerial practices. Each of these dimension categories deserves elaboration.

A major trade-off in strategy concerns time. Essentially much of strategy is clearly a balancing act between the present and the future. Strategy has, almost by definition, a long-term perspective. It is a proactive task in anticipating the future and in suggesting ways for firms to position themselves to take advantage of future opportunities, including technological ones, and to avoid future threats. However, firms must also use current resources effectively. Short-term issues and decisions are also part of strategy since they provide the foundation and resources for future-oriented decisions. Indeed this key trade-off—the present versus the future—is recognized in the strategy field and is at the heart of many well-known strategic portfolios: market share (the present) versus growth (the future), company strength (the present or the future) versus industry attractiveness (the present or the future), or company strength (the present or the future) versus position on an industry life cycle (the present or the future).[2]

A second important dimension category in strategy is the internal–external perspective. Strategy obviously requires close attention to the relevant external environments of a firm, be they economic, technological, political, or cultural. A host of literature deals with the need and processes for adjusting to changes in the external environment.[3] But the internal perspective of strategy is just as important. The internal aspects include structure, decision support systems and processes, and various business systems that are installed in a firm. All of these internal elements need to support strategy.[4]

The final major set of dimensions refers to the way strategic behavior is manifested in a firm. The two extreme types can be referred to as explicit and implicit. Explicit refers to formal, systematic, and analytical procedures for developing strategy. Strategic planning, modeling, strategic formulation, and competitive analysis fall under this type of strategic behavior.[5] Implicit strategy refers to the more intuitive, informal, and action-oriented side of strategy. The leadership and personality of the chief executive officer, corporate culture and history, nonmarket stakeholder management, and strategic implementation are examples of implicit strategy.[6]

It is the blend of these three dimension sets that forms much of the scope of strategy. Successful strategy means that a firm is operating effectively in the relevant blocks, as indicated in figure 4–1. Moreover, the recent elevation of technology to a strategic variable means that technology-related concerns are now increasingly permeating and affecting the various diverse elements of modern strategy.

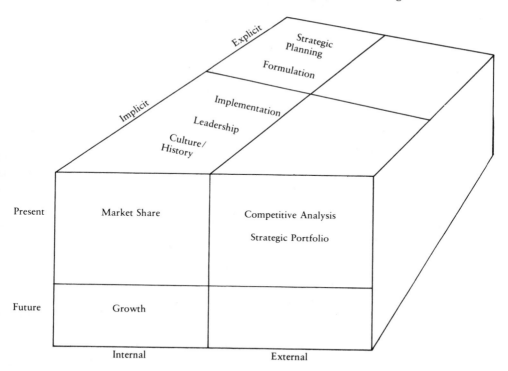

Figure 4–1. Dimensions of Corporate Strategy

The actual and active blending of strategy and technology began in the 1970s. For much of the postwar period in the United States, technology and corporate strategy were distinctly separate fields and areas of activity. The primary reason for this separation was the traditional dichotomy in the private sector between small-company and large-scale-corporation innovation. Corporate strategy was simply not part of the small firm's management repertoire. Instead strategy, if it related to technology anywhere, belonged to the realm of the large-scale corporation and, hence, its R&D activities. But even in this case, technology usually was not yet a strategic variable in its own right.

This is not to say that technology needed to be strategic in order to generate vigorous technological innovation and innovative vitality. On the contrary, until the current blending of technology and strategy and of the various forms of technological innovation began, the key ingredients for technological vitality were the vigorous functioning of each of the distinctive kinds of technological innovation and the active interplay of two distinctly separate forms of private-sector technological innovative activity. When these features did not exist, the level of technological innovation was relatively low. Later in the postwar period, during the 1970s, the boundary between these two major forms of private-sector technological innovative activity began to fade, and in fact the two major types partially merge at times. The blurring of differences was at least concurrent with and probably partly caused by the elevation of technology to a strategic variable. I will illustrate these points using the postwar history and evolution of three industries: semiconductors, machine tools–manufacturing process technology, and personal computers. Two of these industries, semiconductors and personal computers, show the importance of each type of technological innovation and of the interplay of the two distinct forms in the earlier period. One industry, machine tools–manufacturing process technology, demonstrates the lack of vitality when these two conditions are absent. Furthermore, all three industries illustrate the current dissolution of the two distinct private-sector types of technological innovative activity as technology becomes a key part of modern corporate strategic decision making.

Technological innovation has, correctly, been studied as a subject traditionally separate from other management practices, including strategy. Technology has been studied in considerable depth as part of R&D management and the process of technological innovation; it has been reviewed as a determinant of organization structure; and it has been seen as a critical factor in influencing the evolution of the international product life cycle.[7] Modern technological innovation, furthermore, is now recognized as a complex activity. One important aspect of our growing understanding is the realization that technological innovation is a process made up of diverse parts, varied participants, complicated patterns of evolution and information feedback loops, and potentially lengthy time durations. Moreover, great emphasis is now placed on the role of market pull and user needs. Finally, important research continues to highlight the key role of people as champions, entrepreneurs, or technology-familiar managers in effectively promoting and accelerating innovation.[8]

The importance of the distinction between small, high-technology firm entrepreneurship and large-scale, corporate innovation and of the interplay between them has not been given the kind of scholarly attention it deserved. Until approximately the mid-1970s, private-sector U.S. technological innovation could logically be viewed as comprising two paradigms or ideal types: mode I, or small, high-technology firm entrepreneurship, and mode II, large-scale, corporation R&D.[9] (See table 4–1.) Mode I might well be designated the Silicon Valley model of innovation. It represented in the early postwar period a fundamentally new and dramatic phenomenon in U.S. business history, where highly trained and well-educated technological entrepreneurs during the period from the 1950s through the 1970s created high-technology small firms in regions known for high-quality universities, such

Table 4–1
Comparison of Modes I and II

Key Mode Attributes	Inputs			Internal Processes			Output
	Technology and Skills Available	Environment	Market	Goal Setting	Communication System	Organization Structure	Innovation: Product Line or Systems
Mode I	Emphasis on exploiting existing and known technologies Technological capabilities restricted to few areas Key technological skills reside in top management	Contained and definable	Markets for the product are few and definable	Goals are set by top person Goal setting is informal, with few actors involved Options open to the firm are few	Informal Few people Dissemination of information does not demand complex system due to few recipients	Organization structure emphasizes few subunits and informality Top management gets involved in all activities in the organization	Typically a product or a product line scope tends to be limited by the technological capabilities of top management
Mode II	Complex in defined product or process areas Skills consist of technological as well as nontechnological, line marketing, in these areas. Mode II is concerned with existing and nonexisting technologies that they help to develop	Multiple and complex but still definable	Markets for innovations are multi-user markets and complex	Innovation goals are partially set by formal systems Firm has several technological options to choose from Top management may or may not be directly involved in identifying or pursuing technological options	Complex due to several organizational levels, formal and informal Affecting communication is possible but difficult to achieve	Organization tends to be complex, divided into product groups divisions, etc. Often different subunits have conflicting attitude and priorities Corporate boundaries are definable	Large number and/or complex products and processes

as Silicon Valley, Route 128 in the Boston area, the Research Triangle in North Carolina, and Route 1 near Princeton.

The salient features of mode I include a strong commitment generally to a single, narrow, or focused technology area; a comparatively small, informal, and changing organizational structure; a technological champion as head of the firm or part of the top management team; and an overall climate and style of entrepreneurship and risk taking. The key weaknesses of mode I organizations are also apparent: an absence of basic business skills; the huge and sometimes negative role that the personality traits of the founder can play; a lack of various kinds of resources; and the dependence on usually a single technology area or product market area.

Coexisting with mode I firms and even predating them are mode II corporations and the technological innovation process within them. Technological innovation in the mode II multidivision, multiproduct, and multimarket context presents a very different set of behavior patterns and challenges from those found in a typical mode I environment. Generally the major managerial challenge for mode II technological innovation until the 1970s was one of making strategic choices or trade-offs along at least three sets of dimensions: types of technological innovation on which to focus, such as product or process, incremental or radical innovation; the selection of which specific technologies to develop; and the timing or positioning of technology introduction into the marketplace (figure 4–2). (I employ Freeman's classification terminology for this last dimension—offensive, defensive, imitative, dependent, traditional, and opportunist—but other classification schemes may be equally appropriate.)[10]

Even after the strategic decisions are more or less established, the mode II corporation still has to deal with a number of complex internal strategic decisions, including resource allocation, monitoring and evaluation, structural issues and location of the innovating activity, internal technology transfer, and the relationship among the early R&D work, developmental work, and the operating divisions. The linkages between technological innovation activity and ongoing and pervasive formal procedures represent a particularly important difference between mode II and mode I environments. Similarly the significant and often novel opportunities for technological synergies are also a major aspect of mode II technological innovation. Finally, a glaring weakness that is often attributed to mode II conditions is the absence of the key entrepreneurial and risk-taking behavior patterns that are associated with mode I. This latter negative aspect of mode II innovation became a major challenge for modern technology strategy.

The major argument to be made regarding the earlier phase of postwar U.S. private-sector technology strategy is that two distinctive paradigms functioned separately, coexisted, and yet had important kinds of interrelationships. A second argument I make is that during this earlier phase, successful

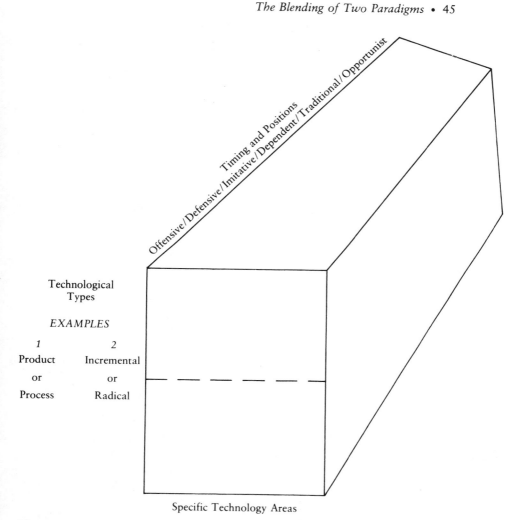

Figure 4–2. Mode II Concepts for Technological Strategic Choices until the 1970s

technology strategy usually required the existence of vigorous mode I activity and often the interplay of mode I and mode II firms. In other words, effective mode I work was usually essential, and often the interplay of mode I and mode II activity was quite helpful. These points are demonstrated using the early U.S. semiconductor industry in the 1950s and 1960s and the U.S. personal computer industry in the 1970s. When there was no vigorous mode I activity, private-sector technology strategy usually stagnated in this earlier postwar period. This point is illustrated using the traditional U.S. machine tool industry as an example.

The First Postwar Phase of Technology Strategy: Two Distinctive Paradigms

Semiconductors

The early semiconductor industry is perhaps the best example of the pattern and vitality of the first postwar phase. Indeed much of our perception and ideas regarding technological innovation and strategy derive from our experience with semiconductors, a critical and explosive technology-based industry.[11] The distinguishing features of the early semiconductor industry include rampant innovation, rapid growth, close conformity with both the traditional international product life-cycle and international diffusion-of-technology models, relatively easy and plentiful access to such critical resources as skilled people, entrepreneurs, venture capital, and technology, and the key but indirect role of government as the main state of the art market for semiconductors.[12]

The most relevant characteristic of the early semiconductor industry for purposes of illustrating the dual paradigm of early postwar private-sector technology strategy was the great variety and fluidity of what might be termed the industry's corporate demography during this period. The early semiconductor industry exhibited great diversity in terms of the types of firms participating in the industry (table 4–2). One analyst distinguished the following types of firms: (1) AT&T alone; (2) receiving tube firms (such as General Electric, RCA, and Sylvania); (3) new entrants—established and large firms (examples are Hughes, Motorola, and IBM); (4) new entrants—established small firms (Texas Instruments); and (5) new firms (Transitron).[13] Of course, not all early semiconductor firms would completely conform to this categorization, but this typology does reflect at least two key important attributes of the early semiconductor industry. First, mode I and mode II firms could clearly be distinguished from each other. Start-ups and spin-offs, generally mode I entities, emerged but did not necessarily thrive. Transitron, perhaps the prototypical mode I firm in the early semiconductor industry, failed to grow and fulfill its early promise, largely due to the absence of key business skills and counterproductive interpersonal factors.[14] But other start-ups or spin-offs did grow and become established, such as Fairchild, National Semiconductor, Intersil, and later Intel.

A second key point is that these new firms were not alone. Larger, established corporations, mode II organizations, were also playing key roles in the semiconductor industry from the beginning. Occasionally some of these large firms did not become significant commercial successes at this time, even when they possessed semiconductor technology, as was true for Sylvania and General Electric. In other cases, however, such as AT&T, IBM, and RCA, mode II firms remained successful in the growing semiconductor industry.

Table 4–2
U.S. Semiconductor Market Shares of Major Firms, Selected Years,
1957–1966
(percentage of market)

Type and Name of Firm	1957	1960	1963	1966
Western Electric	5	5	7	9
Receiving tube firms				
General Electric	9	8	8	8
RCA	6	7	5	7
Raytheon	5	4	a	a
Sylvania	4	3	a	a
Philco-Ford	3	6	4	3
Westinghouse	2	6	4	5
Others	2	1	4	3
Subtotal	31	35	25	26
New firms				
Texas Instruments	20	20	18	17
Transitron	12	9	3	3
Hughes	11	5	a	a
Motorola	a	5	10	13
Fairchild	a	5	9	a
Thompson Ramo Wooldridge	a	a	4	a
General Instrument	a	a	a	4
Delco Radio	a	a	a	4
Others	21	16	24	12
Subtotal	64	60	68	65
Total	100	100	100	100

Source: John E. Tilton, *International Diffusion of Technology: The Case of Semiconductors* (Washington, D.C.: Brookings Institution, 1971), p. 66.
Note: Market shares are based on company shipments and include in-house and government sales.
[a]Not one of the top semiconductor firms for this year. Its market share is included under "others."

But still the mode I and mode II firms operated largely in very different contexts; however, the interplay between these two worlds was critical. First, there was the all-important flow of people, often starting with Bell Laboratories. There were also buy-and-sell and merger-and-acquisition relationships. For example, Shockley Laboratories obtained its initial funding by becoming a wholly owned subsidiary of Beckman Laboratories. A little later, eight of Shockley's scientists started their own firm with the backing of Fairchild Camera and Instrument. In fact, in 1967, a number of investors and entrepreneurs from Fairchild bought National Semiconductor and soon were able to turn around that firm.[15]

Ignoring the important role of government, it was, first, the critical existence of mode I entrepreneurship and then the rich variety of mode I and mode II institutions and the interplay between these two separate paradigms of technology strategy that helped give the early U.S. semiconductor industry its well-known dynamism.

Personal Computer Industry

A similar phenomenon can be discerned in the early personal computer industry, though this was a much later period in the postwar era, the last half of the 1970s.[16] The true spark for this industry came from a mode I environment that was made up of hobbyists, publicists and promoters, technological champions, and entrepreneurs. All three of the major initial start-up firms in the personal computer industry—MITS, IMSAI, and Processor Technology —failed to succeed in the marketplace and to create a sustainable business (table 4–3). Although they were very different kinds of firms in many ways, like Transitron in semiconductors, these early mode I personal computer firms lacked essential business skills, and their fates were too dependent on the personal traits of the founding entrepreneurs.

There was an important second wave in the early personal computer industry, beginning with the appearance in 1977–1978 of one new firm, Apple, and two large, established firms from other industries, Radio Shack-Tandy and Commodore. All three firms—one typical mode I firm (Apple) and two more or less mode II firms (Radio Shack-Tandy and Commodore)—entered the personal computer industry at about the same time. For different reasons all three were successful. Apple reflected the best of mode I behavior: an innovative and adaptable technology and product design, skilled technology champions at the top, a strong entrepreneurial drive, and a remarkably effective,

Table 4–3
Market Share of the U.S. Personal Computer Industry, by Dollar Shares

Company	1976	1978	1980	1982
MITS	25%			
IMSAI	17			
Processor Technology	8			
Radio Shack		50%	21%	10%
Commodore		12	20	12
Apple		10	27	26
IBM				17
NEC			5	11
Hewlett-Packard			9	7
Other	50	28	18	17
Total number of units	15,000	200,000	500,000	1,500,000

Sources: Gary N. Farner, "A Competitive Analysis of the Personal Computer Industry" (Master's thesis, MIT, 1982), p. 18; Deborah F. Schreiber, "The Strategic Evolution of the Personal Computer Industry" (Master's thesis, MIT, 1983), p. 7.

informal, and spirited organization. Radio Shack-Tandy had a good product design, excellent service and support, and a superb marketing and distribution system. Commodore had good marketing and low-cost production through vertical integration.

Like the early semiconductor industry, the early personal computer industry possessed that all-essential mode I entrepreneurial spark. But the mode I factor appeared as a two-phase process. The firms in the first phase (from 1975 to 1978) were not successful in a commercial sense. All failed. This first phase, however, built a foundation by developing technology, designing products, and selling, for the more successful second phase of early personal computer industry. Like its successful counterpart, the early semiconductor industry, during this second wave mode I and mode II personal computer firms remained more or less distinct. But there was again a vital interplay between them as people flowed from one firm to another, and with this flow, the transfer of technology and relevant managerial knowledge and technique took place. Thus, although the evolutionary pattern was somewhat more complex and less neat, like semiconductors, the rise of mode I innovation, the coexistence but separateness of mode I and mode II activities, and the creative interplay between these two paradigms resulted in the rise of another explosive and vigorous industry: personal computers.

U.S. Machine Tool Industry

What happened when these essential ingredients for early postwar private-sector technology strategy did not exist? The experience of the U.S. machine tool industry postwar until the end of the 1970s provides at least a partial answer.

The U.S. machine tool industry has an important and venerable role in U.S. technological development and business history. During much of the nineteenth century, the industry served as the vital link for developing and transferring technology to much of U.S. industry.[17] But by the mid-twentieth century, the U.S. machine tool sector was clearly in a mature phase and had lost much of the technological vitality and importance as a salient industry that had characterized it earlier.

The basic characteristics of this industry during much of the postwar era until about 1980 paint a not very glamorous or exciting picture from the point of view of technology strategy.[18] Encompassing "power-driven, not hand held, machines used to cut, form or shape metal," the machine tool industry itself is a relatively small sector of the U.S. economy, comprising about 0.12 percent of the gross national product and 0.10 percent of U.S. employment in 1982. Most U.S. machine tool firms have traditionally been small, closely held companies with narrow product lines. The industry is not highly concentrated, with the four largest firms in 1977 accounting for 22 percent of industry shipments. Both sales and, to a lesser extent, employment are highly cyclical. R&D expenses, capital investment outlays, and growth and productivity are all relatively low. In 1982, in constant dollars, R&D expenses fell to about the same level that they were in 1975. The global market share of the U.S. machine tool industry fell from 25 percent in 1968 to 20 percent or less in the 1970s. In terms of growth and productivity, the U.S. machine tool industry during the 1973–1981 period fell significantly behind U.S. manufacturing as a whole and, in the case of productivity, behind durable goods manufacturing. During the postwar period, until perhaps very recently, it exhibited a short-term outlook, concerned mostly with annual financial goals.

In the meantime, the U.S. machine tool sector has increasingly seemed to resemble a smokestack or sunset industry. Under the impact of effective global competition and the failure perhaps to exploit or keep up with various new technologies in manufacturing such as new materials, software, computer-aided design and manufacturing and automation, U.S. machine tool firms have become progressively less profitable and have lost significant market share. Even more relevant was the complete absence of significant mode I innovation activity, with the possible exception of the robotics field.[19] Even in robotics, however, much of the technological leadership during the 1970s shifted to Japanese firms.

Moreover, the relatively large mode II firms also did not generally exhibit significant technological R&D activity or leadership. In machine tools during the 1970s, there was very little of the creative and vital interplay between distinctly mode I and mode II institutions that was manifested in the early semiconductor industry or in the second wave of the early personal computer industry. Instead the U.S. machine tool industry stagnated, and vigorous global competitors took quick advantage of this situation.

Private-Sector Technology Strategy: The Blending of the Dual Paradigm Model in the Late Postwar Period

Emerging Strategic Context in Semiconductors, Personal Computers, and Manufacturing Technology

Until recently in the United States there have been two distinct private-sector paradigms for technological innovation and technological strategy. This situation is changing and has been since the 1970s. The demarcation between modes I and II is becoming blurred as small, high-technology firms increasingly establish linkages with large mode II corporations and as mode II corporations create explicit linkages with other large firms and with mode I firms as well. This strategic action, in effect to make continuous trade-offs between competition or cooperation, represents a major current breakdown of the various modes as distinct types of technology strategy activity and a key transformation of modern technology strategy. These trends are presented in table 4–4.

Table 4–4
Direction of Evolution of Technology Strategy, 1960s–1980s

1960s	1980s
Distinctly separate centers of activity	New forms of linkage
Autonomy of firms	Intraorganizational
Various modes remain separate	Interorganizational—domestic
Mode I: Small, high-tech firm	Interorganizational—multinational
Mode II: Large corporation	Public–private
Mode III: Multisector and multi-	Various modes are increasingly
organization enterprise[a]	consciously connected and coordinated
	for strategic purposes

[a]Not discussed in this chapter.

There are at least four kinds of linkages: intraorganizational, domestic interorganizational, multinational interorganizational, and private sector–public sector. All such linkages are becoming more important and more managed as the various modes of technological innovation, by design, increasingly overlap and interrelate. (For purposes of this chapter, the business–government interaction in technology strategy is ignored.) For example, many mode II institutions are now attempting to gain the benefits of the successful mode I firm, such as an entrepreneurial spirit, a dedicated set of champions, a drive to be close to the market and to users, and a familiarity with the relevant technology and products at the highest decision-making levels. To achieve these ends, top management is employing such intraorganizational linkage mechanisms as extreme decentralization (such as at 3M), managed autonomy (such as at Hewlett-Packard), a matrix-type organizational structure based on long-term and short-term criteria (such as OST at Texas Instruments), and new venture groups (such as Exxon Enterprises).[20] Similarly an array of interorganizational linkages, both wholly domestic and multinational, has emerged, including joint ventures, research contracts, equity relationships, and licensing or marketing agreements. Indeed, earlier notions of a pure international product life-cycle model now need major revision.[21]

The prevalence of this new private-sector technology strategy context, the breakdown and blurring of the two distinct paradigms, and the establishment of complex linking relationships across intraorganizational and interorganizational boundaries can be seen in the current patterns of the three industries already discussed: semiconductors, personal computers, and machine tools. In all three industries, this major transformation is manifested. This new pattern is also seen in a fourth industry, biotechnology.

In the semiconductor industry, the linkages between the firms and various modes are clearly becoming increasingly numerous and complex. This characteristic is indicated in table 4–5, which documents the extent of noninternal corporate investment in the U.S. semiconductor industry. Clearly

Table 4–5
Corporate Investments in U.S. Semiconductor Companies

U.S. Semiconductor Company	Corporate Investor	Percentage Ownership[a]	National Base
Advanced Micro Devices	Siemens	20	West Germany
American Microsystems	Robert Bosch	12.5	West Germany
	Borg Warner	12.5	United States
Analog Devices	Standard Oil of Indiana		United States
Electronic Arrays	Nippon Electric		Japan
Exar	Toyo	53	Japan
Fairchild Camera	Schlumberger		Netherlands Antilles
Frontier	Commodore International		Bahamas
Inmos	National Enterprise Board		United Kingdom
Interdesign	Ferranti		United Kingdom
Intersil	Northern Telecom	24	Canada
Litronix	Siemens		West Germany
Maruman IC	Toshiba[b]		Japan
Micropower Systems	Seiko		Japan
Monolithic Memories	Northern Telecom	12.4	Canada
MOS Technology	Commodore International		Bahamas
Mostek	United Technologies		United States
Precision Monolithics	Bourns		United States
SEMI, Inc.	General Tel. & Elec.		United States
Seintech	Signal Companies		United States
Signetics	Philips	Merger	Netherlands
Intel	IBM	13.7	United States
Siliconix	Electronic Engr. of Calif.		United States
	Lucas Industries	24	United Kingdom
Solid State Scientific	VDO Adolf Schindling	25	West Germany
Spectronics	Honeywell		United States
Supertex	Investment Group		Hong Kong
Synertek	Honeywell		United States
Unitrode	Signal Companies		United States
Western Digital	Emerson Electric		United States
Zilog	Exxon		United States

Sources: Morgan Stanley Electronics, December 31, 1979; Dataquest, Inc., January 1979, for percentage of ownership; the consulting group BA Asia Ltd., 1980, for Maruman IC data; *Wall Street Journal,* August 17, 1983, p. 10; U.S. Congress, Joint Economic Committee, *International Competition in Advanced Industrial Sectors: Trade and Development in the Semiconductor Industry*, Study Prepared for the Joint Economic Committee (Washington, D.C.: U.S. Government Printing Office, February 18, 1982), pp. 40, 41.
[a]No percentage indicates 100 percent (wholly owned) or presumed to be wholly owned in the absence of data.
[b]Purchased in 1980 from Mansel KK, pending litigation.

the linkages—both domestic and international—between mode I and mode II firms and between various mode II firms are increasing and becoming an important part of corporate strategy.

A fascinating and important example of this pattern is IBM's equity investment in a leading state-of-the-art semiconductor company, Intel. In December 1982, IBM announced that it would buy a 12 percent stake in Intel for $250 million, which it did in February 1983. In August 1983, IBM boosted its position in Intel to about 13.7 percent. Most observers believed IBM was doing more than making a good financial investment; it appeared to be taking strategic action to protect its and the U.S. technological base by strengthening a key U.S. innovator in semiconductors. IBM had no intention of letting the United States lose semiconductors as the country had lost, say, consumer electronics. Furthermore Intel was already a key outside supplier to IBM, with IBM accounting for about 13 percent of Intel's 1981 revenue.[22]

The same trend is increasingly manifested in the personal computer industry. A dramatic development in the personal computer occurred with the entrance of IBM (table 4–3.) The firm quickly captured a huge market share, particularly in the business market. A sample survey of thirty-seven *Fortune* 500 companies found that 95 percent reported that the primary personal computer hardware to be IBM PC, PC/XT, or PC compatible.[23]

Even more remarkable than IBM's market success in personal computers is the novel way in which IBM structured itself to enter the personal computer industry. The firm went outside its mainstream R&D processes to establish an independent business unit (IBU) for work on personal computers. The IBU worked separately from the rest of IBM and created a totally different kind of product and product strategy. The IBM PC would use off-the-shelf components and an outside operating system, MS–DOS. Also, its operating system would be open so that third parties could develop software. Finally, instead of solely selling through its own sales force, IBM would also sell through retail outlets.[24] In effect, IBM had created a mode I-like organization within its overall mode II structure.

More generally, an increasing number of key linkages, spanning modes, countries, and organizations, were taking place in the personal computer industry (figure 4–3). AT&T had bought 25 percent of Olivetti, and Olivetti quickly produced an IBM-compatible machine for AT&T to sell beginning in July 1984. AT&T also has contracted with Convergent Technologies, a small firm in Silicon Valley, to produce a Unix-based personal computer.[25] Meanwhile, the Japanese ceramics firm Kyocera was building highly successful lap computers for Radio Shack-Tandy, NEC, and Olivetti.[26] Sanyo was building a lap computer for Mitsui.[27] Finally, Apple has Sharp making its flat LCD display for its trim IIc computer. In addition, Apple is said to be negotiating with Canon to market Apple's Macintosh computer in Japan. Both firms are working on software for Macintosh for the Japanese market.[28]

The current machine tool industry, which as late as 1980 appeared to be a stagnant sector, is also exhibiting many of the new patterns in technology strategy that are in view in other sectors. In fact, if the definition of machine tools is broadened to encompass manufacturing process technology as a whole rather than just metal bending, then the industry is now experiencing a major restructuring. The development of software, computer-aided design

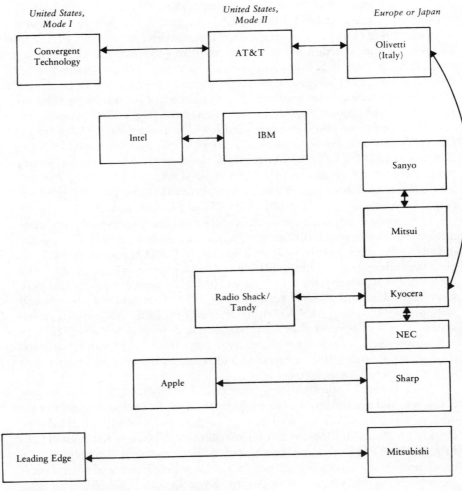

Sources: Various issues of *InfoWorld*, 1983–1984.

Figure 4–3. Selected List of Linkages in the Personal Computer Industry, 1983–1984

and manufacturing, robots, systems, and ultimately full-scale factory automation is dramatically changing what had seemingly been a stagnant sunset industry into a technologically vigorous one. The industry is becoming more complex in terms of proliferating "strategic groups"[29] and is attracting a whole set of new entrants, from new mode I-type ventures to establish large manufacturing firms like General Electric, Westinghouse, and IBM (figure 4–4).[30]

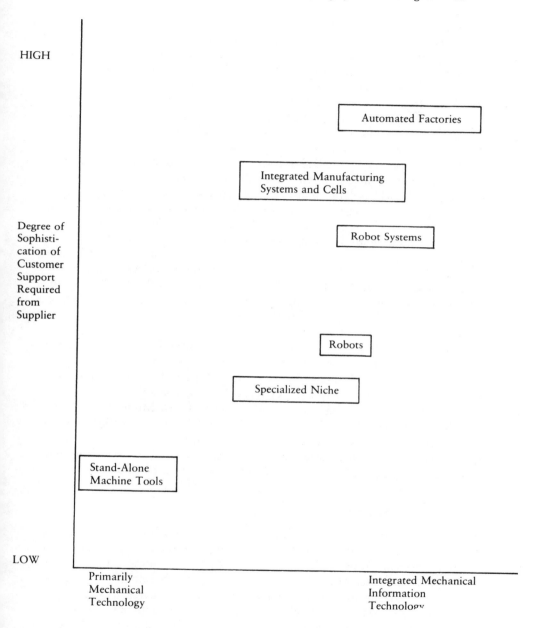

National Research Council, *The U.S. Machine Tool Industry and the Defense Industrial Base* (Washington, D.C.: National Academy Press, 1983), p. 25.

Figure 4–4. Strategic Groups of the Machine Tool Industry

But as in the other modern technology-intensive industries that have been examined, the current pattern of technology strategy in the manufacturing process technology industry is also one of increasing blurring of the distinctions between the various private-sector modes of technological innovation and of establishing linkages between modes and firms.

These trends can be seen by focusing on one strategic group within the whole manufacturing process technology industry, robotics.[31] We find a technology-based industry on the verge of a probable takeoff. In the early 1980s, the rate of growth of the U.S. robotics industry began to increase significantly. But the whole U.S. effort to develop robotics until about 1980 was fragmented, limited to a few players, and it lacked the support of crucial stakeholders, such as large industrial concerns and the government. Until recently, practically all robotics activity in the United States was concentrated in a few companies, with two firms, Unimation and Cincinnati Milacron, together accounting for a U.S. market share of over 50 percent through 1982 (figure 4–5). Like machine tools, robotics in the United States was in the industrial R&D backwater and, except for Cincinnati Milacron and a few small firms, was largely a low-priority R&D item until the 1980s. The involvement of large manufacturing enterprises and corporations with strong capabilities in the key technologies and often huge captive markets was practically nonexistent until the 1980s.

By 1980, however, the situation was beginning to change. The growth rate of U.S. robot sales was accelerating, and, just as significant, a whole set of new entrants had appeared. The new entrants are not primarily new start-up ventures (table 4–6). Instead they represent large, established enterprises with strong manufacturing and/or technological skills. Modes I and II are now fully represented. In addition, suddenly a rich array of linkages is being established through licensing agreements, joint ventures, and mergers and acquisitions, many of them international in character (table 4–7). The new technology strategy context has arrived in the U.S. robotics industry.

Biotechnology Industry

The biotechnology industry is another type of technology-based industry.[32] It is young and global. Almost from the start, it has possessed a full set of complex strategic relationships. All forms of modern technology strategy are represented in this sector in abundance. The major U.S. small firms, such as Genentech, Biogen, and Cetus, have equity and/or research linkages with several large corporations throughout the world. A number of major large corporations, such as Eli Lilly, Monsanto, and even to a limited degree DuPont, in addition to sizable internal R&D activity, are actively linked in diverse ways with other firms. These intertwining relationships are global in nature, as shown in figure 4–6, which illustrates U.S.–Japanese strategic connections.

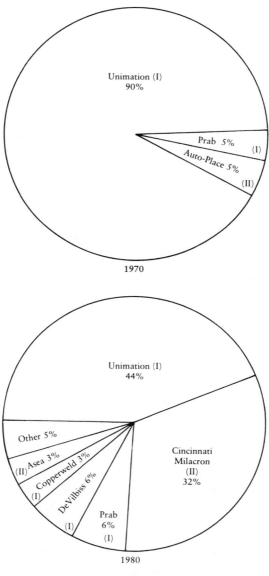

Unimation (I)
90%

Prab 5% (I)

Auto-Place 5%

(II)

1970

Unimation (I)
44%

Other 5%

(II) Asea 3%

Copperweld 3%

(I)

DeVilbiss 6%

Cincinnati
Milacron
(II)
32%

Prab
6%
(I)

1980

U.S. SALES, $90 MILLION

Source: L. Conigliaro, in *Robotics Newsletter*, no. 9 (1982).

Note: Symbols in parentheses refer to mode of innovation.

Figure 4–5. U.S. Robotics Industry Sales and Market Share

Table 4–6
Market Share of U.S.-Based Robot Vendors, 1980–1983
(percentage)

Vendor	1980	1981	1982	1983
Unimation	44.4	43.8	32.1	22.8
Cincinnati Milacron	32.2	32.2	21.0	16.2
DeVilbiss	5.5	4.2	7.4	6.7
Asea Inc.	2.8	5.8	8.7	7.2
Prab Robots Inc.	6.1	5.3	4.2	4.2
Cybotech			1.4	2.3
Copperweld Robotics	3.3	2.3	2.3	1.8
Automatix	0.4	1.9	4.2	7.6
Advanced Robotics Corp.	1.9	0.5	3.5	3.2
Mordson	0.8	1.6	2.5	2.5
Thermwood		0.6	1.6	1.4
Bendix			1.4	2.3
GCA Industrial Systems			1.0	2.9
IBM			0.7	3.0
GE			0.9	1.1
Westinghouse			0.4	1.5
U.S. Robots			0.6	1.5
Graco			0.6	1.5
Mobot	0.9	0.4	0.8	0.8
GM/Fanuc			1.5	3.0
American Robot				0.6
Textron				0.3
Nova Robotics				0.3
Control Automation			0.1	0.3
Machine Intelligence				1.1
Intelledex				0.6
Other	1.7	1.3	1.5	1.7

Source: L. Conigliaro, in *Robotics Newsletter*, no. 9 (1982).

Blending of the Two Paradigms as Seen at the Firm Level

The blending of the two technology strategy paradigms is also supported by data at the firm level. A recent study examined the changes in technology strategy of the U.S. large corporations that spent $80 million or more on R&D in 1983.[33] The data were collected from public reports in the *Wall Street Journal* in 1978 and 1983 and from in-depth interviews.

Between 1978 and 1983 there was a significant increase in the use of a variety of approaches for technology planning, development, and acquisition (tables 4–8 and 4–9). Furthermore, the external-oriented methods have become especially prevalent. Finally, technology strategy is clearly now a multilevel and multifaceted activity (table 4–10). However, there was considerably less enthusiasm expressed by managers in the large technology-intensive corporations who were interviewed for predicting that all of these

Table 4–7
Interfirm Linkages in the U.S. Robotics Industry, 1983

Licensing Agreements

License	Licensor
Kawasaki Heavy Ind. (Japan)	Unimation
RN Eurobotics (Belgium)	Arab
Can-Eng. Mfg. (Canada)	Arab
Murata Machinery (Japan)	Arab
Binks (U.K.)	Thermwood
Cyclomatic Ind.	Thermwood
Diddle Graphics Co.	Thermwood
DeVilbiss	Trallfa (Norway)
Nordson	Taskawa (Japan)
Admiral Equip. Co.	Taskawa (Japan)
Bendix	
Automatix	Hitachi (Japan)
General Electric	Hitachi (Japan)
Interred	Hitachi (Japan)
Graco	Nolaug (Norway)
United Technologies	Nimak (W. Germany)
RCA	Dainichi Kiko (Japan)
IBM	Sankyo Seiki (Japan)
General Electric	DEA (Italy)
General Electric	Volkswagen (W. Germany)
Westinghouse	Ollivetti (Italy)
Westinghouse	Hisubishi Electric (Japan)
Westinghouse	Komatsu (Japan)
Lloyd Tool and Mfg.	Jobs Robots (Italy)

Joint Ventures

Joint Venture	Parents
Unimation	Condac, Pullman Corp.
GMF Robotics, Inc.	General Motors, Fanuc
Cybotech	Renault, Randsburg Industries
Int'l. Machine Intell.	Machine Intelligence, Yaskawa
Graco Robotics	Graco Inc., Edon Finishing

Mergers and Acquisitions

Subsidiary	Parent
Unimation	Westinghouse
PAR Systems	GCA
U.S. Robots	Square D. Corp
Copperweld Robotics (formerly Auto-Place)	Copperweld Corp.

Source: David Schatz, "The Strategic Evolution of the Robotics Industry" (Master's thesis, MIT, 1983), p. 119.

newer approaches would continue to grow in use during the next decade. Indeed in what may indicate an important trend, they tended to anticipate a stabilization or consolidation in the range of technology strategy techniques that would be employed by large corporations in the future.

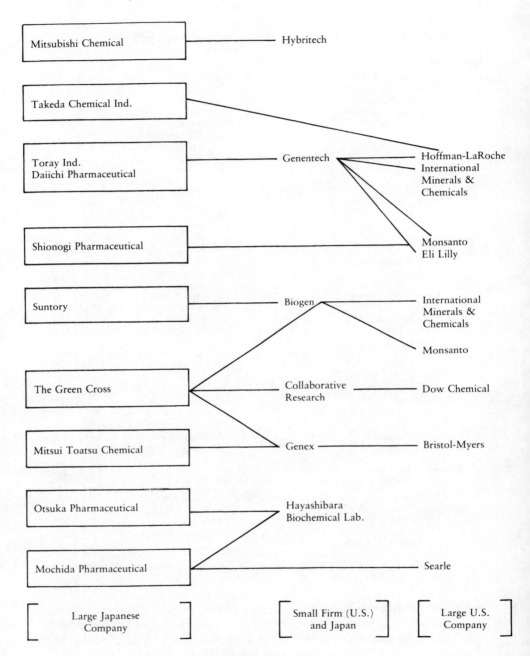

Figure 4–6. Relationships between U.S. and Japanese Biochemical Companies

Table 4–8
Technology Development Activity of Selected Sixteen Firms Spending over
$80 Million on R&D
(number of publicly reported major instances of technology strategy
activities)

Approaches for Technology Development and/or Acquisition	1978	1983
R&D laboratory		1
Internal venturing	0	4
Contracted research	1	7
Acquisition of firms	10	18
Licensee	5	9
Joint venture	1	16
Equity participation	0	8
Other	5	14
Totals	21	72

Sources: *Wall Street Journal Index*, 1978 and 1983. John Friar and Mel Horwitch, *The Current Transformation of Technology Strategy: The Attempt to Create Multiple Avenues for Innovative within the Large Corporation*, MIT Sloan School Working Paper 1618–84 (December 20, 1984).

Conclusion

Private-sector technology strategy is undergoing a major transformation in the United States and probably worldwide. The earlier context, in the first phase of the postwar era, had as one of its most salient features the coexistence

Table 4–9
Directional Change in Relative Significance for the Eight Approaches for Ten of the Sixteen Companies in Table 4–9

	1978–1984		
Approach	Increase in Relative Significance	No Change in Relative Significance	Decrease in Relative Significance
R&D laboratories	0	5	5
Internal venturing	4	6	0
Contracted research	2	8	0
Acquisition of firms	6	3	1
Licensee	4	5	1
Joint venture	5	5	0
Equity participation	3	6	1
Other	3	7	0

Source: Personal interviews. John Friar and Mel Horwitch, *The Current Transformation of Technology Strategy: The Attempt to Create Multiple Avenues for Innovative within the Large Corporation*, MIT Sloan School Working Paper 1618-84 (December 20, 1984).

Table 4–10
Location of Technology Planning Activity

Location	A	B	C	D	E	F[a]	G	H	I	J
Headquarters	X	X	X	X			X	X	X	X
Group				X						
	X		X							
Division				X	X					
Strategic business unit	X	X	X	X			X		X	X
Separate technical planning	X									
Laboratory	X		X	X						
Other										X

Source: Personal interviews.
Source: John Friar and Mel Horwitch, *The Current Transformation of Technology Strategy: The Attempt to Create Multiple Avenues for Innovative within the Large Corporation*, MIT Sloan School Working Paper 1618-84 (December 20, 1984).
[a]Would not divulge information.

of two very different paradigms for private-sector technology strategy: mode I, the entrepreneurial, small, high-technology firm, and mode II, the R&D process in large-scale, multidivision, multiproduct, and multimarket corportion. Although there are some important common characteristics, generally the two modes were very different from one another.

Another major feature of this earlier postwar phase was the extreme importance of mode I behavior. In both the semiconductor and personal computer industries, risk-taking entrepreneurship was perhaps the key engine of change. The early postwar machine tool industry shows the sorry state in which a sector can find itself when mode I activity is missing.

But mode I by itself may not be sufficient. Appropriate and early mode II involvement in both semiconductors and personal computers seemed to be important for sustained innovation and long-term commercial success. The contrast between the total commercial failure of the first wave of the early personal computer industry, when only mode I firms participated, and the more successful second wave when both mode I and mode II firms played important roles, is especially instructive. The early postwar machine tool industry provides a useful negative example of the stagnant conditions that can develop when vigorous mode II practices are also lacking.

The current transformation of technology strategy seems to be a general one. Similar patterns are evolving in all four industries that have been examined, regardless of their different historical patterns or technologies. These trends are also seen at the firm level. As technology now becomes a strategic variable, a whole and complex array of trade-offs, relationships, and linkages has to be managed. One way of conceptualizing these trade-offs is presented in figure 4–7.

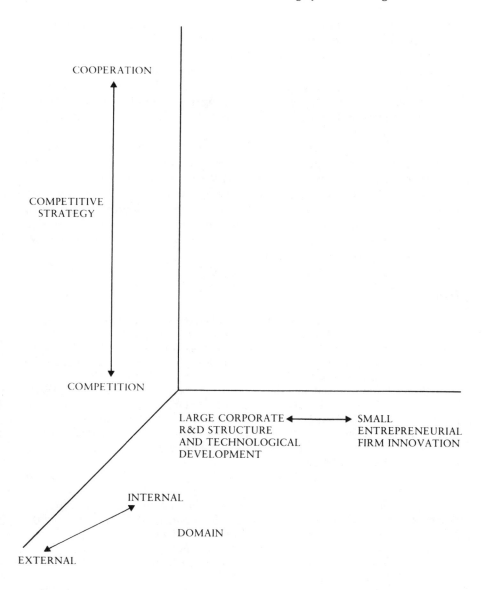

COOPERATION

COMPETITIVE
STRATEGY

COMPETITION

LARGE CORPORATE ←——→ SMALL
R&D STRUCTURE   ENTREPRENEURIAL
AND TECHNOLOGICAL   FIRM INNOVATION
DEVELOPMENT

INTERNAL

DOMAIN

EXTERNAL

Source: John Friar and Mel Horwitch, *The Current Transformation of Technology Strategy: The Attempt to Create Multiple Avenues for Innovative within the Large Corporation*, MIT Sloan School Working Paper 1618-84 (December 20, 1984).

Figure 4–7. Elements of Modern Technology Strategy

Modern technology-intensive corporations are making technology strategy decisions along three dimensions: competition versus cooperation (competitive strategy); internal versus external (domain); and traditional R&D organizations (for example, the industrial laboratory) versus decentralized entrepreneurial units (structure). The appropriate blend of trade-offs along these dimensions is one of the major challenges in technology strategy today, which is a manifestation of the current blending of the two paradigms.

Beginning in the mid-1970s there was a tremendous flurry of experimentation, creativity, and variety in technology strategy. The earlier and simpler situation of primarily separate spheres of technology development in the private sector is probably gone; however, there are indicators that there may also be limits on this exciting wave of managerial development. Complexity may be too great. The desire to internalize or to gain total proprietary control may strengthen. Perhaps by the 1990s a backlash may develop. But even then, with some consolidation, technology strategy will remain more varied and more complex than it was two decades ago.

Notes

1. The critics of the 1980s include Robert Hayes and William Abernathy, "Managing Our Way to Economic Decline," *Harvard Business Review* (July–August 1980). For an overview of the literature that deals with the relationship between technology and corporate strategy, see Alan M. Kantrow, "The Strategy–Technology Connection," *Harvard Business Review* (July–August 1980).

2. See Boston Consulting Group (BCG), *Perspectives on Experience* (Boston: BCG, 1967); R.V. Buzzell, B.T. Gale, and R.G.M. Sultan, "Market Share—Key to Profitability," *Harvard Business Review* (January–February 1975); P. Haspeslagh, "Portfolio Planning: Uses and Limits," *Harvard Business Review* (January–February 1982).

3. For the external-oriented strategy literature, which uses very different approaches, see Michael Porter, *Competitive Strategy* (New York: Free Press, 1980) and R. Edward Freeman, *Strategic Management: A Stakeholder Approach* (Marshfield, Mass.: Pitman, 1984).

4. For an emphasis on the need for strategy to be supported by internal structures, systems, and processes, see Alfred D. Chandler, Jr., *Strategy and Structure* (Cambridge: MIT Press, 1962) and Jay Galbraith and Daniel A. Nathanson, *Strategy Implementation: The Role of Structure and Process* (St. Paul, Minn.: West Publishing, 1978).

5. See BCG, *Perspectives*; Buzzell, Gale, and Sultan, "Market Share"; Porter, *Competitive Strategy*; Haspeslagh, "Portfolio Planning."

6. Chester Barnard, *The Functions of Executive* (Cambridge: Harvard University Press, 1968); Kenneth R. Andrews, *The Concept of Corporate Strategy* (Homewood, Ill.: Richard D. Irwin, 1980); Thomas Peters and Robert Waterman, *In Search of Excellence* (New York: Harper & Row, 1982); Freeman, *Strategic Management*; J. Brian Quinn, *Strategies for Change: Logical Incrementalism* (Homewood, Ill.: Richard D. Irwin, 1980).

7. For the process of technological innovation, see Donald G. Marquis, "The Anatomy of Successful Innovations," *Innovation*, no. 7 (1969); *Success and Failure in*

Industrial Innovation: Report on Project Shappho (London: Centre for the Study of Industrial Innovation, n.d.); R. Rothwell et al., "SAPPHO Updated: Project SAPPHO Phase II," *Research Policy* 3 (1974); and James Utterback, "The Process of Technological Innovation within the Firm," *Academy of Management Journal* (March 1971):75–88. For the technology–organization structure discussion, see J. Woodward, *Industrial Organization: Theory and Practice* (London: Oxford University Press, 1965); D. Hickson, D.S. Pugh, and D. Pheysey, "Operations Technology and Organizational Structure: An Empirical Reappraisal," *Administrative Science Quarterly* 14 (1969):378–396; and G.G. Stanfield, Technology and Organization Structure as Theoretical Categories," *Administrative Science Quarterly* 21 (1976):489–493. For the role of technology in the international product life cycle, see Louis T. Wells, Jr., "International Trade: The Product Life Cycle Approach," in Louis T. Wells, Jr., ed., *The Product Life Cycle and International Trade* (Boston: Division of Research, 1972), p. 3–33.

8. For necessary interactions with the market and with the user, see Donald G. Marquis, "The Anatomy of Successful Innovations," *Innovation,* no. 7 (1969); *Success and Failure in Industrial Innovation;* Rothwell et al., "SPPHO Updated"; and Eric Von Hippel, "The Dominant Role of Users in the Scientific Instrument Innovation Process," *Research Policy* 5 (1976). For discussions about the need for champions, entrepreneurs, and technology-familiar managers, see Donald A. Schon, "Champions for Radical New Inventions," *Harvard Business Review* (March–April 1963); Schon, *Technology and Change* (New York: Delacorte, 1967); Edward B. Roberts, "Entrepreneurship and Technology," *Research Management* (July 1968); Edward B. Roberts, "Generating Effective Corporate Innovation," *Technology Review* (October–November 1977); and Robert Hayes and William Abernathy, "Managing Our Way to Economic Decline," *Harvard Business Review* (July–August 1980).

9. Mel Horwitch and C.K. Prahalad, "Managing Technological Innovation—Three Ideal Modes," *Sloan Management Review* (Winter 1976).

10. Christopher Freeman, *The Economics of Industrial Innovation* (Cambridge: MIT Press, 1982), chap. 8.

11. For a history of the early semiconductor industry, see John E. Tilton, *International Diffusion of Technology: The Case of Semiconductors* (Washington, D.C.: Brookings Institution, 1971), and Ernest Braun and Stuart MacDonald, *Revolution in Miniature: The History and Impact of Semiconductor Electronics* (Cambridge: Cambridge University Press, 1978).

12. Mel Horwitch, "Changing Patterns for Corporate Strategy and Technology Management: The Rise of the Semiconductor and Biotechnology Industries" (paper presented at the Mitsubishi Bank Foundation Conference on Business Strategy and Technical Innovations, Ito City, Japan, March 26–29, 1983); Mel Horwitch and Kiyonori Sakikabara, *The Changing Strategy-Technology Relationship in Technology-Related Industries: A Comparison of the United States and Japan,* MIT Sloan School Working Paper 1533–84 (January 5, 1984).

13. Tilton, *International Diffusion of Technology,* pp. 49–55.

14. Personal interviews.

15. Tilton, *International Diffusion of Technology,* p. 51; personal interviews.

16. Information on the early history of the U.S. personal computer industry comes from the following sources: Paul Freiberger and Michael Swaine, *Fire in the Valley* (Berkeley, Calif.: Osborne/McGraw-Hill, 1984); Gary N. Farner, "A Competitive

Analysis of the Personal Computer Industry" (master's thesis, MIT, 1982); and Deborah F. Schreiber, "The Strategic Evolution of the Personal Computer Industry" (master's thesis, MIT, 1983).

17. For the key role of the machine tool industry in U.S. business history, see Nathan Rosenberg, "Technological Change in the Machine Tool Industry, 1840–1910," *Journal of Economic History* 23 (December 1963).

18. For a comprehensive industry analysis of the traditional U.S. machine tool industry, see National Research Council, *The U.S. Machine Tool Industry and the Defense Industrial Base* (Washington, D.C.: National Academy Press, 1983), chap. 2.

19. For robotics, see Horwitch and Sakikabara, *Changing Technology–Strategy Relationsip.*

20. "The Technological Strategy of 3M: Start More Little Businesses and More Little Businessmen," *Innovation,* no. 5 (1969); *Texas Instruments* (A) 9-476-122 (Boston, Mass.: Intercollegiate Case Clearinghouse, 1976); "Exxon's Next Prey: IBM and Xerox," *Business Week,* April 28, 1980; Edward B. Roberts, "New Ventures for Corporate Growth," *Harvard Business Review* (July–August 1980).

21. For examples of those reappraisals and revisions, see Raymond Vernon, "The Product Life Cycle Hypothesis in a New International Environment," *Oxford Bulletin of Economics and Statistics* 41, no. 4 (November 1979):255–267, and John H. Dunning, "Explaining Changing Patterns of International Production: In Defense of the Eclectic Theory," *Oxford Bulletin of Economics and Statistics* 41, no. 4 (November 1979):269–295.

22. "IBM and Intel Link Up to Fend Off Japan," *Business Week,* January 10, 1983, pp. 96–97; *Wall Street Journal,* August 17, 1983, p. 10.

23. "Microcomputer Use Doubles in Past Year in Leading Organizations," Research and Planning, Inc. press release, circa June 1984.

24. "Personal Computers and the Winner Is IBM," *Business Week,* October 3, 1983, pp. 76–95; Lawrence J. Curran and Richard S. Shuford, "IBM's Estridge," *Byte* (November 1983):88–97; Vrian Camenker, "The Making of the IBM PC," *Byte* (November 1983):254–256.

25. "AT&T Introduces Personal Computer," *New York Times,* June 27, 1984, p. D5; "AT&T's Long-Awaited Micro," *InfoWorld,* July 16, 1984, pp. 46–47.

26. "A Real Computer on Your Lap?" *InfoWorld,* April 2, 1984, p. 13.

27. "Kaypro Lap-Size Portable to Run IBM PC Programs," *InfoWorld,* March 26, 1984, p. 14.

28. *InfoWorld,* May 14, 1984.

29. For a general discussion of strategic groups, see Michael E. Porter, *Competitive Strategy* (New York: Free Press, 1980), chap. 7.

30. For the restructuring and broadening of the machine tool industry, see National Research Council, *U.S. Machine Tool Industry,* chap. 2.

31. See Horwitch and Sakikabara, *Changing Technology–Strategy Relationship.*

32. For a comprehensive discussion of the biotechnology industry, see ibid.

33. For a comprehensive discussion of these findings, see John Friar and Mel Horwitch, *The Current Transformation of Technology Strategy: The Attempt to Create Multiple Avenues for Innovation Within the Large Corporation,* MIT Sloan School Working Paper 1618-84 (December 20, 1984).

5
Frameworks to Increase Trade

W.H.C. Simmonds

C urrent trading difficulties were not resolved at the 1978 Bonn summit
conference, and few new approaches are discernible. Contrary to the
goal of the summit, in practice governments are competing to gain for
themselves, shifting losses elsewhere if possible. Masanori Moritani (1983)
has aptly termed this the "all-take, no-give" attitude. There is concern that if
this sink-or-swim approach is pushed too far, adjustments will be made but
at costs that may entail long-term difficulties or unforeseen consequences.
The purpose of this chapter is to propose one way of breaking out of this box
by changing our perception of trade and thus acquiring new options. Such an
approach may enable the full potential for trade between two nations to be
estimated, something not apparently possible at present.

Proposal

Trade is usually discussed within either the framework of the GATT (General
Agreement on Tariffs and Trade) rules or within the free trade concept of
economics. Neither is adequate. As Cantley (1981) has pointed out, attempts
by one nation to improve its internal affairs by stimulating or restricting demand creates a prisoners' dilemma for a second country that trades with it,
leading to a zero-sum situation. On the other hand, the free trade approach
omits consideration of power, cultures, and histories and to the extent that it
rests on comparative advantage has been shown to be incomplete; comparative
advantages can and are being changed, notably in the Pacific Rim region.

As Iacocca (1985) emphasized in his recent speech to the American
Chamber of Commerce in Tokyo, "Trade has to be a win–win situation."
One step toward this is to change the framework within which we look at
trade. The kind of framework needed is one that does not see trade simply as
a transaction between two isolated nations but rather as one that encompasses both nations (similar to the approach being adopted by Chrysler and
Mitsubishi, for example). This framework frees the mind from the roadblocks

of single-nation thinking and attitudes by looking at the market, production, and investment potential of their combination first. Obviously this will make little difference in many cases—Canada has resources, and Japan manufacturers—but could have a significantly beneficial effect in others. There are also trade items in which both countries want to be first, have the first plant, and control the development. This leads to distinctive competition and the likelihood of delay or stalemate. By looking at the market as a whole, however, the development sequence for some profitable business may become clearer; cooperation by some companies across the two countries may be beneficial to both. Bit by bit, item by item, a less nationally focused, more realistic approach can develop, in the manner proposed by the Business Council on National Issues for Canada–U.S. trade (d'Aquino, 1984).

Technological advance is a second reason for changing our trade framework. Existing GATT rules do not deal adequately with service industries, which are rapidly expanding. Japan, the United States, and Canada have recommended that negotiations to update these rules start in 1986, but France is opposed. Change is inevitable, however. As major new technologies emerge, they always require changes to and enlargement of national and international frameworks; examples are the histories of the steam engine, the railroad, the car, electric power, and radio.

A third factor compelling us to change the way we think about trade stems from changes in the nature and structure of companies as the consumer society of yesterday gives way to the information–knowledge–experience society of tomorrow. These companies are not so much international or multinational as transnational, shipping goods among operations in many countries. Governments are becoming more aware of such footloose firms and intercompany trade and of the magnitude of this trend and its effects.

Finally, by looking at the maximum possible trade when the markets, productive capacity, and investment of two countries are pooled, an estimate of their maximum trade potential can be obtained. Is, for example, the $11 billion Canada–Japan trade close to its potential or, say, only half of it? If the former, no action is required. If the latter, both nations and both governments have incentives to encourage more trade since both have problems of employment, growth, deficit, welfare, and ageing to solve.

As Bateson (1972) has pointed out, we all use psychological frameworks that include some things and exclude others. Similarly, when trade is perceived within too narrow a framework, opportunities are missed. The trick is to enlarge the framework sufficiently to release energies and restore growth. The result will not be a millennium, but it can and should lead to a shift from zero-sum behaviors toward a more win–win situation. Moreover, the first step—looking at the total market, production, and investment situation of two countries—can be done now and does not have to wait for the negotiation or renegotiation of new treaties. Initial explorations can be made using national econometric and international trade models such as Akira Onishi's (1983) FUGI macroeconomic international trade model. Two examples of trade framework creation and enlargement follow.

Transatlantic Submarine Cable

The retroactive technology assessment study of the transatlantic submarine cable by Vary Coates and Bernard Finn (1979) reveals the interplay of entrepreneurship and technological advance, the enlargement of government frameworks, and the resulting benefits. It began in 1854 when a U.S. entrepreneur, Cyrus Field, succeeded in applying short-distance cable technology to a long-distance cable that would span the Atlantic. Both of Field's attempts to bring his idea to fruition failed. At this point the British government stepped in and constructed a different framework for what would become a public monopoly. Top scientists established the more stringent quality control needed for long-distance cables, manufacture was standardized, financing organized, and the world's largest ship commandeered to lay the cable under rigorous conditions. Success was achieved in 1866.

As had been anticipated, the results were staggering. Owners, not ship captains, were now in control of their cargoes. Price and volume movements were known at once on both sides of the Atlantic. International trade became routinized. Arbitrage and futures trading developed rapidly. New York's status as a financial center rose immeasurably. But the monopolies of the merchant houses were eroded, middlemen lost their influence, and competition in world markets increased enormously.

At the same time, cooperation also increased in the exchange of news and information, and a new balance evolved. Increased competition and trade resulted, and greater wealth accrued to most. Without consciously seeking to do so, business and government had helped each other, but with one unforseen twist: the cable that brought commercial wealth also centralized war making. Fifty years later, the centralized war machines slid inevitably into World War I after the assassination of an archduke.

Marshall Plan

The largest and best example of trade framework enlargement is the Marshall Plan at the end of World War II. The United States took the daring and unusual decision to put both its allies and its former enemies back on their feet as quickly as possible. The institutions that were to implement the plan were set up with the cooperation of the other nations involved: GATT, the World Bank, the International Monetary Fund (IMF), and the Bretton Woods agreement on exchange rates. These clear-cut and mutually accepted rules created for the first time a free world international trading area. It lasted for some twenty-five years and gave the world the highest rates of economic growth ever experienced. War technologies served as the foundation for civilian technology advances, and competition grew as nation after nation got back on its feet. The highest return was to the United States itself, where the multinational company was developed to take advantage of world rather than national markets. U.S. multinational corporations controlled about half of total nonagricultural trade among nonsocialist countries (Muller 1977). Subsequent events in South Vietnam also showed what might have happened if the United States had acted unilaterally or in the punitive manner adopted by the Allies after World War I. The pockets of communism that existed in France and Italy might have coalesced if economic conditions had deteriorated sufficiently. The profoundly farsighted decision of the United States prevented this.

Japanese Example

Japan provides another but quite different example of the evolution of trade frameworks, born in this case out of necessity. In 1945, Japan was in more serious condition than Europe. Two-thirds of a million of its inhabitants had been killed in air raids, food was short, and industry was virtually at a standstill (Reischauer 1977). There was an urgent need for government, business, and labor to set priorities and get Japan back to some semblance of normal conditions as quickly as possible.

Aided by the Marshall Plan, the Japanese accomplished this by what Kikushi (1983) calls hard work and "leg" (staying) power. The basic plan was to use the United States as a working textbook for Japan's reindustrialization, termed by Yamauchi (1983) the "leader-follower relationship." Implementation was facilitated by the movement of Japan's skilled workers from military industries into civilian ones. Aeronautical engineers moved into the automotive industry, military engineers into construction and railroads, naval engineers into shipbuilding, and optical experts into cameras and precision measurement.

The Japanese made two important business discoveries: that personal use markets could be differentiated from household and family markets (notably in electronics) and that product quality could be used as a competitive element separate from price. (Contrary to popular belief, the Japanese are and always have been quality conscious.) From this background, they applied themselves vigorously and with great thoroughness to the business of catching up. As Gold (1978) has documented in detail for the steel industry, they succeeded.

When the catch-up process began in 1945, Japan was technologically deficient. Technology had to be acquired and put in place, and exports had to be developed to buy raw materials, energy and food. Moritani (1983) recently summarized these developments in his theory of progress in trade and technology (figure 5–1). The horizontal axis in figure 5–1 represents technology, which can be imported, neutral (no imports or exports), or exported, and the

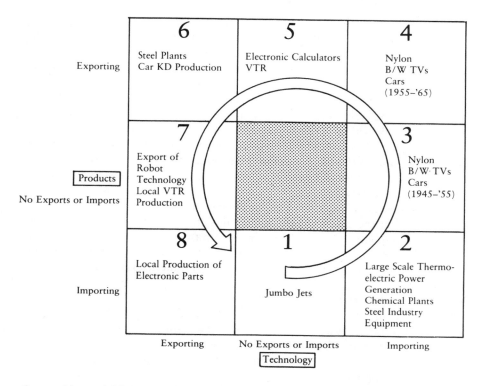

Source: Masanori Moritani, *Advanced Technology and the Japanese Contribution* (Tokyo: Nomura Securities Co., 1983). Reproduced with permission.

Figure 5–1. Theory of Progress of Trade and Technology

vertical axis represents the products of that technology, which can also be imported, neutral, or exported. The overall direction of Japan's postwar development is indicated by the counterclockwise arrow.

Like other countries, Japan imported, and still imports, products like large aircraft with their contained technology (although it now manufactures some components) (stage 1). As soon as they could, however, the Japanese adopted the policy of importing the products and their associated technologies at the same time and then set about producing these products. In 1952–1953 their priorities were for large-scale thermal power plants and chemical and steel plants (stage 2). This led on to stage 3 in which only the technology was licensed, as in the cases of black and white television sets, transistors, and Toray's license for nylon. The automotive companies signed agreements with car companies in other countries for the same purpose. Once international competitiveness had been reached, exporting from Japan began (cars in 1955, black and white televisions in 1957) (stage 4).

As the original licenses began to run out, Japanese companies became freer to develop and export their own new products, such as the Sharp calculator in 1964 and videotape recorders in 1975 (stage 5). The next step was to export both the product and its associated technology (stage 6, the opposite of stage 2). Exports of steel plants began with the Usimas steelworks sale to Brazil in 1960, followed by the overseas production of knockdown cars. In stage 7 only the technology is exported. Rising exports of technology finally overtook imports of technology in 1973 and by 1980 exceeded the latter by a factor of 2.7 on a new contract basis (Abbeglen and Etori 1983; Moritani 1983; Yamauchi 1983). A similar picture can be given of technological development in other Western nations, but these have taken place over a longer period of time.

Japan has now caught up with the leader, the United States, in most areas of technology; the main exceptions are in defense or defense-related areas. Japanese companies are therefore adapting to the consequences of becoming leaders themselves. Narusawa (1984) has documented the changes made by the Japanese in their financial structures and in the financial instruments used. Their reliance on Japanese banks has been drastically reduced; there is less indirect internal financing and more direct and foreign financing. Moritani (1983) sums up Japanese progress to date: "Technology is the lifeblood of trade." He might have added that the heart that is pumping the blood is competition: competition between Japanese companies for first place in the Japanese market and the extension of this competition into world markets.

Japanese companies, however, have been hesitant to advance to stage 8, where U.S. companies have been for some time. Stage 8 is the point at which a technology is exported and the exporting country imports back the products made with its own technology. Moritani notes the proclivity of Japanese industry to make everything in Japan, but he believes wiser counsel will prevail on two counts: by allowing Japanese resources to be deployed more efficiently overseas, a surplus is created that becomes available to assist Japan to move more quickly into the coming information–knowledge economy and society (Masudam 1975, 1983); and second, "the best course will be for Japan to bear its share of responsibility for overall world security not by a build-up of its military power but through its technology" (Economic Planning Agency 1983).

Although the hardships overcome have unified government, industry, labor, and the people of Japan, the younger generation has begun to question some aspects of this unity. Japan currently faces a more formidable combination of simultaneous changes than those facing any Western nation: continuing dependence on imported resources, energy, and food; problems in world trade; leadership in technology; changes in education; becoming the world's financial center in the Far East (internationalizing the yen has immense consequences for Japan's internal financial structure and domestic interest rates); social welfare problems posed by the most rapidly ageing society in the industrialized world (along with Sweden); threats to its "mom-and-pop" activities, which support older people; and the move to the information society, which seems to require a redefinition of work for one of the world's hardest-working nations.

Japan's framework for trade must evolve congruently with its changing needs and help to fulfill them. From the rest of the world's point of view, it is highly desirable that the second-largest single market should continue to function well, not only for itself but for the sake of the social and economic success of all (McMillan 1984).

Application of the Moritani Model

Moritani's method of analyzing trade and technology can be used to track changes in the use and development of technologies and their products in other countries, states, and provinces. Since it is an operational analysis (that is, it relates actions to effects), it adds a dimension to conventional analyses based on the Standard Industrial Classification (a nonoperational classification) or on levels of technology (high, medium, low). However, the situation is usually more complex when technological development has taken place over many years. All eight Moritani stages are usually present, as shown in table 5–1 for central Canada.

Stage 1 is the same as in Japan—for example, the import of large aircraft and mainframe computers but not their technologies. Stage 2 shows that Canada imports products like microchips and machinery and some of their technology. Stages 3 and 7, in which technology is imported or exported but no products are exported or imported, appear to be mostly missing in Canada in view of its open markets as compared to Japan. Stage 4 represents

Table 5–1
Moritani Picture of Central Canada

Stage	Technology E	No E/I	I	Products E	No E/I	I	Examples
1		+					Large aircraft
2			+			+	Microchips, machinery, autos
3			+		+		
4			+	+			Autos, subway cars
5		+		+			Candu, snowmobiles
6	+			+			Northern Telecom
7	+				+		
8	+					+	Northern Telecom

Note: E: exports from Canada; I, imports into Canada; no E/I = no exports or imports.

imports of technology and exports of products, of which the Bombardier-Kawasaki Heavy Industries subway cars are an example.

Stage 5 includes Canada's own technology developments, such as the Candu reactor, cobalt 60, Bombardier's snowmobile, and the de Havilland short takeoff and landing aircraft. Stages 6 and 8 reflect the position of companies such as Northern Telecom that do R&D in Canada but have to set up manufacturing facilities in the United States for much the same reasons as Japanese companies have. The position of the automotive industry and parts industry is obviously complex due to the Canada–U.S. auto pact, with both technology and products moving both ways across the border. Developed economies clearly contain a wide variety of technology–product arrangements arising from past competition and from governmental regulations, tariffs, taxes, and other agreements.

Nevertheless, by analyzing a province's trade according to Moritani's eight categories and tracking the changes in them, a picture of that province's use of technology emerges. Does it generate enough technology itself, utilize imported technology successfully, export technology or technology products? The standard for comparison is other provinces or states in similar circumstances. This analysis pins down the good and bad points by relating the technological situation directly to the trade situation.

Canada's Trade in a Wider Framework

The framework proposed here suggests that Canada's trade can be looked at from viewpoints other than the customary ones. Canada's trade with Japan is an example; its growth is shown in table 5–2 (Hay 1983; Canada–Japan Trade Council 1985).

Trade to Japan represented 5.4 percent of Canada's exports; trade to Canada represented 2.8 percent of Japan's exports. Eighty-two percent of

Table 5–2
Canada–Japan Trade
(billions of dollars)

	Canada Exports	Japan Exports	Bilateral Balance	Total Trade
1970	0.81	0.58	0.23	1.39
1975	2.14	1.20	0.94	3.34
1980	4.36	2.80	1.56	7.16
1982	4.57	3.53	1.04	8.10
1983	4.76	4.41	0.35	9.17
1984	5.53	5.47	0.06	11.10

Source: Canada–Japan Trade Council, 1985.

Canadian exports originated in the West, the chief items being coal, softwood lumber, rapeseed, and woodpulp. British Columbia and central Canada, respectively, received 33 percent and 58 percent of Japanese exports, for a total of 91 percent. The chief items were cars, communications equipment, trucks, and photographic goods. Canada wishes to increase the value-added in its resource exports, while Japan wishes to continue to manufacture and export as much as possible under the GATT rules (Dubota 1985) without investing more than necessary abroad.

A typical example of the benefits of an expanded trade framework might be in the development of splinterwood, a new forest product for construction arising from R&D in Canada. What might happen if its development is looked at from the total (Canada plus Japan) market point of view as opposed to that of two national markets? Investigation using, for example, Akira Onishi's FUGI macroeconomic international trade model can compare the first-order and further-order effects of investment in Canada, investment in Japan, or joint investment in both countries to maximize the joint market and establish further markets.

Trade Potential

The same approach can be extended to estimate the full potential for trade between two countries such as Japan and Canada. By looking at successive economic activities from the point of view of the total (combined) markets, the inefficiencies attributable to national boundaries can be identified and estimated. The existing GATT rules and other regulations, tariffs, and costs are assumed to remain unchanged, although the effects of changing them can be studied separately. It would seem best to do this with a neutral team (nongovernment, nonbusiness) from both countries. The effect of increasing Japanese investment abroad is already being investigated (Onishi 1985). If such studies indicate the possibility of significantly increased trade, then the next stage would be reached.

As the Japanese government is already doing in relation to its discussions with the U.S. government, two countries can create a loose, flexible framework designed to increase trade within existing rules. (The governments might not describe it this way, but this is in fact what they are doing.) This includes the provision of information, discussions between organizations, and the setting up of agencies or institutions designed to make the increase of trade easier, smoother, and better known (as Japan is doing). The function of business is then to compete for the new opportunities. Governments provide the framework; companies supply the action and the results. All of this takes place without the need for negotiation of any treaty since it falls within the existing rules. Clearly this is a low-cost way to encourage entrepreneurship and international competitiveness and lessen unemployment.

Grouping Commodities

The Canada–Japan case suggests also that we look at exports to another country as a single group and not divide them into commodities in the usual way. When this is done, it is clear that Vancouver occupies today the same position with regard to Japan and the Far East that Winnipeg occupied in regard to the development of the prairies a hundred years ago. Vancouver is the portal to the Pacific and should therefore possess all the skills and services necessary for such a position. Even if Canada does not go the *sogoshosha* route (Tsurumi 1983), there are potential gains in handling goods according to their destination rather than by commodity. A start is being made in the redesign of the western Canadian rail system on this basis.

If it pays to look at exports to one country as a group, then perhaps we should also start to look at Canada as a whole. For some time this has not been popular, but it is doubtful if Canada will be able to afford the luxury of separatism and protectionism for much longer. International competitiveness requires efforts to be consolidated, not scattered. What are the advantages of exporting splinterwood versus importing cars? Questions such as this, which mean balancing intercountry as well as intracountry trade, need to be asked. By combining Japanese international trade models with Canadian econometric models, it should be possible to look at internal and external balances. Such calculations cannot give precise answers, but they can indicate the directions of change and second-order effects.

Does it follow that in an information–knowledge society the sharp separations between east, west, and central Canada will continue unchanged in their present form? It may be time for a joint Canadian–Japanese team to start looking at the potential for more trade and its possible effects in both countries. Such studies commit nobody but assist in freeing minds from the stereotypes of the past.

New Companies

Implicit in a changing trade framework are changing kinds of companies. If adaptability and flexibility are the key characteristics for survival in a changing world, what forms of company might be best suited? Put another way, how can one maximize capabilities and minimize liabilities? This prompts the following ideas about the company of the future:

Capital: As little as possible confined to the key steps of the operation; twenty-four-hour-use of money by suitable location of activities.

Labor: None. The concepts of labor, blue–white collar, wages–salaries, empoyer–employees, and grievances belong to the nineteenth century.

People: Yes. Few but good; members, not employees, of the company; preferably shareholders–partners and similar forms of ownership to maximize personal commitment and identification and protect against takeovers.

Operations: Key ones only. The risks of money, labor, competition, and interference will be pushed on to suppliers; international competitiveness will be demanded from them for other components. Assemble against orders to avoid too much inventory and working capital in the electronic age (Stulman 1972). Electronic delivery to consumers just in time (Ito-Yokado 1985). Use customers' storage where possible.

Location: Probably many rather than in one or two countries.

Management: Minimal and adaptable. People manage themselves and are paid accordingly. But key areas (technologies, marketing, manufacturing and assembly steps, machines, procedures, and finance) will be controlled and accurate knowledge of the business situation (taxation and costs, for example) around the world maintained.

Technology: Active R&D in key areas; up-to-date tracking of technologies in related areas; twenty-four-hour R&D by suitable location of R&D facilities in Far East, North America, and Europe.

Size: Dictated by the nature of the business (no merit in being small or big in real terms).

Note: For billionaires to be. You can have more than one of such companies, but please do not mix them up. There is no need to repeat the mistakes of the multinationals and the conglomerates.

Many, if not all, of these possibilities already exist, although not on a large scale. The physical location of a company counts most, and government programs and taxation are based on that. But in tomorrow's world, money, knowledge, and information will seem to be floating over our heads. The aim will then be to tap into these sources as they go by, and the physical location of the company will be somewhat less important. Not all companies will be affected, but enough will be to require further changes in trade frameworks.

Summary

Much of what is happening at the moment can be better understood if we appreciate the value of creating loose, flexible frameworks for increasing trade within the existing rules of international trade. This consists of looking at the total market and examining the new possibilities that this approach, rather than the conventional national one, offers. At the same time this method helps reveal the full potential for trade, something that by itself can stimulate economic activity. It also suggests the value of regarding the countries or regions with which we trade as a bloc and recognizing the need for a total, and not just a commodity, approach. This in turn requires the internal balance of trade and advantage within Canada to be examined as a whole in relation to changes in its external trade. The opportunities in this kind of trade may also facilitate the evolution of a more flexible, less fixed type of company. All the necessary steps, studies, and other arrangements can be undertaken by governments without requiring renegotiation of present treaties or agreements, as current activities show. Canada–Japan trade could well be a suitable candidate for such a study.

References

Abegglen, J.C., and Etori, Akio. 1983. "Japanese Technology Today." *Scientific American* (November).

Bateson, Gregory. 1972. *Steps to an Ecology of the Mind*. New York: Ballantine.

Canada–Japan Trade Council. 1985. Trade data.

Cantley, M.F. 1981. "Scale, Protectionism and European Integration." *European Journal of Operational Research 7*.

Coates, Vary, and Finn, B. 1979. *A Retrospective Technology Assessment: Submarine Telegraphy*. San Francisco: San Francisco Press.

d'Aquino, T. 1984. *The Canada–United States Trading Relationship and the Idea of a Trade Enhancement Agreement*. Ottawa: Business Council on National Issues.

Dubota, Akira. 1985. "Canada's Response to Japan's Economic Offensive: A Japanese Critique." Address given at the Japanese Embassy, Ottawa, February 26.

Economic Planning Agency. 1983. "Outlook and Guidelines for the Economy and Society in the 1980's." Tokyo: Government of Japan.

External Affairs, Department of, Government of Canada. 1985a. "Competitiveness and Security: Directions for Canada's International Relations." Ottawa, Department of Supply and Services.

——. 1985b. "Canada/Japan Businessmen's Conference." Fact Sheets, Issues, Trade Situation, for the May 19–22, 1985, Conference at Calgary, Ottawa.

Gold, Bela. 1978. "Steel Technologies and Costs in the U.S. and Japan." *Iron and Steel Engineering* (April).

Hay, K.A.J. 1983. *Canada's Future Technological Ties with Japan*. Ottawa: Canada–Japan Trade Council.

Hay, K.A.J., and Hill, S.R. 1983. *The Canada–Japan Export-Import Picture in 1982*. Ottawa: Canada–Japan Trade Council.

Iacocca, L.A. 1985. "Japan Should Protect Its Market in America." *Japan Economic Journal* (May).

Ito-Yokado 1985. "This Supermarket Company Has Just Installed a Retail-Business Person of the Just-in-Time System Developed in the Automobile Industry." *Japan Economic Times* (May).

Kikuchi, Makoto. 1983. *Japanese Electronics*. Tokyo: Simul Press.

McMillan, Charles J. 1984. *The Japanese Industrial System*. New York: de Gruyter.

Masudam, Yoneji. 1981. *The Information Society as Post-Industrial Society*. Tokyo: Institute for the Information Society.

——. 1983. "The Information Society and Human Life." *Report of the General Policy Committee of the Social Policy Council*. Tokyo: Economic Planning Agency.

Moritani, Masanori. 1983. *Advanced Technology and the Japanese Contribution*. Tokyo: Nomura Securities Co.

Muller, R.E. 1977. "National Economic Growth and Stabilization Policy in the Age of Multinational Corporations." In *Economic Growth in the International Context*, vol. 12, Washington, D.C.: Joint Economic Committee of the U.S. Congress.

Narusawa, Takashi. 1984. Private communication.

Onishi, Akira. 1983. "The FUGI Macroeconomic Model and World Trade to 1990." *Futures* (April).

Onishi, Akira, et al. 1984. "Global Impacts of Oil Price Reductions and Official Development Assistance." *Developing Economies* 22.

——. 1985. Private communication.

Reischauer, E.O. 1977. *The Japanese*. Cambridge: Harvard University Press.

Stulman, Julius. 1972. "The Methodology of Pattern." In *Fields within Fields . . . within Fields*. New York: World Institute Council.

"The Transformation of American Business." 1985. *Tarrytown Newsletter* 50 (June).

Tsurumi, Yoshi. 1983. *Sogoshosha*. Montreal: Institute for Research on Public Policy.

Yamauchi, Ichizo. 1983. "Long-Range Strategic Planning in Japanese R&D." *Futures* (October).

Part II
The Role of Government in Leading and/or Facilitating Change

6
The Role of Government Action in Formulating Competitive Strategies

Michael Cassidy

T here is a profound sense that the role governments have been playing in formulating and implementing competitive strategies has been misdirected and ineffective. Just how governments are going wrong, however, is very much in dispute. It is much easier to talk about the dilemmas than it is to put forward solutions that prove successful.

In looking at the role of government and competitive strategy, I speak as a politician who has tried to lift my attention from the day-to-day pressures and short-term issues of politics to the longer-term question of technology and its impact on people and competitiveness. We need to look at this question because by constantly focusing on the short term, politicians are not adequately addressing the issue.

Historical Perspective

Up to the early 1970s, broad policies of demand management along with some targeted programs for training, postsecondary education, and regional development had a good deal of success in Canada. Economic growth was strong, unemployment low, and Canada seemed able to afford a comprehensive range of social programs such as medicare and the Canada Assistance Plan.

The idea of government-led competitive strategy did not exist in Canada in the 1960s, when European models of economic planning were considered too interventionist for the North American setting. Nonetheless, there were some extremely successful initiatives in economic management from which Canada still benefits. Most notable was the U.S.–Canada Auto Pact, which, despite its failure to transfer R&D, has had an enormous impact on the industry's productivity and production in Canada and on Canada's trade and balance of payments. Another successful policy was Canada's capital cost tax allowances, which were very generous relative to those in the United States. This may explain why the Canadian steel industry modernized in time to maintain its world competitiveness at a time when the U.S. steel industry was disintegrating.

The last twelve years have seen substantial changes in the role played by governments. Ottawa has turned to monetarism in its efforts to control inflation. Corporate tax rates have been cut and cut again, mainly through the use of tax incentives designed to spur growth and investment. The federal government has become deeply and directly involved in industry through such measures as the takeovers of aircraft manufacturers Canadair and de Havilland and through the National Energy Policy, which was intended to Canadianize the oil industry.

The reasons for the current disillusionment are obvious: none of the recent policy measures seems to be working. Real wages are falling, unemployment has risen despite the new initiatives, real interest rates have reached record highs, and the federal deficit seems to be firmly entrenched at a crippling $30 billion or more per annum. The deficit alone makes it hard to see how a policy of more of the same—more tax cuts and incentives to business—can be afforded.

Current Situation

Although the current Conservative government promised change in Canada's economic policy, little has been achieved in the government's first year of power. Deregulation in the oil industry and the dismantling of the Foreign Investment Review Agency took place as promised; however, the new government's financial support for Domtar's papermaking operations in Quebec and its $70 million bail-out of the Canadian Commercial Bank are more or less just what the previous Liberal government would have done. No fundamental change is yet evident. The May 1985 budget did initiate some major changes, which increase inequity in Canada's tax system in the hope that this may lead to stronger economic growth. In a sense, this too is more of the same, except that the tax exemption for the first half-million dollars of capital gains, which is intended to stimulate investment in small businesses, does represent a shift away from tax policies directed toward large corporations.

One has to ask why this lack of initiative persists and what its consequences are. Can Canada afford to stand still in terms of its national economic policies at a time of rapid change in technologies and more and more intense competition in the world economy? Are there new policies that could help Canada weather the changes now taking place in the world economy?

The basic reason for immobility in Canadian industrial policy is that in Canada, as in many other countries, no consensus exists regarding the role of government in the economy. Hard choices have not been confronted. In fact, Parliament and the political system have played a very minor role in directing the economy due to this lack of consensus.

The idea of intervention by government is relatively well established in Canada, as it is in most European countries, even if it is decried in theory. Fiscal policy is widely used to attain social and economic objectives. Strong incentives and subsidies have been provided to encourage R&D. The government of Canada has traditionally played a substantial role in promoting and paying for investments in regional development and personnel training.

Industry-specific policies are also well established. Examples include the auto pact and the Japanese auto import quotas, the federal program of grants and loans to encourage modernization in certain sectors like the pulp and paper industry, and federal adjustment assistance to threatened industries like textiles and clothing.

The federal and provincial governments create a framework for corporate activity through labor and health and safety regulation, consumer and environmental standards, and social programs like Medicare and the Canada Pension Plan. They set the framework for specific industries through product standards, restraints on certain corporate activities, securities legislation, and competition policy. Finally, and unlike the United States, both the federal government and the provinces play a direct and major part in the economy through crown corporations like Canadian National Railways, Atomic Energy of Canada, Ontario Hydro, the Urban Transit Development Corporation, and Air Canada.

One could consider this list of programs and policies as a portfolio of interventions, just as a company may consider its lines of business as a portfolio of investments. Government should ideally be able to manage its portfolio, weeding out programs that are weak and investing in policies that best meet its long-term goals for growth, equity, employment, and competitiveness. The dilemma of democracy, however, is that it is easier to retard change than to initiate it. Despite the feeling that the present mix of policies is costly and does not meet Canada's needs, consensus about change is lacking, and every program has its defenders. Compounding the problem is the fact that consensus about goals is also lacking. The government machine is slow to react; most bureaucrats are not experienced in formulating competitive strategy and therefore are handicapped in dealing with the accelerating pace of change in the business world.

One of the fundamental problems is that neither govenments nor political parties have worked out what goals they want their economic programs to achieve. The answer seems to vary depending on the time, the place, and who is talking. For example, most crown corporations were originally established for social as well as economic purposes, but their original raison d'être was often very quickly lost. Since governments can create new ventures more quickly than they can divest, this has led to the existence of a number of crown corporations that now have no clear mandate from their owner, the government. Consequently any strategic direction that exists flows only from management.

Difficulties in Building Consensus

Even when government succeeds in articulating its objectives, they often conflict with the objectives that business seeks to achieve through technology policies. The payoffs for business lie in such areas as growth, profits, and market development. Governments are likely to place greater emphasis on social values and on political payoffs such as perceived benefits for particular regions or groups or simply the perception that some action to solve a problem is being taken.

In order to develop and carry out competitive strategy, government, like business, must engage in economic planning. This fact is accepted in Europe and many other parts of the world, but in Canada it is not. If government planning for industry is not seen as legitimate, then government is confined to acting as a mere handmaiden to industry rather than being a partner. Yet if government is not seen to be reconciling social and economic goals, it runs the risk of losing its political base of support.

There are other reasons why consensus is hard to achieve in Canada. Domtar illustrates the kind of double standard that prevails: business spokesmen condemn government handouts to industry yet rush to take them if they are available to their own corporation. Then there is the fact that Canada is regionally diverse. Different regions want different strategies because their industries and markets differ. The conflict between the resource-based interests of western Canada and the secondary manufacturing interests of Quebec and Ontario is a classic example.

Finally, Canada is not alone is trying to find new tools for economic policy. Since the oil shortage crisis of 1973, all Western countries have been having problems trying to achieve the goals of full employment, economic growth, and minimum inflation. Western governments have experienced strong and specific pressures from industry, labor, and affected regions to take defensive measures in favor of declining industries adversely affected by technological and competitive change. On the other side of the balance, the payoffs from promoting new industries and new technologies tend to be diffused, hard to measure, and hard to exploit in political terms. The payoffs from defending old industries tend to be larger and more focused and are aided by the tradition of logrolling found among politicians in most countries.

When political leaders succeed in imposing a strategy in the absence of consensus, the side effects can be very costly. Margaret Thatcher's hard-nosed monetarism and her rejection of the British tradition of muddling through have devastated the industrial landscape in northern England (which normally votes Labour). In social terms these policies have left the country deeply divided. Much of industrial Britain is now in a permanent state of economic depression. The dynamic new economy that the Conservatives anticipated has yet to emerge, and Britain remains a sick partner in the European Economic Community (EEC).

In the United States, social values are not as well entrenched in political life as they are in Canada and in Western Europe. The policies of economic regulation that have had a substantial impact in such industries as air transport and trucking have been carried through with bipartisan support. Hence there has been more apparent consensus for President Reagan's supply-side policies than they would have received in Canada. Despite the success of these policies in reducing unemployment and stimulating economic growth in the United States, they carry a heavy long-term cost that is reflected in the enormous increase in the manufacturing trade deficit. In terms of competitive strategy, short-term gains in employment are being achieved at the expense of permanent long-term damage to U.S. competitiveness.

Alternatives

What kind of alternatives can one see for government action in formulating competitive strategies?

Clear the way for the free market. This approach, which is often argued by the private sector, usually calls for tax cuts, deregulation, decreases in social spending, and a promise of stable policies from government. It may also include direct action to weaken the strength of labor and other groups concerned with the social responsibilities of government because of their perceived negative impact on industry costs and competitiveness.

Such an approach has been used in both Great Britain and the Canadian province of British Columbia but with extraordinarily divisive results and no dramatic evidence of success in terms of investment or jobs. Although this approach was advocated by many Conservatives in the 1984 Canadian election campaign, the will of the new Conservative government to act in this direction is weakening. Despite its massive majority, the new government perceives that it must try to balance economic and social values in order to maintain power. A free market approach would not have permitted federal government assistance to Domtar, despite the perceived importance of the project to Quebec in both regional and political terms.

Support the growth of individual firms and industries. This is the traditional Canadian approach. Policies in the areas of education, manpower training and mobility, export finance, and trade promotion fall in this category. So do specific programs to help industries adjust to new competition, to help bail out companies like Chrysler and Massey-Ferguson if they are threatened with competitive collapse, or to promote technology diffusion in specific industries through programs such as the technology centers, which Ontario began to establish in 1981.

As we have learned from experience, however, these policies are no longer sufficient to keep the economy growing and Canadians employed.

Governments can no longer count on getting enough revenues to pay for the rising costs of social programs or for the increasing cost of tax incentives and concessions to business. At the federal level in Canada, this kind of tax expenditure has grown just about to equal the $35 billion annual deficit. Moreover, many of these policies are not adequate to meet the needs for which they are designed. There is widespread criticism of education in Canada, for example, for failing to meet the needs of industry and for failing to graduate even close to half the young people who enter high school. Federally financed manpower training falls far short of providing the skills needed in industry, and training and apprenticeship within industry are hopelessly inadequate. Federal aid for specific industries cannot resolve the problem; new alternatives must be found.

Develop a national strategy for competing in the world. When people talk about an industrial strategy in Canada, they generally mean having the federal government, perhaps in conjunction with the provinces, determine which industries should grow and then put policies in place to bring this about. But with limited public resources, the selection of winners generally means deciding which industries should be losers, and for political reasons, that task has been just about impossible. To acknowledge Canada's textile and clothing industry as a loser, for example, would mean pronouncing a death sentence on many plants that are major employers in small and medium-sized communities. Hence this industry and its jobs are being cushioned with adjustment assistance. Market forces are still forcing closures and layoffs, but at least governments can say that something is being done. However, no strategy is in place to redeploy the resources of the textile and clothing sector into new growth industries.

The idea of a national strategy has worked best in Japan and in Sweden where much closer institutional links joining government, major industries, and banks exist than in Canada. The result is that national economic strategy is being carried out along the lines of a large conglomerate moving resources into emerging sectors of the economy and out of declining sectors as a matter of deliberate policy and not just as a consequence of market forces.

The harmony that permits that kind of strategy is lacking in Canada, for reasons already given. While some sense of unity can occasionally be achieved, as with Quebec's commitment to the James Bay power project in the 1970s, implementation can be difficult unless the strategy is carried out by the public sector. For both financial and ideological reasons, that is seldom possible.

Canada's Response

I am pessimistic in reviewing the various options for a national competitive strategy. I do not doubt that they can do some good; some industries may in fact achieve world-scale competitiveness because of public intervention. However, I doubt this will be enough to keep Canada abreast of a difficult and changing competitive environment and to overcome unacceptable levels of unemployment. An added reason for pessimism is the fact that while Canada hesitates, the world economy is evolving at an increasingly rapid rate. New technologies are changing the way work is performed and the way industry needs to be structured. Each year, traditional industries based on mass production in the developed countries are becoming more and more vulnerable to competition from Asia and the rest of the third world.

In the meantime, Canada has wasted its time with interest rate policies that have shaken many industries to their roots and has tolerated the paper entrepreneurship and speculative dealings of financiers like Peter Pocklington and Conrad Black, while real productive investment declined and labor force skills became degraded and obsolete due to new technologies.

Even if all the traditional answers seem to be inadequate, I am arguing that the changes occurring in the world economy are so important that Canada may not survive as an advanced economy if it does not develop a strategic response within government as well as within industry. If it allows its future to be directed by market forces alone, Canada may emerge as a resource-based economy with a manufacturing sector that approaches the third world in income levels and technology.

The key to a successful response by government is to seek to change the framework of management, particularly at the level of the firm, in order to create an economy that is more flexible and able to respond to change. Changes in the world economy already are having substantial impact on the form of enterprise. Organizations are becoming flatter, more flexible, more innovative, and more knowledge based in order to survive and evolve in a technologically advanced world. The most successful organizations and societies are those that best learn how to cope with change.

There is no guarantee that Canadian business and economic institutions will evolve in the direction that is needed quickly enough to survive as an advanced economy. That is why governments will need to provide leadership. They already provide the framework of policies, laws, and programs within which business operates. That framework can be changed in order to provide for more flexibility and more partnership by putting into place the concepts of a new economic democracy.

The political environment in which governments work tends to respond to those parts of society where the political and economic power is greatest. The kind of changes I am talking about are therefore likely to be resisted by economic power groups who see their short-term interests seriously affected. But the old approaches are not working, and a new line of attack must be developed if Canada is to survive.

Governments are clearly involved with change in almost every area of policy. Programs to create jobs often include encouragement of new industries and new technologies. The social safety nets of government welfare programs are in large measure directed toward people adversely affected by changes such as the decline of outmoded industries or the closure of non-competitive firms. Government has had less to do with the other factors that affect how the economy responds to change but should become involved now because it relates so directly to the question of competitive strategy.

In 1983–1984 when I was in the Ontario legislature, I chaired a New Democratic party caucus task force, Work, People and Technological Change. Ours was the first group of politicians in Canada to give serious consideration to the issue of how government policy should respond to the impact of new technology. Although this task force began with a goal of how to achieve and maintain full employment, we found we had to deal with the question of competition because of the degree to which Canadian jobs and Canadian industry are affected by changes in the world economy.

New technology is finding its way into Canadian markets through imports and domestic competition. Few Canadian industries are sheltered anymore. Industrial change is becoming more severe, so what is at stake is more than just a pay raise or a dividend; in many cases, it is the survival of the plant or firm and the jobs attached to it. Hence there is a common interest among Canadian workers, the enterprises for which they work, and the communities in which these firms are located to respond to new technology. That common interest, however, is seldom identified or acknowledged by leaders in business, labor or government.

Economic Partnership

How, we asked, would it be possible to achieve the kind of consensus about the survival of enterprises in the face of new technology, which is now so evidently lacking? By extension, if such a consensus began to be built at the level of individual communities and firms, could this in time form a stronger consensus about regional and national goals than now exists in Canada? We concluded that for firms to respond successfully to change, a great deal more consensus about goals is needed. But to achieve that consensus, there needs to be a remarkable change in the way that the workplace is organized and, in particular, in the role that employees and their representatives play in the direction of their work and of the enterprise.

Achieving consensus on goals and coping with change require a much greater sense of partnership than is the norm in most Canadian enterprises today. If companies are to cope with change, they are more likely to succeed if they have the cooperation of the work force. With greater partnership, many more people within a firm will be promoting and encouraging the implementation of change than if change is generated by a few executives and imposed on the entire organization.

The concept of partnership is an old one, but success in achieving it has been limited. Most of Canada's manufacturing enterprises are organized, but the common pattern of labor management relations has tended toward confrontation rather than cooperation. In the growing white-collar sector of the economy, there has been little structure, either in the form of unions or otherwise, through which employees can play a role in their firm beyond doing what they are told. Canada has not had a tradition of the kind of works councils that in Europe have provided many firms with a forum for sharing information and developing patterns of cooperation.

In a firm, consensus about goals needs to be based on a two-way flow of obligation: the responsibility of employers for their employees and the responsibility and involvement of workers for the survival and success of the enterprise where they work. Some of these obligations are obvious; workers are paid, and they normally put in a full day's work. Many managements, however, have accepted little responsibility for job security or for upgrading their workers' skills by training. The obligations of employers have tended to be enforced by government actions such as labor standards and collective bargaining laws. Equally, many workers have viewed their responsibility as just doing their job rather than working smarter. During times of full employment, workers could easily move to another job if they were laid off or dissatisfied with the way their job was managed. With unemployment now beyond 10 percent, these options are no longer available, but the opportunity for workers to have input into their jobs has not expanded.

Our task force concluded that employees must be given more participation in running their firm and must be willing to take more responsibility as well. But if workers are to share in responsibility for the future of their firm, they need adequate information and the means to be consulted and involved in crucial decisions. This can obviously create problems, such as how workers are to participate when almost all fundamental decisions are made at foreign head offices. Nonetheless, sharing information is essential if there is to be a sharing of responsibility with workers and by workers. If companies are to be cost competitive, workers will need detailed information about costs so they can help bring them under control. If workers are to adapt to new technology being introduced, they need advance notice and consultation about the implications. If the competitive environment requires rapid changes of product line or development of new technology, with consequent impact on the jobs of employees, then a good deal of employee input into strategic planning and into decisions about training will be required so that employees will buy in to a consensus about future directions for the firm and be prepared to cooperate in implementation.

This kind of changed relationship between managers or owners and employees is needed even in enterprises that are not unionized. It may be needed even more within government bureaucracies, since these have traditionally been more hierarchical and more resistant to change than the private sector.

The new models of work organization that Canada will need and that governments can help to put in place recognize that private corporations will likely remain the dominant form of economic organization but seek to redefine their role. The fact that corporations generally respond to more than just the interests of their shareholders is widely recognized in both management literature and in sociology but less so in political ideology and practice. Yet it is governments that have created the corporate form of organization through which the economy operates. Therefore it is entirely appropriate for governments to consider changes in the framework of corporate organization if such changes would increase Canada's ability to respond to an era of rapid change.

Our task force reaffirmed the central value of work in Canadian society, not just as a means of earning an income or of distributing wealth but also because it gives purpose and social significance to human lives. This is as true for routine jobs as it is for the professions or in management. The profound social value of work must be recognized alongside its economic value. The policies that flow from this realization can probably be achieved only through government action. If jobs are maintained mainly for their social value, inefficiency could result. This must be weighed against the turbulent competitive environment in which more and more businesses now work. Our task force favored a substantial reduction in working time, achieved through shorter hours, longer holidays, and other means, as the best way to achieve and maintain high employment and high productivity.

Our task force pointed the way to a new kind of partnership between workers and management—one that does not yet exist in Canada—within a new framework of corporate structure. These alternatives exist but only in a modest way. West Germany has works councils and codetermination. The quality of work life movement has been preaching the need for a changed relationship in the workplace, and this concept is catching on in the form of company-inspired programs of worker involvement. Yet the depth of labor–management distrust makes it unlikely that without outside intervention, new corporate structures will evolve at the pace needed to cope with the acceleration of change. Canada still suffers from a management world view that does not recognize how the environment has changed and that barely tolerates such instruments of economic democracy as trade unions.

Some firms now practice information sharing and consultation. Too often, however, the story is the opposite. Employees become aware, for example, that the branch plant where they have worked for years is running into difficulties. Investment in new machinery tapers off, and managers who are appointed by head office show no interest in the operation or are themselves shut out of corporate decision making. Sometimes the information that workers need is shared—but only when the plant or company is on the brink of disaster.

What Government Can Do

To go beyond that kind of last-minute sharing of responsibility will require major changes in corporate culture. Such changes cannot be achieved by direct government action, but governments can accelerate the process of change by laws and by example. Through legislation, governments can insist that companies share information, provide advance notice of new technology, create works councils, and provide regular reports of the strategic position of a company or a particular plant. The intent of such legislation would be to create a climate of cooperation sufficient to allow greater consensus about goals and common action to achieve them.

Canada has a mixed economy in which private industry, governments, and other institutions often work together to resolve problems or to seek common objectives. The approach I have described at the microlevel would also apply in creating programs for whole industries or in harmonizing action by government and a particular industry. A model for such an approach already exists in Canada, in Quebec. One of the most creative initiatives of the Parti Québécois government was the initiation of socioeconomic summit meetings for particular industries or regions in many parts of the province. Taking a particular region or industry, the Quebec government brought together employers, employees, industry associations, unions, affected communities, and other interest groups in seeking to understand the problems and opportunities facing the region or industry and to develop initiatives to resolve those problems or exploit those opportunities. The process of preparation, planning, and consultation takes a number of months, but that time is not wasted if it results in a genuine consensus on which actions can be based. This is an example of how the process of consensus building at the level of the firm can be expanded to enable whole industries or regions to respond to the changing competitive environment. It is a much more positive role for governments than the present practice of leaving bureaucrats to devise industrial policy or adjustment programs with limited input from those who are affected and with limited direction from the political level.

Would Canadians respond to the kind of approach I have described? I think so. In spring 1985, when I traveled across the country with a New Democratic party task force on jobs, we found a surprising sense of optimism and initiative even from communities with chronic high unemployment. Many of the people we met doubted whether central planning and national programs could help their economic development. They wanted local initiatives encouraged and resources put into the hands of small business, cooperatives, and municipal enterprises. They believed regional institutions should replace unwieldy central bodies like the Federal Business Development Bank in providing finance for economic development. If the money was made available locally, then strategy could also be developed locally.

The reaction we got supports what I call a microapproach to competition strategy. People were looking for different forms of enterprise to complement private corporations and wanted far more bottom-up involvement of employees and local communities in economic planning and development. Some centralized initiatives would still be required, but a bottom-up strategy should help to speed up the response to change by clearing issues off the crowded agenda of governments. Politicians and governments can deal with only a few issues on their agenda at one time. Issues that are seen as less pressing will be deferred unless there is some means for them to be resolved, such as the one I have devised.

Economists have argued for decades that certain major Canadian industries such as textiles should be written off because they cannot be competitive. Governments have resisted those arguments because too many jobs are at stake in communities where there is no readily apparent alternative source of employment. The case for trying to preserve jobs in traditional industries is becoming stronger because we now know that the emerging high-technology industries are unlikely to generate a great deal of employment. But the strategy for preserving traditional industries cannot be to maintain them unchanged through public subsidy or the use of import quotas. The experience of recent years shows that such a policy will not work. An industry like textiles will have to evolve and find the market niches where there is room for Canadian protection. That process is far more suited to the microapproach to strategy than to the broad national programs Canadian governments have tended to use.

Conclusion

I believe that a bottom-up approach to technological change in an increasingly competitive world would succeed in Canada. It is a peaceable nation with a well-educated and technologically adept, if not well-trained, work force. It has ample resources, ample supplies of capital, and almost unlimited access to the largest single market in the world.

In governments and at the political level, however, Canada's ability to recognize and encourage adaptation to change is sadly lacking. Politicians debate in slogans drawn from past generations and fail to recognize where the future is heading. The structures of government are even more resistant to change than those of private industry. In Parliament and in lesiglatures, almost no time is given to the issue of science, technology, or the future direction of economic development.

Can politicians change their spots? Can they look beyond the issues of today and start dealing with the future? Will politicians who are aligned with the prevailing power structure have the courage to create new structures for economic democracy in workplaces so that industries and bureaucracies are more flexible and able to respond to the changes of a dynamic environment? I hope so, and one of the reasons I am in politics is to make those kinds of changes come about.

7

Technological Change and Reindustrialization: In Search of a Policy Framework

Roy Rothwell

Need for Innovation Policy

While governments in the advanced market economies have, throughout the postwar years, been involved in implementing policies designed to stimulate scientific advance and technological and industrial change, there are features of the current world economic crisis that render the adoption of such policies especially important today. Increasingly, it is being suggested that the current recession is part of a long-term cycle of industrial structural change characterized by the maturing, more or less simultaneously, of the new industries of the postwar era, and that the products of these industries, now generally rather mature and increasingly standardized in form, are suffering from demand saturation (Freeman, Clark, and Soete 1982; van Duijn 1983; Rothwell 1984a). Indeed some would claim that the recessionary trend of the 1970s and early 1980s is the direct result of a paucity of radical innovations capable of spawning major new product–market opportunities (Mensch 1979).

While stressing the structural nature of the current economic crisis, these neo-Schumpeterians are at the same time pointing to the future, and in particular to a cluster of emerging technoeconomic combinations that represent the leading edge of a new economic upswing:

Biotechnology (biomass, single cell protein, bioengineering, new drugs).

Energy-related technologies (heat pumps, solar energy devices).

Electronic office equipment.

Advanced information technology (including fiber-optics, electronic mail, and satellite communications).

This chapter is based on R. Rothwell and W. Zegveld, *Reindustrialization and Technology* (London: Longman, January 1985). I would like to acknowledge the financial support of the Leverhulme Trust Fund during the preparation of this chapter.

Advanced medical electronics and new forms of implants (biocompatible materials).

Photochemistry.

Coal gasification and liquefaction.

Exploitation of ocean resources (the ocean bed, aquaculture).

Robotics technology and FHS.

New agrochemicals for the regeneration of marginal land.

Of course, emphasis on stimulating the growth of new sectors does not mean that existing sectors can be ignored. Thus while postwar prosperity owed much to the rapid growth of new technology-based industries, such as semiconductors, synthetic and composite materials, electronic computers, aerospace and consumer electronics, long-established sectors, such as steel, textiles, and construction, also played an important part. Moreover, in all three industries, major innovations played an important role: continuous casting of steel and oxygen steelmaking, synthetic fibers, carpet tufting machinery and shuttleless weaving in the textile industry, and systems building in the construction industry. Today policies in the advanced economies should aim simultaneously at stimulating the emergence of the new technoeconomic combinations and revitalizing existing sectors through major innovation. In other words, we need policies of reindustrialization:

> We would define reindustrialization as "the structural transformation of industry into higher added value, more knowledge-intensive sectors and product groups, and the creation of major new technology-based industries and products serving new markets". A good example of the former can be found in the structural shifts in Japanese industry during the past thirty years; an example of the latter is the emergence in the United States in the 1950s and 1960s of a group of new, high-technology industries. (Rothwell and Zegveld 1985, p. 1)

Designing and implementing national policies for reindustrialization through technological change is no easy matter, and policymakers are likely to encounter many problems and constraints. For example, technological potential varies considerably from country to country; financial and technological institutions well adapted to the support of existing firms and sectors may be inappropriate to the generation of new sectors; the adoption of new (labor-saving) production technology may encounter vigorous resistance from workers; accumulated capital in one form of production may inhibit the movement to new and better production techniques; and social resistance to change may hinder diffusion. Despite the many problems, reindustrialization remains an indispensable task for governments, and, in the long term, greater unemployment and social disbenefit will surely accrue to those of the advanced market economies that fail to grasp the new technological possibilities and achieve the necessary structural industrial adaptation.

Innovation Policies in the 1970s and 1980s

During the latter half of the 1970s, governments in many of the advanced market economies began to adopt explicit innovation policies rather than the more traditional science and technology and industrial policies. If we define innovation as "the technical, financial, managerial, design, production and marketing steps involved in the commercial introduction of a new (or improved) product or the first commercial use of a new (or improved) manufacturing process or equipment" (Freeman 1974)—a process that involves the whole gamut of activities from invention through to the marketplace—then we can see that innovation policy is essentially an integrative concept. In other words, innovation policy represents the combination, in a coordinated manner, of elements of science and technology policy and industrial policy. A list of innovation policy tools is given in table 7–1.

Table 7–1
Classification of Government Policy Tools

Policy Tool	Examples
Public enterprise	Innovation by publicly owned industries, setting up of new industries, pioneering use of new techniques by public corporations, participation in private enterprise
Scientific and technical	Research laboratories, support for research associations, learned societies, professional associations, research grants
Education	General education, universities, technical education, apprenticeship schemes, continuing and further education, retraining
Information	Information networks and centers, libraries, advisory and consultancy services, data bases, liaison services
Financial	Grants, loans, subsidies, financial sharing arrangements, provision of equipment, buildings, or services, loan guarantees, export credits
Taxation	Company, personal, indirect and payroll taxation, tax allowances
Legal and regulatory	Patents, environments and health regulations, inspectorates, monopoly regulations
Political	Planning, regional policies, honors or awards for innovation, encouragement of mergers or joint consortia, public consultation
Procurement	Central or local government purchases and contracts, public corporations, R&D contracts, prototype purchases
Public services	Purchases, maintenance, supervision and innovation in health service, public building, construction, transport, telecommunications
Commercial	Trade agreements, tariffs, currency regulations
Overseas agent	Defense sales organizations

Source: Rothwell and Zegveld 1981.

An analysis several years ago of innovation policy recommendations by type of tool in six advanced market economies, taken from national innovation policy statements published in the late 1970s, illustrated a number of important differences among countries in the types of tool adopted (Rothwell and Zegveld 1981). In Great Britain, the greatest emphasis was on financial and taxation measures, which appeared to reflect a preoccupation with obtaining a healthy environment for industry to operate in. In the case of the United States, 50 percent of the measures were in the category "legal and regulatory," which reflected a deep concern about the economy's being over-regulated. These two contrasted with the other four nations (Japan, the Netherlands, Canada, and Sweden), which preferred to deal more directly with the inputs to the process of innovation. Thus, in the United States and the United Kingdom, policy emphasis was on the creation of a climate conducive to firm-based innovatory endeavors, government leaving the choice of technology in the hands of individual managers with market forces dictating patterns of resource allocation.

This difference in approach to innovation policy reflects the different roles that governments play in the economy and in industrial development generally. In some countries, such as Japan and France, state intervention in industry is seen as a major part of a process of indicative planning. Innovation policy is seen as an important instrument for economic policy, and the objectives of innovation policy are formulated within a framework of economic and social development plans, which are indicative for the private sector. In other countries, most notably the United States but also West Germany and the United Kingdom, innovation policy is seen as part of general economic policy, aiming to create a favorable climate for industrial development. Although these latter countries use innovation policies and instruments or even sectoral policies, they are not formulated within the framework of a national plan, nor are they used as selective policies in an intensive or systematic way. Other countries generally lie on a spectrum, with France and Japan at one extreme and the United States at the other.

An important feature of innovation policy in countries such as Japan and France is that it involves the deliberate choice for public support of certain key technologies and main priority areas. Japan and France both have clear-cut, long-term strategies toward the development and exploitation of specific, selected high-technology product groups and new technologies (tables 7–2 and 7–3). Such policies have a strong reindustrialization flavor, and the reindustrialization process as seen through the eyes of Japanese policymakers is clearly illustrated in figure 7–1.

The distinction between the two main ways of approaching innovation policy should not be seen as a model for describing two totally different worlds, and in practice differences are often not as great as they may at first sight appear. For example, despite the current British government's stated

Table 7–2
Areas of Interest to Japanese Industry

New Products	Energy Industries	Advanced, High-Technology Industries
Optical fibers	Coal liquefaction	Ultra-high-speed computers
Ceramics	Coal gasification	Space developments
Amorphous materials	Nuclear power	Ocean developments
High-efficiency resin	Solar energy	Aircraft
	Deep geothermal generation	

Source: Japanese Ministry of International Trade and Industry.

Table 7–3
Strategic High-Technology Priorities in France

Strategic Industry	Objectives	Overall Actions Planned
Electronic office equipment	To achieve 20–25 percent world market share and avert an anticipated $2 billion trade deficit in 1985	In strategic sectors, government will negotiate development contracts with individual companies, setting specific goals for sales, exports, and jobs. Firms that make such commitments will receive tax incentives, subsidized loans, and other official aids
Consumer electronics	To create a world-scale group including TV set and tube makers that will each rank among the top three globally; to eliminate the $750 million trade deficit in such products	
Energy-saving equipment	To ensure that government grants to companies and households to install such equipment are spent primarily on French products	
Undersea activities	To recapture second place in the world after the United States	
Bioindustry	Objectives not yet defined	
Industrial robots	Objectives not yet defined	

Source: Reprinted from the June 30, 1980, issue of *Business Week* by special permission, © 1980 by McGraw-Hill, Inc.

Note: These six industries together are expected to add $10 billion in sales and to double their work force to 135,000 by 1985.

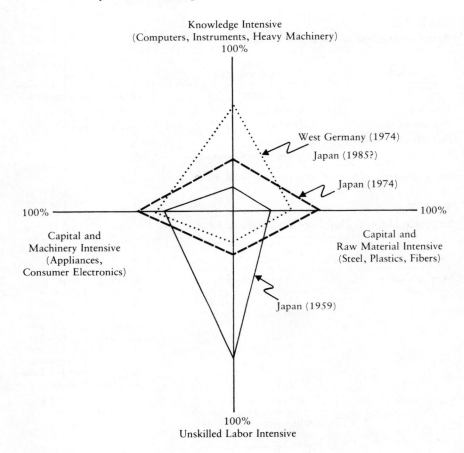

Source: Japanese Economic Planning Agency.

Figure 7–1. Evolution of Industrial Structure: A Comparison of Japan and West Germany

commitment to a market forces policy, the Department of Trade and Industry has established a set of strategic aims that include the adoption by British industry of certain (selected) key technologies (table 7–4).

Regarding technology choice, there appears recently to have been some convergence of national policies in this respect. For example, it is probably true to say that more or less all the advanced market economies now have explicit policies toward the development and exploitation of information technology (English and Watson Brown 1984). Even in the United States, where political factors largely preclude the adoption of comprehensive, indicative national

Table 7–4
U.K. Department of Industry Strategic Aims

Climate	Efficiency	Innovation
Social climate that values productive industry	Human skills in industry equal to competitor	Gear research and inward technology to U.K. needs
Fiscal regime that encourages new enterprise	Expose state-owned industries to competition by privatization	Standards to raise U.K. design and quality performance
Regulatory framework to promote competition and new firms	Reduce U.K. regional disparities in resource utilization	Awareness and rapid adoption of key technologies
Elimination of trade obstacles	Inward investment and collaboration with foreign companies	Public purchasing to promote innovation and competitiveness
	Technical support for U.K. companies in world markets	
	Selective aid to raise U.K. output and performance	

Source: J. Elliot, *Financial Times*, November 16, 1982.

innovation policies (Roessner 1984), it has been argued that covert or informal policies are pursued by the funding and procurement activities of the Department of Defense:

> The R&D programmes of the U.S. Department of Defence contribute significantly to the country's civilian technology and to its industrial base. In the past the Department of Defence spokesmen have generally referred to this contribution in terms of dual technology and ensuring an adequate industrial production capacity to satisfy military requirements. In recent years there has begun to be reference to civilian applications per se and the importance of a competitive advantage over other countries particularly Japan. Dr Richard DeLauer, Under Secretary of Defence for Research and Engineering, is reported to have made the following statement to representatives of the semiconductor industry in February, 1983: "The nth-generation development programme is the US answer to Japan's government supported fifth-generation computer program". The US program to which Dr DeLauer referred is formally titled Strategic Computing and Survivability. (Rothwell and Zegveld 1985, p. 139)

Publicly funded institutions have undoubtedly played a key role in the United States in the past in stimulating the emergence of new technology-based industries, a good illustrative example being the crucial role of the National Aeronautics and Space Administration (NASA) in the emergence of the U.S. civilian satellite communications industry. This has been comprehensively documented by Teubal and Steinmuller (1983). The point is, in addition to creating a considerable source of civilian R&D funding and enabling successive U.S. administrators to circumvent the dogmatic issue of direct (formal) government involvement in technological and industrial development, organizations such as the Department of Defense and NASA have effectively played a key role in the selection, development, and diffusion into use of new technologies and product groups in the United States.

Finally, Aubert (1984) has summarized succinctly the main features of current innovation policies in Japan, Europe, and the United States (figure 7–2).

Some Past Problems of Innovation Policy

With a few notable exceptions such as the Experimental Technology Incentives Program in the United States (Herbert and Hoar 1982) and several small-firm policy initiatives in West Germany (Meyer-Krahmer, Gielow, and Kunze 1982), few innovation policy initiatives have been subjected to systematic and objective evaluation (Gibbons 1984). As a result, innovation policy today can be said to be as much a matter of faith as of understanding (Rothwell 1982). Despite the paucity of systematic assessments, it is nevertheless possible to identify a number of rather general problems from which innovation policies have suffered in the past (Rothwell and Zegveld 1984).

First, there has often been a lack of market know-how among public policymakers, and according to Golding (1978) and Little (1974), there exists evidence to suggest that government funds often have gone to support projects of high technical sophistication but of low market potential and profitability. As well as often having lower market potential, projects funded by governments have also tended to present higher technical and financial risks than those funded wholly by industrial companies. The fact that projects pose high technical risk might, of course, be taken as justification for government involvement; the problem governments face is to identify high-risk projects that also have high market potential, yet it is doubtful whether government policymakers generally possess the competence to assess market prospects satisfactorily.

Second, subsidies in the past have tended to assist mainly large firms, an imbalance that can and should be redressed. This tells us nothing, of course, about the effectiveness of those subsidies that have been made to small firms. In the case of large firms, evidence from Canada and Germany suggests that funds often have gone in support of projects that are relatively small and sometimes of dubious merit such that the companies would not by themselves

FOCAL POINTS FOR NATIONAL INNOVATION EFFORTS

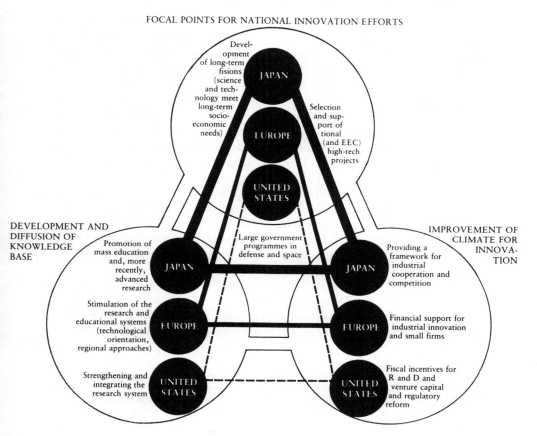

Source: Aubert 1984.

Note: The lines joining the three circles indicate the links and interactions among the three government policy areas. The dotted lines indicate weak interactions, the solid line stronger ones.

Figure 7–2. Government Innovation Policies: Main Features

finance them (Little 1974). The Enterprise Development Program in Canada (Rothwell and Zegveld 1981, p. 199), which will support only projects that represent a significant risk to the firm, represents an explicit attempt to avoid financing marginal projects in large firms. More recently, many governments have attempted to redress the large firm bias and have promulgated many measures aimed specifically at augmenting the innovatory potential of small and medium-sized firms (Rothwell and Zegveld 1982).

Third, governments often have tended to adopt a passive, rather than an active, stance toward information dissemination. As a result, policy measures have been taken up largely by a limited number of aware (usually large) companies.

Fourth, there has sometimes been a lack of interdepartmental coordination—and sometimes cooperation—between the relevant organizations and agencies involved in the policy process. This can result in lack of complementarity between different initiatives and might also lead to the propagation of contradictory measures. That this is true in other areas of public policy is amply demonstrated in table 7–5 for the United States.

Fifth, there has been a tendency for innovation policies to be subjected to changes in political philosophy rather than to changing national or international economic needs or conditions. Thus, in many countries, policies have been subjected to a political cycle rather than to the dictates of economic, industrial, or technological cycles.

Finally, there has been a general lack of practical knowledge or imaginative conceptualization of the process of industrial innovation by public policymakers. As a result, they have tended to adopt an R&D-oriented view of innovation (more R&D equals more innovation), to the detriment of other important aspects of the process, such as using innovation-oriented public purchasing on the demand side.

If a new cluster of technoeconomic combinations is emerging that will form the basis for future industrial and economic growth, it is crucially important that governments formulate coherent policies toward this end. In order to achieve this, policymakers must adopt an appropriate policy framework.

Table 7–5
Some Contradictory Policies Affecting Industry in the United States

The Environmental Protection Agency is pressing hard for stringent air pollution controls	The Energy Department is pushing companies to switch from imported oil to dirtier coal
The National Highway Traffic Safety Administration mandates weight-adding safety equipment for cars	The Transportation Department is insisting on lighter vehicles to conserve gasoline
The Justice Department offers guidance to companies on complying with the Foreign Corrupt Practices Act	The Securities and Exchange Commission will not promise immunity from prosecution for practices the Justice Department might permit
The Energy Department tries to keep down rail rates for hauling coal to encourage plant conversions	The Transportation Department tries to keep coal-by-rail rates high to bolster the ailing rail industry
The Environmental Protection Agency restricts use of pesticides	The Agricultural Department promotes pesticides for agricultural and forestry use
The Occupational Safety and Health Administration chooses the lowest level of exposure to hazardous substances technically feasible, short of bankrupting an industry	The Environmental Protection Agency uses more flexible standards for comparing risk levels with costs

Source: *Business Week*, June 30, 1980.

Three Approaches to Innovation Policy

Supply, Environment, Demand

Although it is clear from the many empirical studies of innovation at the level of the firm that success or failure is determined largely by the qualities and actions of firm's management, it is equally clear that public policies can play an important role. First, if companies lack the technical expertise or the financial resources to enable them to undertake risky R&D and innovation endeavors, then it is unlikely that they will enter the innovation race. In such cases governments can assist through technology transfer schemes and by providing financial support for innovation. Indeed most governments currently operate schemes to these ends.

Second, companies do not exist in a vacuum. On the contrary, they operate in an environment on which governments have a major influence through, for example, taxation policy, general macroeconomic policy, and regulatory policy. Thus governments have a significant role in creating an environment that might stimulate (or inhibit) innovatory endeavor at the firm level. There is, for example, considerable evidence to suggest that perceptions by U.S. managers that they were overregulated during the 1970s considerably reduced their propensity to invest in technological innovation (Rothwell 1979; National Academy of Sciences 1978). It was for this reason that, during its first hundred days in office, the Reagan administration made seventy-nine separate regulatory changes "to fulfill the president's commitment to 'take government off the back of business' " (Leone and Bradley 1981).

Third, governments have an important market role. Given that public authorities purchase between 30 and 50 percent of all goods and services produced in the advanced market economies, it is surprising how few explicit attempts have been made to utilize public purchasing as a means to stimulate supplier innovations. To be sure, most governments have relevant experience in the defense sector where procurement has been highly successful at stimulating innovations (Nelson 1982), but few systematic attempts have been made at innovation-oriented procurement in the civilian sector. Since evidence from the United States suggests that public procurement can be particularly effective in influencing the rate and direction of technological change during the early stages in the development of a new technology (Herbert and Hoar 1982), it would appear to be a potentially potent tool in the context of reindustrialization policy.

We can present the first innovation policy framework in table 7–6, which lists some policy tools. A number of these tools are concerned not only with the generation of innovations, but also with their diffusion, a crucially important aspect of innovation policy. Finally, it should be emphasized that tools in the three categories should be applied in a coordinated manner; they do not represent alternative approaches to intervention but rather complementary paths of intervention.

Table 7–6
Supply-Side, Demand-Side, and Environmental Tools for an Innovating Company

Supply-Side Tools	Environmental Tools	Demand-Side Tools
R&D grants	Regulations	Volume of public purchasing
Technological know-how	Planning procedures	Creating quality demand for existing products (not the cheapest buys)
Skilled personnel	Patent policy	Innovation-oriented public purchasing (diffusion-stimulating policies)
	Fiscal policy	
	Attitudes toward industry	Military and space
	Macroeconomic policy	Telecommunications
	Stimulating social acceptance of new technology (diffusion-stimulating policies)	Hospitals
		Transport
		Energy
		Education
		Offices
		Underwriting cost of purchase of innovative new equipment (diffusion-stimulating policies)

Strategic and Tactical Tools

A second approach to innovation policy, and one that would perhaps fit better with our definition of reindustrialization, is to list policy tools under the general headings strategic and tactical. Strategic policy tools are of long-term perspective and are concerned with stimulating the emergence of new or sunrise industries and with inducing major structural industrial shifts. Examples of strategic policy tools include the following:

Funding long-term projects in the science and technology infrastructure (such as in universities and government laboratories).

Venture capital schemes for new technology-based start-ups.

Funding major national technology programs involving collaborative research (such as university–industry or industry–industry).

Strategic public purchasing, such as in aerospace, telecommunications, and health care.

The adoptions of such tools would imply the need for governments first to formulate long-term innovation (reindustrialization) strategies.

Tactical policy tools are concerned with improving the innovatory potential of existing firms and upgrading product quality and manufacturing productivity. Tactical tools include the following:

Grants for R&D and innovation.

Technology transfer schemes involving collective research institutions and other infrastructural elements, such as the manufacturing advisory scheme for small firms in the United Kingdom.

Preproduction purchasing of new models.

Establishment of stringent performance standards.

One useful feature of tactical tools is that they often enjoy a low political profile.

For each of the two broad categories of strategic and tactical policy tools, the tools can be subclassified as demand side, environmental side, and supply side according to their operational focus.

Although throughout Europe governments for many years have promulgated a battery of tactical tools, recently there has been increased emphasis on the use of strategic tools. More specifically, governments have become involved increasingly in venture capital schemes (Rothwell 1984a) and in funding national collaborative technology programs. Examples of the latter are the Alvey Programme for advanced information technology in the United Kingdom (Department of Trade and Industry 1982) and the EEC-wide ESPRIT Programme on information technology (Mackintosh 1984). These programs are designed to create technological capacity in the broad area of information technology, providing a technological envelope for the specific, product-oriented innovatory activities of individual companies.

Three Broad Areas Approach

A third policy approach, and one that is the most relevant to the theme of reindustrialization, considers three broad areas of policy intervention and the relationships between them: technological opportunity, the structure and dynamics of the industrial sector, and the size and nature of demand.

Technological Opportunity

An important factor in reindustrialization and technology policy is the tranfer of scientific knowledge to the market sector. "Knowledge", as an input factor, is transferred to industry in two main ways. First, knowledge is incorporated in the labour supply to industry via the labour market. The currently perceived importance of education can well be illustrated—and measured—by the considerable allocation of financial resources to this area, which represent a significant share of overall government budgets. At the same time, little attention has been paid to coupling mechanisms between the educational system and its "clients", an important client being industry. These relationships clearly require reinforcement.

The second priority transfer path consists of the direct transfer of knowledge and hardware to industry from the technical and scientific infrastructure, wholly or partially publicly funded R&D institutions including universities and collective industrial research institutes. Reindustrialization and technology policy should pay considerably greater attention to industry-infrastructure links. Empirical research shows, for example, that links between industry and the scientific and technical infrastructure are substantially stronger in countries with high innovation performance. (Ergas 1983, in Rothwell and Zegveld 1985, p. 254)

Thus governments need to give closer attention to both the volume and structure of infrastructural R&D and to the links between the infrastructure and industry. This is especially important during a period in which basic research is becoming increasingly important to the strategic needs of industry, most notably in the generic areas of information technology and biotechnology. It is, moreover, no easy task to change the orientation (culture) of infrastructural institutions or the structure of their skills and research. Evidence from the United Kingdom, for example, suggests that the structure of British university research has failed to adapt to match the evolving strategic needs of industry; British university research strengths are becoming increasingly locked into areas of diminishing strategic commercial potential (Martin, Irvine, and Turner 1984).

Industrial Sector Structure and Dynamics. Just as infrastructural institutions need to adapt to satisfy better emerging industrial needs, so too may the structure of the industrial sector require adaptation to accommodate better the requirements of radical new technologies. Current industrial organizations may lack both the flexibility and the culture to enable them rapidly to adapt to exploit the new technomarket regimes. This point has been emphasized by Nelson in his discussion of revolutionary technological changes in the United States:

> These sharp shifts in technological regimes often were marked by changes in the nature of the predominant companies. Thus, as jets replaced piston-driven planes, Boeing replaced Douglas as the leader in the design and production of airlines. With the advent of the integrated circuit, the old electronic equipment producers, like General Electric and Westinghouse, failed to stay competitive and were replaced as technological leaders by such companies as Texas Instruments and Intel. (Nelson 1984, p. 9)

The importance of obtaining the appropriate industrial structural dynamic is underlined by consideration of the evolution of the semiconductor industries of the United States, Japan and Europe (Rothwell 1984b). In the United States where the industry originated, the early radical inventive activity came about in the R&D laboratories of large corporations, most notably Bell Labs. These companies then produced semiconductor devices mainly for their own use. The rapid diffusion of semiconductor devices throughout the U.S. economy came about through the dynamic, entrepreneurial activities of new firms, some of which grew rapidly to national and international importance. Moreover, these entrepreneurial newcomers were often founded by workers spinning off from the large corporations, bringing with them a great deal of state-of-the-art technical expertise and adding to it their own entrepreneurial flair and market dynamism. A similar pattern occurred during the evolution of the U.S. computer-aided design industry (Kaplinsky 1982).

In Japan, the semiconductor industry began much later than in the United States and evolved very differently. Technology was acquired (mainly from the United States) by existing large R&D-performing companies in a coordinated, industry-wide manner under the guiding hand of MITI. Assimilation of the technology was aided by publicly funded collaborative research. The Japanese companies quickly built up their in-house R&D expertise and rapidly caught up with their counterparts in the United States. Capitalizing on their genius for total quality control and highly efficient mass production, Japanese firms rapidly gained market share to become a major force in world semiconductor markets.

In Europe, in comparison with the United States, the semiconductor industry developed only slowly. Here semiconductor devices were introduced later and largely by established electronics companies, which, partly through lack of dynamism and entrepreneurial flair, exhibited laggard behavior. As a result, European companies have enjoyed only a minor share of world semiconductor markets. Few new technology-based firms along U.S. lines were established in Europe (Little 1977).

From the late 1960s on, the output of the U.S. semiconductor industry began increasingly to be concentrated in the top ten or so companies. Production economies of scale grew in importance (and plant size increased), as did production learning, and firms began actively to seek rapid movement down the production learning curve. According to Sciberras (1977), the prime motive for rapid cost reductions was to deter new entrants by creating significant scale barriers to entry in addition to technological entry barriers. This might at least partially explain why semiconductor technology was exploited in Europe mainly by large electronics companies: Europe entered the race at a late date, by which time existing scale and technological barriers together largely precluded entry by small firms.

This description suggests that established, large technology-based companies can be extremely effective in creating new technological possibilities; they are highly inventive (table 7–7). Although they are adept at utilizing the results of their inventiveness in-house (new technology for existing applications), they are less well adapted to the exploitation of their inventions in new markets

Table 7–7
Patterns of Evolution of the Semiconductor Industry in the United States, Europe, and Japan

United States
  Leading-edge R&D in major companies
  Invention and innovation geared mainly toward own use
  High rate of spin-off and vigorous entrepreneurship
  Entry barriers initially relatively low
  Rapid market diffusion and the emergence of new technomarket paradigms
  Rapid growth of NTBFs
  Technological and market leadership

Europe
  Technologically laggard behavior by major companies
  Inadequate attempts at in-house catching up
  Late market entry, at which time there are few possibilities for NTBF formation because
    entry barriers are now too high
  Technological and market backwardness

Japan
  National policies for technology acquisition
  High degree of coordination and cooperation
  Existence of large R&D-capable companies
  Technology acquired for whole industries and not individual companies
  Long-term development strategies at company, industry, and national levels
  Emphasis on quality control and production efficiency
  Rapid catching up in determinate (well-specified) markets and technologies

(new technology for new applications). It appears that new firms initially are better adapted to exploit new technomarket regimes, breaking out from existing regimes within which established corporations for historical, cultural, and institutional reasons might be rather strongly bound. Today we can see how the new wave biotechnology industry is being pioneered by new, small firms (in this instance, university spin-offs), albeit that established chemical, food, and pharmaceutical companies are now entering the race, often through equity investments in the newcomers and through joint ventures with them.

In terms of industrial structure and dynamics, it seems that the presence of leading-edge R&D performing institutions (companies, universities) coupled to vigorous spin-off entrepreneurship leading to the creation of new, dynamic, fast-growing firms, is a system well adapted to the creation of new technoeconomic combinations. A system of large, R&D-capable corporations with coordinated, long-term, explicit strategies toward technological acquisition and know-how accumulation is a system well adapted to rapid catching up within established technoeconomic regimes. A system in which neither leading-edge R&D activity (at least on an appreciable scale) nor coordinated national policies toward technology acquisition exist seems doomed to technological and market backwardness within existing regimes.

Size and Nature of Demand

> The size and structure of demand are clearly key elements in determining innovative performance. Consideration of market structure and dynamics is thus an important element in reindustrialisation and technology policy. Compared with Europe, the USA and Japan both have large internal markets and ones which adapt rapidly to, and indeed which help to create, a technically sophisticated supply. From the standpoint of achieving international competitiveness, firms in these countries have first to compete successfully in their national markets because of the severe levels of internal competition existing there. In the effectively fragmented markets in Europe, fierce competition on a more than national level is often lacking, largely because of the existence of many non-tariff barriers. Even within the EEC, many obstacles prevent the functioning of one "common" market. (Rothwell and Zegveld 1985, p. 257)

Governments are in a good position to open up more technologically demanding markets for industry through their military and civilian procurement activities. In the context of regional development policy, local authority procurement might be utilized to stimulate supplier innovations and new start-ups in areas largely deficient in innovation-oriented demand (Rothwell 1984c). One of the primary aims of reindustrialization policy must be the identification, stimulation, and diffusion into use of new technologies on which future economic growth can be based. The more traditional policies of support, encouragement, and experimentation should be complemented by more ambitious long-term procurement strategies for stimulating technological change.

Governments might also develop policies designed to stimulate the social acceptance of new technologies, thereby influencing the rate of diffusion of innovative new products (Rothwell and Wissema 1985). In the United Kingdom, for example, the public-sector BBC showed in prime time its Computer Program, which was associated with the sale of the so-called BBC Computer. At the same time the government established a scheme to underwrite the purchasing cost of small computers in schools (to date something like 200,000 mcirocomputers have been installed in British schools). As a result of these two initiatives, Britain now has more home computers per capita than any other nation. An approach that combines knowledge (software) with hands-on experience (hardware) can be extremely effective in stimulating public acceptance of and demand for new technology-based devices.

To summarize, our third approach, innovation policy, should aim in a coordinated manner at creating technological opportunity and forging the appropriate linkages with industry, achieving the appropriate industrial structure, and favorably influencing the size and structure of demand. Many

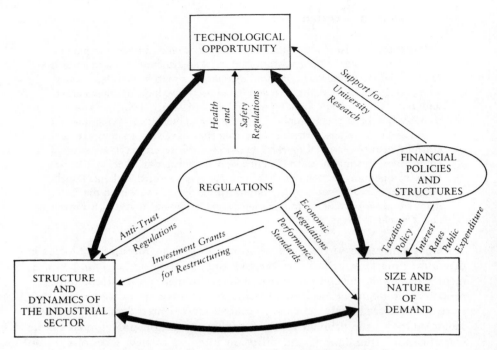

Figure 7–3. Three Broad Areas Approach

of the policy tools listed previously can influence each of the three broad areas in a variety of ways, as illustrated in figure 7–3 in the case of regulatory and financial policy tools.

Finally turning briefly to the specific area of financial policy:

> Finance is an integral element of reindustrialisation policy since it can greatly influence all other main elements. For example, public finance can significantly influence the rate of infrastructural (and firm based) technological change; financial systems (including grants for equipment, innovation, etc.) can influence the structure and operations of the industrial sector; and the size and structure of market demand is to an extent influenced by capital availability and public policies affecting interest rates, tax levels, public sector expenditures and so on. In this respect, it is perhaps government financial policies that act as the main link between technology and reindustrialisation policies and macroeconomic policies. (Rothwell and Zegveld 1985, p. 259)

Additional Considerations

A number of potential problems and constraints are likely to be met by policymakers working to establish an appropriate innovation policy framework.

Base to Build On

Research on diversification in manufacturing companies suggests that successful firms tend to move into new areas that are in some way related to one or more of their existing core strengths (Rumelt 1982; Ergas 1983). In other words, the direction in which a firm is able to move is to some extent determined by where it has already been. Similarly, from the point of view of national policies for structural adjustment through technology, the question of where a nation is going is very much determined by where it is today, the possibilities being largely determined by the national store of technological skills and expertise. Acquiring new technological capability is a costly, cumulative learning process; new know-how cannot be picked simply off the shelf. Only on the basis of a detailed assessment of national industrial capabilities, a knowledge of infrastructural scientific and technological expertise and potential, and an estimation of the financial resources available can a nation begin realistically to establish a set of aims and to identify what resources (volume and structure) are required and how to allocate them.

The richer the nation and the fuller and more varied its scientific and technological endowment, the greater are the possibilities open to it. Table 7–8 shows the share in total R&D expenditure by the Organization for Economic Cooperation and Development (OECD) taken by the United States, the EEC, Japan, and other OECD member countries in 1981. These data suggest that, with the exception of the United States, few countries can hope to be technological leaders across the board. This implies for most nations the need for policies of technology choice; the need, where possible, for international collaboration; and the need for policies of technology importation as well as technology generation.

Technology Trade and Dependency

Table 7–9 shows cumulative receipts and expenditures in international trade in technology for four major market economies. (In 1982 Canada had a nega-

Table 7–8
Total R&D Expenditure in 1981 within OECD
(percentage)

	1981	1975–1981
United States	46	− 1.0
EEC	29	− 2.0
Japan	17	+ 3.0
Other	8	Same

Note: Total R&D expenditure for 1981 was approximately $102,000 million.

Table 7–9
Receipts and Expenditures on Patents, Inventions,
Processes, and Copyrights
(millions DM)

	1972	*1980*
United States		
Receipts	8,833	12,696
Payments	938	1,375
Balance	+7,895	+11,323
United Kingdom		
Receipts	1,079	2,185
Payments	978	1,681
Balance	+101	+504
West Germany		
Receipts	674	1,101
Payments	1,574	2,624
Balance	−900	−1,523
Japan		
Receipts	226	643
Payments	1,741	2,411[a]
Balance	−1,518	−1,768

[a]Mainly from the United States.

tive technology trade balance of $270 million.) Japan, perhaps the competitively most successful nation during the past twenty or so years, has been extremely adept not only at importing foreign technology but also at assimilating it. Successful assimilation occurs when a nation also builds up national expertise in the areas of technology importation (table 7–10). Thus, successful assimilation is a process of establishing technological complementarity between the imported technology and in-house expertise. Attempting to substitute national capability through technology importation is not a viable policy in the long term.

Table 7–10
Policy Coordination in Japan, 1974

Fees and Royalties Paid[a]		*Total R&D Expenditure*[b]
Electrical Machinery	24.6%	25.0%
Chemicals	16.9	1.1
Machinery	12.9	9.2
Transport	16.7	15.2
Total	71.1%	68.5%

[a]Total was 159,932 million yen.
[b]Total was 1,589 billion yen.

In 1982, OECD technology exports totaled $12 billion, and the United States was the source of between 50 and 75 percent of technology for most importing countries. There appears to be a trend that countries with comprehensive and broadly based domestic technological capacity have reduced their level of direct reliance on imported technology. For example:

> Japanese firms have consistently increased their own R and D efforts to use, improve, develop and perfect imported technology. Technology imports of firms performing R and D fell from 25 per cent of the value of R and D expenditures in the early 1970s to 10 per cent in 1982. . . . During this period many Japanese firms closed the technology gap between themselves and leading foreign firms. As this occurred, internal R and D has been an increasingly important part of firm expenditures.
>
> On a more limited scale the same phenomenon occurred in Canada. Payments for technology by firms performing R and D have dropped from 30 per cent of the value of Canadian business R and D expenditures in the early 1970s to 20 per cent now (1984) as R and D expenditures rose sharply in the aircraft, communications and petroleum industries. (OECD 1984)

There is a second feature of technology trade, one that is currently the cause for some concern in Europe: an increasing tendency toward national appropriability of R&D results by the United States. This might herald a general tendency for nations to hang on more tightly to the results of state-of-the-art R&D exclusively for domestic companies to exploit. If this trend does become established, then the implications for heavily technology-importing countries are serious.

A third significant feature of technology trade is that it occurs largely between affiliated companies, and payments to the United States are mainly from affiliates to U.S. parent companies. In the case of Canadian, German, and U.K. payments to the United States in 1982, the percentage going to affiliates was 94 percent, 78 percent, and 89 percent, respectively (OECD 1984). In addition, in 1977 the percentage of total business enterprise R&D expenditures performed by U.S. firms in Canada, Germany, and the United Kingdom was 32, 6, and 10 percent, respectively. Thus, in the case of countries such as Canada, in addition to the battery of problems faced by policymakers in all other countries, policymakers have to face the crucial issues of technological dependency and foreign control of R&D resources when formulating national technology policies. This clearly represents a major constraint on the range of future actions that can be taken.

In most cases governments would have to opt for a policy of technology choice that, in the case of smaller countries, means a policy of technomarket specialization: the niche-strategy approach. Choosing the appropriate technologies is no easy task, and a simple formula to govern choice simply does not exist. However, there are a number of questions policymakers might sensibly ask themselves when attempting technology selection (Rothwell and Zegveld 1985):

What is the long-term market potential of each technoeconomic combination?

Can public markets influence the rate and direction of development?

To what extent do we bias resource allocation in favor of the limited set of technologies chosen from the broader range of alternatives?

Is it possible to back fully a limited number of primary selections, while at the same time offering limited support (maintaining a limited capability) over a broader range of technologies?

To what extent will the ensuing pattern of resource allocation—locked largely into a handful of primary technologies—effectively reduce our national technological flexibility and hence our ability to respond to new technoeconomic threats and opportunities to arise?

Are some technologies inherently more expensive or more difficult to develop than others? If so, to what extent should this influence our primary selection?

How does each technology match with our national stock of human capital and with our identified set of comparative national technical, industrial, and market strengths and weaknesses?

How appropriate to the nation are the benefits to be derived from each particular stream of technology?

How can we achieve a reasonable balance between the resources devoted to industrial renewal and those devoted to the creation of new combinations?

To what extent will each combination be subjected to especially stringent and difficult regulatory requirements in other countries?

At what stage in the chain of technological development can we even begin to make rational choices among a variety of emerging technoeconomic options?

How broad is each technological stream in terms of its range of potential technoeconomic alternatives and combinations?

Which actors and institutions should be involved in the selection process?

To what extent are there interdependencies among the different technological streams?

To what extent are we able to capitalize on potential synergies among the chosen streams of technology?

Which institutions will play the major role in developing each of chosen fields, and/or which phase of development will each concentrate on?

Who will play the major coordinating role?

How far should government involvement go, from the choice of broad technologies to the choice of individual products?

At what stage will government's role begin to diminish in each area as private industry begins increasingly to dominate R&D activity?

Toward an Innovation Policy Framework

Although it is not the purpose of this chapter to suggest a definitive set of innovation policies and tools appropriate to reindustrialization, it can be said with some confidence that whatever policies are adopted should contain at least five important features (Rothwell and Zegveld 1985).

Coherence

The actions of the various institutions that formulate and implement policy should be coordinated in order to avoid the promulgation of contradictory measures, especially between innovation and other policies. More positively, potential synergies must be sought and capitalized upon. Innovation policies and general macroeconomic policies must pull together.

Consistency

Innovation policies must be insulated from the dictates of the short-term political cycle. While this might not be too difficult to achieve with tactical policies, it might be more difficult with strategic policies that affect major programs of restructuring. Innovation policy should not be the creature of party dogma.

Flexibility

While innovation policies should be consistent, they should not at the same time be inflexible. Policies must be capable of responding to changing industrial needs, threats, and opportunities. Greater inherent flexibility might be acheived if the policy initiative has in-built learning by doing. In other words, policy measures should incorporate continuous evaluation, with positive feedback to the policy system in order to improve policy effectiveness.

Complementarity

Policies should not only complement each other, but they should complement also the strategic interests of domestic companies. This means that policymakers should be aware of the long-term strategic thinking within major national companies.

Realism

Policymakers must recognize the inherent limitations of public policy and accept them. Overoptimistic expectations, unmet, might result in disillusionment and the termination of promising initiatives. Policies should thus be based on a realistic assessment of industrial potential. Public policymakers should also recognize their own limitations. While, in consultation with industry, public bodies might be involved in the selection of rather broad areas of technoeconomic activity, the choice of individual projects is probably best left in the hands of industrial managers.

As Rothwell and Zegveld (1985) have emphasized, innovation policies by themselves are not enough; they must go hand in hand with the appropriate general economic and social policies. Governments must strive to create a favorable overall economic climate (for example, by low interest rates and moderate corporation tax regimes), a favorable social climate (perhaps by stimulating the social acceptance of new technology and helping to overcome social and institutional rigidities and resistances to change), a relatively stable political climate (dramatic political swings create uncertainty), and avoid rapid policy changes (stop–go policies can deter the adoption by firms of the necessary long-term development strategies). In other words, reindustrialization can occur effectively only when government achieves overall policy coherence. Well-thought-out and -implemented technological innovation policies are a necessary but not sufficient condition for successful reindustrialization.

References

Aubert, J.E. 1984. "Innovation Policies: A Three-way Contrast." *OECD Observer*, no. 131 (November).

DTI. 1982. *A Program for Advanced Information Technology*. London: HMSO.

English, M., and Watson Brown, A. 1984. *National Policies in Informtion Technology: Challenge and Responses*. Brussels: Intelligence Unit, ITTTC, EC Commission.

Ergas, H. 1983. "Corporate Strategies in Transition." Mimeo. Paris: OECD.

Freeman, C. 1974. *The Economics of Innovation*. Penguin Modern Ecnonomic Texts.

Freeman, C.; Clark, J.; and Soete, L. 1982. *Unemployment and Technical Innovation*. London: Frances Pinter.

Gibbons, M. 1984. "Evaluating Policies For Innovation." *Policy Studies Review* 3, nos. 3–4.

Golding, A.M. 1978. "The Influence of Government Procurement on the Semiconductor Industry in the U.S. and Britain." Six Countries Programme Workshop on Government Procurement Policies and Innovation, Dublin.

Herbert, R., and Hoar, R.W. 1982. "Government and Technology: Experimenting with Change." NBS-GCR-ETIP 82–100. Washington, D.C.: Bureau of Standards.

Kaplinsky, R. 1982. *The Impact of Technical Change on the International Division of Labour: The Illustrative Case of CAD*. London: Frances Pinter.

Leone, R.A., and Bradley, S.P. 1981. "Towards an Effective Industrial Policy." *Harvard Business Review* (November–December).

Little, B. 1974. "The Role of Government in Assisting New Product Development." Working Paper Series no. 114. London: School of Business Administration, University of Western Ontario. March.

Little, A.D. 1977. *New Technology-Based Firms in the United Kingdom and the Federal Republic of Germany*. London: Wilton House Publications Ltd.

Mackintosh, I.M. 1984. "A Survey of Community Support Programmes and Strategies in Information Technology." Luton, U.K.: Mackintosh International Ltd.

Martin, B.; Irvine, J.; and Turner, R. 1984. "Trends in British Research Performance: Some Myths Exploded." *New Scientist*, November 8.

Mensch, G. 1979. *Stalemate in Technology*. Cambridge, Mass.: Ballinger Press.

Meyer-Krahmer, F.; Gielow, G.; and Kunze, U. 1982. *Innovations-forderung bei kleinen und mittleren Unternehmen*. Frankfurt: Campus Verlag.

National Academy of Sciences. 1979. *Antitrust, Uncertainty and Technological Innovation*. Washington, D.C.: National Academy of Sciences.

Nelson, R. 1984. *High Technology Policies: A Five-Nation Comparison*. Washington, D.C.: American Enterprise Institute.

———, ed. 1982. *Government and Technical Progress*. Elmsford, N.Y.: Pergamon Press.

OECD. 1984. "The Structure of International Flows of Technology." DSTI/SPR/84.67. Paris, November 13.

Roessner, D. 1985. "Prospects for a National Innovation Policy in the United States." In *Design and Innovation: Policy and Management*, edited by Langdon and Rothell. London: Royal College of Art, Department of Design Research.

Rothwell, R. 1979. *Government Regulations and Industrial Innovation*. Report to the Six Countries Programme on Innovation. (TNO, PO Box 215, 2600 AE Delft, the Netherlands.

———. 1982. *Evaluation the Effectiveness of Government Innovation Policy*. Report to the Six Countries Programme on Innovation.

———. 1984a. "Technical Innovation and Long Waves in Economic Development." Prepared for International Seminar on Cambio y Desarrollo Economico, University Internacional Merendez Pelayo, Santandar, Spain, September 10–14.

Rothwell, R. 1984b. "Venture Finance, Small Firms and Public Policy in the UK." Prepared for Conference on Venture Capital and Innovation Policy, University of Pisa, Italy, July 6.

——. 1984c. "The Role of Small Firms in the Emergence of New Technologies," *OMEGA* 12, no. 1.

Rothwell, R., and Zegveld, W. 1981. *Industrial Innovation and Public Policy.* London: Frances Pinter.

——. 1982. *Innovation and the Small and Medium Sized Firm.* London: Frances Pinter.

——. 1984. "An Assessment of Innovation Policies." *Policy Studies Review* 13, nos. 3–4.

——. 1985. *Reindustrialization and Technology.* London: Longman.

Rothwell, R., and Wissema, H. 1985. "Technology, Culture and Public Policy." Mimeo. Science Policy Research Unit, University of Sussex, February.

Rumelt, R.P. 1982. "Diversification Strategy and Profitability." *Strategic Management Journal* 3, no. 4.

Sciberras, E. 1977. *Multinational Electronic Companies and National Economic Policies.* Greenwich, Conn.: JAI Press.

Teubal, M., and Steimuller, E. 1983. "Government Policy and Economic Growth." Research Paper 153. Jerusalem: Maurice Falk Institute for Economic Research in Israel.

van Duijn, J.J. 1983. *The Long Wave in Economic Life.* Assen, Netherlands: Van Garcum.

8
Strengthening the Technological Competitiveness of Industries: Potential Contributions of Government

Bela Gold

T he development of effective policies to strengthen the competitiveness of domestic industries that are already under severe pressure from foreign products, as well as of industries likely to face such increasing pressures, must be based on more precise diagnoses of the factors undermining their market shares than have emerged in generalized public and governmental discussions. Only then can the potential contributions of government and private industry to improving such competitiveness be clarified.

Major Sources of Competitive Advantages in Industry

Analysis of the factors that seem to have been most influential in affecting the relative market strength of foreign and domestic competitors in a variety of industries highlights product design and service capabilities, cost advantages, marketing superiority, and governmental aids and restrictions (Gold 1983b).

Product design advantages are of two kinds. One includes the attractiveness of appearance, the variety of available types and sizes, and the provision of features offering greater convenience in use—none of which need involve any technological superiority. But the latter may be a source of the second kind of advantages: those involving the level and consistency of product qualities, as well as such aspects of performance capabilities as operating efficiency, durability, reliability, safety, and ease of maintenance.

Cost advantages may similarly be traced to two different sources. First, advantages derive from the availability and price of inputs, including natural resources, energy, labor, and investment funds, which need not involve any technological superiority. But cost advantages may also derive from superiority with respect to one or more of the following determinants of efficiency in production operations:

More highly trained and experienced management combined with more aggressive managerial pressure for productivity improvements.

Larger and more advanced technical staff with greater incentives and pressure to keep improving technological capabilities.

Greater productive efforts by the labor force combined with greater willingness to accept technological innovations and greater mobility among tasks.

More modern, technologically advanced, and effective scale of facilities and equipment.

More limited product mix, more highly standardized products, longer production runs, and higher rates of capacity utilization.

Among these five, technological superiority is likely to play a major role only with respect to facilities and equipment, although the technological sophistication of engineering personnel may play a significant supporting role.

Marketing advantages seem to center around four factors:

1. More effective market research, with more precise identification of current or prospective shortcomings in meeting customer requirements.
2. Greater responsiveness to customer preferences relating to product design, availability, servicing, and financial arrangements.
3. Matching or shading competitive price–quality–order size combinations.
4. More aggressive selling efforts.

These obviously do not require technological superiority, nor do the remaining sources of major competitive advantages, which are traceable to such governmental aids as subsidies and tax relief, as well as restrictions on foreign competitors.

Most of the numerous factors grouped under the headings of cost and marketing advantages are essentially nontechnological and clearly the responsibility of managements alone. Major potential contributions to competitiveness derived from technological superiority relate only to product capabilities, production efficiency, and technical manpower. It is obvious, however, that increasing competitive disadvantages with respect to these and attendant costs cannot be overcome for long by intensified marketing efforts or financial expedients. Thus, technological competitiveness alone may not be a sufficient condition for achieving and maintaining a strong market position, but it is an essential condition.

Because technological development efforts in industry are controlled by management decisions, it is easy to underestimate the powerful influence of governmental actions on such decisions. In fact, however, a number of governmental tax, regulatory, and trade policies may discourage industrial commitments to major innovational programs by reducing their prospective profitability. In addition, the normal incentives for undertaking long-run, risky programs in the hope of achieving important technological advances may be blunted by the apparent inadequacy of governmental efforts to control inflation, to maintain expectations of vigorous economic growth, and even to minimize the risk of substantial imminent recessions. Consideration should also be given to the effects of possible shortcomings in governmental contributions to developing the precommercial structure of science and technology. This represents a national resource rather than a privately appropriable asset to be left to profit-seeking development efforts alone. Hence, its inadequate development has left domestic industries with more meager foundations for undertaking advances with commercial potential than is being provided by various foreign governments to their own producers.

Governmental efforts could therefore make major, and certainly necessary, contributions to reinvigorating the technological development efforts of many industries, although these would have to be strongly reinforced by managerial commitments and by trade union support if adequate progress is to be achieved.

Potential Governmental Contributions to
Increasing Industrial Competitiveness

Governmental efforts to strengthen the technological capabilities of domestic industries should be focused on two channels of improvement: helping to reduce the technological advantages of foreign competitors by encouraging the more rapid and fuller domestic adoption of available superior technologies and helping to generate significant technological advantages over foreign competitors by encouraging heavier commitments to long-term R&D programs promising major advances (Gold 1980). Measures seeking to support such objectives should be focused on the following needs:

1. Developing an information base for diagnosing and monitoring the technological competitiveness of various industries.
2. Increasing the financial attractiveness of innovational efforts by individual firms.
3. Reducing certain risks to the realization of expected innovational benefits.
4. Increasing the array of promising innovational opportunities.
5. Encouraging needed increases in basic research and the entry of more scientists and engineers into hitherto neglected industrial sectors.
6. Strengthening governmental capabilities for evaluating technological improvement needs and progress.

Developing an Information Base

The economic importance of industrial competitiveness and the modest rate at which its technological determinants can be changed emphasize the importance of developing a program for periodic mapping of the pattern of technological advantages and disadvantages relative to foreign competitors, covering domestic industries that still enjoy some technological superiority as well as those that have already fallen behind (Gold 1985a). Such biennial or triennial surveys would help to alert government and trade union officials as well as industrial executives to changes in the technological underpinnings of their competitive positions. Resulting findings would help to identify sectors of significant improvements or slippage, provide evidence of the relative effectiveness of the measures taken to strengthen competitiveness, and call attention to sectors that may require more far-reaching or differently oriented measures to prevent further deterioration of competitiveness.

Such surveys might also be broadened to encompass nontechnological factors affecting competitiveness or future technological pressures. These might include current or prospective changes in the availability and prices of important input factors, the quality specifications of products as well as in product mix, the emergence of new sources of competition, and foreign government policies affecting the competitiveness of their producers in export markets. Such broader coverage would provide the basis for a more effective assessment of changes in the current and prospective market competitiveness of industries than a narrow focus on technological capabilities alone.

It is often assumed that all firms are fully aware of the potentials and limitations of the technological advances already utilized by their competitors. This may be true in large measure for familiar domestic competitors but much less so for foreign competitors. Even large domestic firms with substantial international interests often appear to be inadequately informed about significant advances abroad. Trade journals often report the introduction of major new technologies abroad, but they seldom track their rate of diffusion or provide serious economic analyses of their effects—as differentiated from the enthusiastic claims of their innovators. Moreover, because competitive pressures tend to be evaluated by each firm in terms of its own experiences with customers, with a tendency to remain quiet about unfavorable outcomes, awareness of general industry-wide declines in competitiveness is likely to emerge only gradually. Correct identification of the factors actually involved is likely to take even longer, especially when attributable to technological shortcomings, because of the reluctance of engineers and managers to admit inadequacies regarding such a widely accepted requirement of competitiveness. Indeed even when a decline in competitiveness has become widely recognized, industry and trade union representatives are often likely to place all or most of the blame on nontechnological factors. Such diagnoses may be justified, at least in part, but so long as they obscure the contributory role of technological shortcomings, which may already be significant and growing, they encourage continued neglect of what may be one of the primary sources of potential remedial developments.

The formulation of effective remedial policies requires identification of the specific needs to be met and their relative importance in different market sectors, analysis of their causes, and at least preliminary exploration of alternate measures to achieve objectives. Policy recommendations proposed for application to industry at large imply that most, if not all, industries share the same shortcomings and that these are attributable to common pressures and hence are likely to be responsive to the same measures. But the existing wide differences in the international competitiveness of domestic industries, including their relative technological competitiveness, emphasizes the substantial limitations of such assumptions. Policies to deal with industrial problems having serious implications for the national welfare must be rooted in more solid foundations.

Increasing the Financial Attractiveness of Innovational Efforts

The most common recommendations for improving the technological competitiveness of domestic industries seem to center around the need to improve profitability and cash flow through various kinds of changes in tax and depreciation policies (Gold 1982a, chap. 17). Such recommendations rest on two implicit assumptions. The first is that increased innovational efforts by domestic industries require more attractive incentives for greater investment in research, development, and the capital facilities and equipment needed to utilize resulting technological advances. The second assumption is that increases in profitability and cash flow would ensure at least comparable increases in needed innovative efforts.

The first assumption seems reasonable, although sight should not be lost of the fact that intensified innovational activities are also not infrequently traceable to decreasing profits, increasing threats to survival, and the absence of less unattractive managerial options. But the assumption that increases in profitability and cash flow would generate proportionate increases in needed innovational efforts is open to more serious question.

The overriding objective of private industrial firms is not to maximize their technological capabilities but to improve or maintain profit rates. Proposals for strengthening technological capabilities must therefore compete with many other managerial options. Among these alternatives, allocations for innovational undertaking seem to have been consistently inadequate in a variety of industries during recent years of favorable as well as unfavorable profit rates and cash flow. Accordingly merely increasing the magnitude of such flows is not likely to generate substantially increased commitments to innovational efforts unless managerial perceptions of their relative profitability are significantly sharpened.

Four suggestions designed to make such managerial perceptions more favorable seem to warrant further consideration. They obviously apply both to encouraging more rapid adoption of technological advances already developed by others and to undertaking longer-term and riskier R&D projects, bearing in mind management's awareness that these are unlikely to yield commercial benefits until R&D expenditures are supplemented by often large investments in production and related facilities.

First, in order to help offset the discouraging effects of current high discount rates on calculations of the net present value of projects offering only long-deferred profits, consideration might be given to some means of adjusting tax rates on such eventual earnings so as to embody a reverse discount rate. Thus, the profits from recognizedly major innovational projects might be taxed at rates that are progressively lower in proportion to increases in the investment-weighted average time elapsing between project initiation and the probable realization of reasonable net profits. Only through some such overt and financially significant incentives could managements be helped to justify increasing the ratio of longer-term to shorter-term resource allocations.

Second, in order to decrease the net additional investments that might be required to support needed innovational activities, one approach would be to permit depreciation to begin as soon as the construction of relevant facilities is initiated instead of awaiting their completion. This would be especially significant in the case of building projects taking more than three years to complete. Another means would be to allow sharply accelerated depreciation in such investments in order to minimize the risks of early obsolescence through intensified technological competition. Also helpful would be an option to defer some portion of currently due tax payments if they are allocated to needed kinds of innovational activities, carrying such tax liabilities forward for perhaps three years, when resulting innovational benefits might be expected to emerge.

Third, in order to increase the availability of additional investment funds for needed innovational undertakings and in order to reduce their costs, a government agency might be established that would encourage investments in innovational technologies by means similar to those used in the United States by the Export-Import Bank to encourage foreign trade. Important as the latter objective undoubtedly is, its national welfare potentials surely fall far short of those offered by accelerating the technological progress of industry. Indeed fostering such progress would offer a powerful means of improving export potentials. Accordingly such an agency might not only provide loans on favorable terms but might also provide some form of partial insurance to help reduce attendant risks, as is already provided in connection with certain export loans.

Fourth, consideration needs to be given to the means of increasing investor awareness and support of longer-term managerial commitments to advancing technological capabilities. One of the most direct measures would be to adjust taxes so as to increase substantially the incentives for undertaking long-term and risky innovational programs. Another might be to have the government require annual reports to review not only past performance but also current and continuing commitments to technological advances and other programs seeking to safeguard the future competitiveness of the firm. Such public records might help to ease prevailing pressures on managements to maximize current profitability by skimping on resource allocations unlikely to improve short-term results—in addition to providing investors with a broader view of company potentials.

Reducing Certain Risks to the Realization of Expected Innovational Benefits

In order to encourage major innovational undertakings still further, means should also be considered for reducing certain associated risks other than those already noted.

One of the most important of these is the far from uncommon experience of trade union reactions, which tend to reduce and even eliminate the expected cost savings from technological advances, either through resisting reductions in employment levels or through necessitating increases in wage rates that offset any such reductions. It would be undesirable for the government to become regularly involved in labor–management negotiations about the absorption of improvements in productivity and technology. But consideration might well be given to developing means of providing three kinds of contributions to the easing of related problems.

One might involve helping to reduce prospective criticisms of management and union officials by employees and others for introducing major technological innovations through offering to prepare, in response to joint requests, objective and expert evaluations of the prospective effects on competitiveness and employment of rejecting such available advances. Another might be to help reduce labor resistance to employment-threatening innovations by broadening measures available to the victims of import-induced unemployment. For example, the government might consider guaranteeing the past average earning of displaced or downgraded labor for perhaps two years, along with retaining opportunities and job relocation help for younger employees and reasonably attractive early retirement terms for older employees. Displaced employees might be guaranteed preferential consideration for any new job opportunities resulting from the stronger competitive position generated by such technological advances. A third form of governmental contribution might result from developing an early warning center to identify newly diffusing technologies likely to engender labor problems and unemployment as a basis for alerting company and trade union officials, as well as government agencies likely to be dealing with such difficulties.

The government could also help to reduce the risks to innovational undertakings attributable to subsidized exports from abroad as well as to foreign denial of equal access of exports to their domestic markets. One means would be to strengthen antidumping restrictions. In addition, effective tariff penalties might be considered to protect private enterprise from unfair competition by imports relying on direct and indirect governmental subsidies and other aids not available to domestic firms. Such efforts need not, however, discriminate against imports on the basis of lower wages abroad. On the contrary, one of the objectives of improving domestic technology is to permit the domestic labor force to compete with such imports by raising productivity levels sufficiently to make higher wage rates economically viable. But direct restrictions might well be considered against imports from countries that apply direct or indirect restrictions against this country's exports.

Two additional risks tending to decrease allocations for the development of major technological advances require governmental remedial efforts. Patent protection needs to be strengthened so as to minimize the current risk to grantees that they will be subject for many years to the likelihood of heavy legal fees to defend important patent rights and even to the possibility of losing such rights retroactively, along with all benefits received since their issuance. Even when such threats are avoided or overcome, large corporations—which are generally most capable of undertaking major technological development projects—need some reassurance against the looming possibility of being forced to share resulting advances with smaller competitors in order to prevent any increases in concentration.

Increasing the Array of Promising
Innovational Opportunities

In order to increase the array of reasonably attractive potentials for longer-run intrafirm R&D undertakings, the government might provide active leadership in helping to organize and to support intraindustry programs to bridge the gap between available scientific and technological knowledge and the development of intermediate stages of technology to a level within striking distance of commercial applicability. The need is not only to expand the number of industries actively involved in such activities but also to encourage a shift from occasional past reliance on intermittent projects scattered over a wide variety of problems and over a broad array of institutions in favor of larger continuing programs, each concentrated in fewer institutions, which would thus be enabled to achieve more highly developed expertise through building and maintaining highly specialized staffs and facilities.

Consideration might be given to establishing one or more centers of excellence in research and precommercial development for each of a wide array of industries, preferably in association with, if not an integral part of, universities. This would facilitate attracting excellent staff, it would provide ready access to a broad range of specialists in related fields, it would help to ensure concentration on precommercial technological objectives, and it would help to attract undergraduate and graduate students to the industry whose problems are one of the centers of interest on campus. It should also be emphasized in this connection that university-associated research centers are capable of carrying R&D efforts far beyond the bench-scale levels to which they have commonly been restricted. Given the suggested continuing and broader program support, as well as relevant facilities, they might well become national centers for continuing exchanges among academic and industrial specialists concerning the emerging problems and developments of the industrial sectors in which each such institution specializes.

The government's role in encouraging the establishment of such centers might include the following:

Ensuring the legitimacy and promoting the importance of such centers.

Selecting the industries in which such centers are developed on the basis of invited expressions of interest from firms comprising the industry in participating in and helping to finance such centers.

Helping industry representatives to decide where such centers should be located, as well as the planned level of operations over the first five years.

Offering to finance an initially substantial but progressively decreasing share of capital requirements and operating costs, provided that remaining budget requirements are pledged and providing that a reasonable proportion of firms agree to participate.

Continuing participation as a small minority, along with representatives of the associated university, in the executive board directing the activities of each center.

All of the findings of such centers would presumably be available to all participants. Each would also be free, however, to select any finding as the point of departure for its own separate development efforts in the hope of achieving a commercial success whose benefits accrue solely to itself.

The role of government leadership becomes especially critical in developing such centers in industries dominated by relatively small firms, as well as in developing such centers for concentration on problems common to several industries. In the former case, the basic difficulties usually arise from the inadequacy of past experience with R&D, uncertainty or skepticism about what it can accomplish, and stringently limited resources for helping to finance such pioneering. Additional difficulties may be encountered in identifying research foci of wide interest and in defining the limits of precommercial development, in view of the limited capabilities in many small firms for further technical development activities. Accordingly it might prove necessary in such cases to consider a more active role for government in helping to organize, manage, and finance such centers during the first few years of their establishment.

In the case of interindustry research undertakings, it would seem more feasible to organize research centers around particular problem areas than around particular groupings of industries. For example, corrosion, computer-aided manufacturing, robotics, and composite materials are of interest to a wide variety of industries but to quite different groups of them. It is conceivable that far more progress may be achieved for given outlays by concentrating research efforts related to each in a relatively small number of specialized centers committed to a continuing focus on the problem area instead of a continued scattering of such efforts among many short-term projects in changing locations. This would not justify any coercive efforts to centralize activities in each field, but it might justify government exploration with the industries involved of the possible benefits of intensifying certain sectors of such research in given locations as the basis for considering possible changes in organizational direction.

Finally, consideration might also be given to expanding the array of regional research laboratories concerned with the problems of increasing the economic value of a wide variety of local natural resources. Promising possibilities might be realized through improvements in locating new reserves, in extraction methods, in processing and purification methods, and even in transportation and conservation methods. Unlike the other sectors of research, these undertakings may well include national cooperation with local governments as well as with private firms and universities, and they may also involve heavier support by national and local governments. On the other hand, resulting benefits may also be heavier with respect to maintaining or increasing regional employment and income than with respect to the profits of individual firms.

Clearly there are a number of potentials for governmental contributions to increasing the array of promising precommercial technological advances that might attract increasing commitments from firms seeking to profit from developing them to the point of commercial success. It does not seem unreasonable to assume that increasing the array of such attractive possibilities is likely to increase the resources allocated by one firm or another to harnessing these potentials.

Encouraging Needed Increases in Basic Research and the
Entry of Scientists and Engineers into Hitherto
Neglected Industrial Sectors

It should be apparent that even existing basic research programs will have to be expanded to support the early exploration of a wide array of promising new technologies with important potentials for increasing the competitiveness of various industries. The long development periods that are often required, combined with their high costs and risks, have led a large proportion of manufacturing firms to minimize such efforts. As a result, an increasing number of governments have made heavy investments in developing industrial technologies as a means of bolstering the competitiveness of their substantial manufacturing sectors. Under such conditions, governments that fail to strengthen such foundations of continuing technological advances may be handicapping the longer-term survivability of their industries. In expanding support for such programs, government objectives would center around generating more laboratory-level findings, which might then invite precommercial developmental efforts and also help to supply the larger numbers of scientists and engineers needed to staff enlarged technology-improvement programs. Here again it is hoped that governmental leadership would help to establish new aspiration levels in addition to encouraging comparably expanded contributions from industry.

Consideration should also be given to encouraging the entry of scientists and engineers into hitherto neglected sectors of industry. Such past neglect may have been attributable to managerial complacency about existing processes and products, to skepticism about the potential contributions of R&D, or simply to the inadequacy of resources for supporting needed pioneering efforts. Recent experience with the revitalization of technological progress in such long-dormant industrial sectors as textiles, shoes, watches, office equipment, and various types of machinery, however, suggests that impressive gains might be achieved in substantial industries by encouraging the systematic reexamination of long-prevailing technologies in the light of recent advances in scientific and technological knowledge. Toward that end, the government might offer research fellowships and grants for exploratory critiques of the existing technologies in selected industries whose competitive strength seems to be declining. Resulting findings might then stimulate industry support for efforts to develop improvements and also help to increase the interest of scientists and engineers in participating in such programs.

Strengthening Governmental Capabilities for Evaluating
Technological Improvement Needs and Progress

In order to design effectively focused efforts to stimulate needed increases in the technological capabilities of domestic industries, the government will also have to develop expertise in appraising such capabilities and associated short-comings, determining their causes, and estimating their economic and broader effects. In order to assess the strengths and weaknesses of whatever policies and programs are introduced to improve technological capabilities, it would be necessary to organize periodic reviews of the achievements, shortcomings, and still unmet needs of the industries to be helped. Additional valuable perspectives on prospective changes in the pressures facing domestic industries and in relevant government policies could be provided by monitoring alterations in the science and technology as well as trade policies of other nations and by also keeping abreast of any major changes in the technological capabilities of their industries.

Some of these capabilities are already available in the national governments, although they are often scattered among a number of agencies. Other needed capabilities are inadequate or nonexistent. In any case, effective design and implementation of a program dealing with such a complex array of needs, deterrents, and problems may well require new forms of governmental organization.

In considering such organizational possibilities, attention must also be given to potential conflicts among governmental agencies. The government is concerned not only with improving employment and income levels but also with minimizing the social cost of such advances. Because these responsibilities are delegated to a variety of agencies, each tending to emphasize some of these objectives rather than others, effective means must be developed to prevent conflicts among their respective activities that result in frustrating the national objective of achieving reasonably balanced progress toward an array of goals. For example, measures designed to encourage more rapid advances in industrial productivity and technology might well engender direct or covert opposition from agencies concerned primarily with short-term tax receipts, with reducing unemployment, with helping small business, or with reducing obstacles to imports. Even the efforts of agencies seeking needed reductions in pollution ought to be coordinated with, rather than remain wholly isolated from, concomitant pressures to improve the technological capabilities of affected industries.

Potential Contributions by Other Groups

A substantial acceleration of progress in the technological capabilities of domestic industries would also require additional contributions by managements, trade unions, and universities.

Increasing the Contribution of Industrial Managements

The most important stimulus to technological progress in a firm is the degree and continuity of top management's commitment to such objectives (Gold 1982b,

1983a). Even if shifts in government policies should persuade managements to give greater weight to these goals, however, results would depend on the effectiveness of the means introduced for implementing them, as reflected by budget allocations, performance targets, and criteria for determining rewards. In seeking to effectuate such modifications in operating objectives, special consideration might be given to some of the suggestions highlighted by past research concerning means of reinforcing such efforts, as well as key problems to be dealt with.

In order to increase the technological capabilities of production facilities, Japanese experience suggests increasing the ratio of engineers to labor and also setting periodic improvement targets for the engineers as well (Gold 1978). It also seems important that technological improvement goals be defined in terms of physical measures and that performance be evaluated initially in these same terms instead of on the basis of costs effects. Shifting to the latter permits technological achievements to be offset by changes in factor prices and in market demand, thus minimizing recognition and incentives for engineering contributions.

Demonstration of deepening management commitments to improving technological capabilities may also require decreasing the extent of past tolerance for wide differences in such performance among the plants of multiplant firms. Seemingly logical reasons are often accepted without penetrating tests, and persistent differences come to be accepted as somehow unchangeable—as indeed they tend to become when prevailing performance levels have long been accepted by the plant management, their technical personnel, and the labor force. Only powerful new pressures from top management implemented by close monitoring of results and by their reflection in promotions and salaries are likely to overcome such inertia.

Of outstanding importance in this connection is the need for management to develop more effective support from its work force for continuing improvements in technological capabilities. Headway has been made in many industries over the years through incentive payments, bonuses for suggestions to increase effectiveness, and even threats of layoffs. But the tendency for labor to identify with management's need for increased competitiveness is not widespread in most private industries. Even more serious is the pervasive belief in the work force that labor interests conflict with those of management: that management seeks to reduce employment, decrease skills, hold down wage rates, and minimize fringe benefits. There is ample basis for such adversary viewpoints. Nevertheless, the challenge remains—and it is one of the greatest threats to the survival of our present form of economy—to increase evidences of management's concern to minimize the adjustment hardships of its labor force.

The Japanese have gained labor acceptance of innovations by providing long-term employment guarantees and by basing increases in wage rates on years of service to the company rather than on skill grades or seniority in particular jobs. These obviously cannot be transferred directly into Western industrial systems. But unless suitable alternatives can be devised, the potential benefits of technological advances are not likely to be fully realized.

Turning to the R&D component of increasing technological capabilities, the demonstration of intensified managerial commitments would require larger budget allocations for longer-term projects, safeguarding them from substantial budget adjustments from one year to the next and avoiding demands for unreasonably rapid achievements. Such longer-term guiding perspectives, too, may be more common in Japan. In the United States they have been undermined not only by the general pressures for maximizing short-term performance but also by widespread disappointment with exaggerated estimates of R&D profitability, by general underestimation of the actual benefits of such programs, and by continuing doubts about the effectiveness with which R&D resources are utilized (Gold 1975; "Silent Crisis," 1976).

Hence, in addition to suggestions for increasing the prospective profitability of long-term R&D projects, rebuilding managerial support for such commitments may also require the following steps:

1. The development of more effective approaches to evaluating the costs and multiple short-term and longer-term benefits of R&D programs to bolster confidence in the appraisal of such proposals.

2. More persuasive studies of the actual results of R&D programs in the specific industries where government is seeking to encourage increases in such undertakings.

3. Analyses of the potential gains from reallocating R&D resources by narrowing the foci of in-house R&D while increasing reliance on licensing and contracting out projects requiring types of expertise needed only intermittently.

Research findings dealing with R&D management processes also warn of the dangers of excessive reliance on rational, quantitative estimates of probable payoffs from major new developments during the consideration of such proposals and during the early stages of their exploration, for such estimates are likely to be dominated by subjective judgments reflecting biases either in favor of or against proceeding. Equally serious is the danger during later stages of development efforts of allowing an overweighting of attractive market potentials to minimize recognition of the risks represented by continuing technological shortcomings (Gold 1981).

Increasing the Contributions of Trade Unions

Because democratic trade unions must be responsive to their membership, it is especially difficult for their officials, who face periodic reelections, to develop any cooperative relationships with management that may then be challenged by rank-and-file extremists. It seems reasonably clear that minimizing long-run reductions in employment levels and maximizing long-run wage rates and fringe benefits in industries subject to competition from imports or substitute products requires continuing advances in productivity and technology. But this tends to be much less self-evident in the short run, and short-run considerations commonly overshadow long-term implications in the course of periodic elections.

As a result, trade union managements face as challenging a problem as company executives. This will require courageous efforts to explore with management how improvements in productivity and technology can be harnessed so as to save jobs and improve earnings, while also minimizing accompanying hardships. Progress is more likely to take the form of a succession of limited agreements, of course, rather than of an all-embracing program, but each advance may be used both to join with management in seeking any governmental help that may be needed and also to demonstrate to the majority of union members the superiority of such policies as compared with unrestrained opposition to all productivity and technological improvements. It is to be hoped that the higher educational levels and generally improved living standards of the present labor force have increased the possibilities of gaining a sympathetic response to such constructive efforts.

Trade unions, too, have to supplement agreements in principle with supporting actions. Thus, for example, there are current instances of national trade unions' avowing acceptance of all technological innovations, while some of their local branches clearly restrict the implementation of available advances and thus inhibit managerial efforts to develop further advances. Blame for acquiescence in such resistance must be shared by local managements fearful of the effects of labor resistance on their plant's performance. But cooperation between corporate managements and trade union officials is not likely to advance very far if it cannot cope with such early tests.

Increasing the Contributions of Universities

In considering possible means of increasing the contributions of universities to accelerating technological progress in industries, the most promising possibilities may well involve altering conceptions of their role in such efforts. Many universities have long emphasized a monopolizing commitment to basic research, conceived in their science divisions as limited to searching out new knowledge about fundamental relationships in the physical and biological sciences. Such a limited research purview has been reinforced by a tendency to devalue contributions by faculty members that can be characterized as applied and by similarly restricting graduate student research efforts. As a result, industry support for university research has also been heavily concentrated within these limiting confines.

It is not at all clear, however, that such traditional extremist concepts accord with the effective development of the universities' teaching and research responsibilities. Both of these contributions could be substantially augmented if universities expanded their research horizons to cover all stages of the R&D process short of commercialization. Much is to be learned at each successive stage, with new difficulties in later stages triggering deeper explorations of earlier stages. Moreover, the development of means of applying embryonic experimental findings and associated theoretical speculations to the tests represented by real problems often represent challenges as intellectually demanding and as potentially valuable to the understanding and control of natural forces as many kinds of basic research. And encompassing such a broad range of developmental stages would enable universities to develop a fuller array of relevant specialties, would add to the capabilities of university staffs by exposing them to a wider array of interlocking experiences, and would facilitate the buildup and maintenance of an increasingly knowledgeable staff in selected fields. Each of these gains would help to enrich the range of teaching and research experiences communicated to students. Fuller awareness of the problems posed in converting original laboratory-level findings into eventual commercial industrial processes might also lead to the development of more effective teaching and research programs in the related fields of manufacturing technology and research management, as well as the economics and other social science aspects of technological change.

No less important would be the prospect that university research centers thus committed to exploring a broader range of the problems underlying the determinants of increasing efficiency in various industries might well become the centers for continuing exchanges among industry and academic specialists. Resulting increased cooperation in identifying the factors limiting further technological advances, in evaluating new research findings, and in probing newly emerging needs might well bring about a mutual reinforcement that would benefit both as well as the national economy, as has already been demonstrated abroad, especially in West Germany.

More Specific Suggestions for Implementation

One of the most vexing problems faced in seeking to promote greater commitments to accelerating the technological capabilities of industries is the conflict between recognizing the wide differences among the needs and potentials of different industries and responding to the understandable pressures in national governments for dealing with major problems by means of a limited number of relatively standardized measures. Such opposing pressures can never be completely resolved, but some progress toward bridging them can be made by clarifying some guiding principles, trying to group the major kinds of industries according to their most important common needs, and also trying to define some general approaches to particular types of technological improvement needs.

Suggested Guiding Principles

The basic principle guiding all such efforts should be to stimulate technological progress in all industries and firms—advanced as well as lagging, new as well as mature, and large as well as small—in the interests of strengthening the economy at large instead of concentrating primarily on sectors already losing relative position. Hence the major initial effort of the government should be to minimize deterrents to, and to increase incentives for, all investments directed toward increasing the technological capabilities of industries.

A second principle should be to help redress the current overemphasis on short-term performance, thereby bringing managerial objectives into closer alignment with the need to safeguard the longer-run needs of the nation. Such exhortations by the government, however, should be reinforced by its willingness, for example, to shift tax policies from maximizing current receipts to deferring a portion of such claims to later periods. In effect, this would demonstrate the government's confidence in the value of such technology-improvement efforts as evidenced by its own willingness to invest in them now for later returns.

A third principle should be that accelerating the technological progress of industries requires that government reach beyond simply promoting effective competition in developing and utilizing commercially applicable advances in technology. It should also encourage and facilitate cooperation among firms, industries, and universities in enriching the infrastructure of scientific and technological knowledge and personnel. This constitutes an increasingly important national resource, as well as the seedbed of promising opportunities for private efforts to develop commercializable technological advances.

Illustrative Means of Implementation

The investments qualifying for the incentives to be provided by government in the interests of accelerating technological progress should be defined broadly at least during the first several years of trying to generate industry-wide responses. Hence all investments in new facilities and equipment representing efforts to modernize or to advance technological capabilities should be included. In order to encourage larger and longer-term commitments, incentives should be progressively more generous for increasing conformance with such objectives. Accordingly, consideration might be given to the core concepts of such proposals as the following:

Offering progressively greater investment tax credits for technology improvement projects requiring progressively longer periods before yielding substantial revenues.

Allowing depreciation to begin at the same time as construction and allowing it to accumulate up to 50 percent of total investment if significant revenues are not received during the first three years after construction is initiated.

Reducing taxes on the profits from such investments by 20 percent for the same number of years as elapsed between actual construction and the initial earning of profits on that investment (perhaps weighting years by their resepctive investments).

Additional incentives should be considered for contemplated investments by two additional categories of industry: industries already facing very heavy import competition in domestic markets because of past or current capital or operating subsidies to foreign producers from their governments and industries under pressure to ease domestic shortages of necessary goods by developing or testing technologies that have not yet been proved to be reliable and economic.

Industries in the first category may already have fallen behind technologically because of the unavailability of the aids given to their foreign competitors. In addition, they may lack the financial resources either to modernize or to undertake the development of new technologies that might restore their competitiveness. In such cases, it is not at all clear that the managements alone were at fault for being unable to offset the advantages provided by foreign governments. Rather, a case can be made for arguing that the government's failure to safeguard fair competition for domestic producers would justify belated government efforts to restore equality of competitive positions by offering loan guarantees to enable domestic competitors to match the more modern facilities abroad and by providing research assistance at least to offset partially that provided by foreign governments to the competing producers. Although such governmental aids may be considered as means of making up for past forms of unfair competition, it would certainly seem preferable in the future to avoid such special domestic aids by preventing imports from exploiting such aids in domestic markets.

Industries in the second category may lack the capital and may in any event be loath to take the heavy risks involved in developing or relying on hitherto unproved technologies. And if important public needs are involved—such as, energy or medicinals—they may well fear government control of prices and profits if their risk taking should prove successful. It if is clearly in the public interest to encourage such efforts, a reasonable case can be made for providing government loans or even grants to supplement private capital in undertaking such developments—and in sharing attendant risks. It should also be borne in mind, however, that only by enabling the private risk takers to enjoy a generous rate of return on their original risky investments can the government encourage other private investors to undertake similar risks in the future.

These measures would also tend to increase the relative attractiveness of longer-term R&D programs. In view of the critical importance of such efforts to strengthening the future competitiveness of domestic industries, further incentives would seem to be justified. For example, consideration might be given to allowing firms to defer up to 5 to 10 percent of each year's current tax liabilities for five years if such resources are allocated to increasing R&D projects not expected to yield commercial benefits within five years. Firms might be allowed to write off investments in R&D facilities and equipment as current costs. In the case of firms reporting profits of less than 2 to 4 percent of equity investment, future tax credits might be granted for long-term R&D costs up to 1 percent of equity each year.

Turning to cooperative research on subcommercial technologies, the government should not only provide active leadership in helping industries to organize such centers in association with universities but should also ease the burdens of financing them. In this connection, consideration should be given to allowing participants to allocate up to 1 percent of their current tax liabilities to support such centers; to having the government contribute an equal amount to operating funds in the first two or three years, diminishing progressively thereafter to perhaps only 10 to 20 percent of industrial contributions in the tenth year; to meeting initial capital requirements by allowing all participants to double their contributions from current tax liabilities for the first three years and having these matched up to 50 percent by government grants through the associated universities. It would also be helpful if the government offered to finance up to ten research fellowships in each such center for the first five to ten years. Similar contributions might also be offered by the government to development of the interindustry research centers.

In the case of cooperative research centers focused on regional resource problems, however, financial support covering capital as well as operating needs should be provided by the national government and by the local governments directly affected, with the former providing 75 to 100 percent during the first three to five years. Thereafter national financing might gradually decline to 40 to 50 percent, while the local governments increase their respective contributions.

The proposals here add up to considerable sums, but these may come to be recognized as reasonable when regarded as a national investment in reinvigorating the most powerful source of future industrial competitiveness and of rising standards of living. Indeed the most serious threats to the success of such an intensified technological development efforts are less likely to be the magnitude of resources required to support them than the effectiveness of the governmental policies and administrative measures for harnessing such investments to the specific purposes they would be designed to achieve.

Concluding Observations

Need for Long-Term and Broad Perspectives

Recent inadequacies in advancing the technological capabilities of domestic industries portend increasingly serious problems over an extended period (Gold et al. 1985). A number of industries have not only lagged behind foreign competitors but are continuing to fall behind. In part, this is due to the fact that existing facilities continue to age and to resist effective adaptation to changes in product requirements as well as in the supply and prices of inputs. But such lags are also due to continuing advances in the technological capabilities of foreign producers seeking to expand their exports. Indeed such efforts abroad are also tending to expand the array of domestic industries that may be overtaken by overseas competitors.

Realistic efforts to deal with this problem must begin by recognizing that even if governmental and other measures to intensify innovational activities by domestic industries were instituted immediately, competitive benefits could be expected to emerge only gradually over a period of years. Merely to construct new facilities that embody the advanced technologies already in use abroad would take three to six years in many manufacturing industries. And yet this would serve merely to reduce rather than to overcome competitive disadvantages because such competitors are likely to achieve further improvements over these periods and because the addition of some new facilities would still leave most domestic capacity at a competitive disadvantage. A sharp increase in long-term R&D projects seeking significant advances beyond current and already emerging technologies might reasonably be expected to yield some major successes. Experience suggests, however, that attaining commercial applicability, constructing facilities to use them, and achieving a significant competitive advantage in markets would be likely to take considerably more than five years in most cases—even if foreigners were less successful in their concomitant development efforts.

During such extended periods, industrial managers and government officials would have to be encouraged to allocate increasing resources to these innovational activities despite the continued deferment of rewards. Although industrial corporations are legally immortal, most executives and investors tend to have limited planning horizons within which they seek to maximize their performance and rewards. Senior corporate officers are often in command for only five- to eight-year periods and hence tend not to favor undertakings that involve heavy burdens during their tenure, thus reflecting negatively on their performance, while deferring rewards to enhance the achievements of successors. Institutional investors and their advisees are usually prepared to shift their funds every few months in order to take advantage of even modest gains in stock prices and dividends, thus tending to intensify managerial emphasis on relatively short-term results. Only in the case of family-controlled firms and investors with continuing loyalties (or other sources of inertia) are long-term prospects given significant weight in evaluating performance.

But the national interest has a heavy stake in maintaining high-level performance beyond the limited horizons of most executives and investors. Hence it is essential for the government to devise an array of policies and implementing measures powerful enough to motivate larger commitments to longer-term and riskier efforts to advance the technological capabilities of a substantial array of domestic industries over successive decades at least as rapidly as other major nations.

In short, there is an urgent need to develop a virogous program for improving the productivity and technological capabilities of domestic industries. But the prospects for achieving its purposes will depend in large measure on the extent to which its objectives and implementing measures have been brought into reasonable conformity with other policies rooted in powerful domestic and international pressures. Past governmental actions influencing industrial decisions have intended to emerge independently of one another in response to intermittent urgencies. It has become increasingly desirable, therefore, to identify the variety of policies and regulations affecting reinvigoration of the international competitiveness of domestic industries, to resolve conflicts among them, and even to introduce modifications serving to increase their mutual reinforcement. Such efforts would help to lay the foundations for developing an integrated framework of national policies seeking to safeguard the maintenance of a powerful sector of private industries that compete effectively with increasingly numerous, efficient, and aggressive foreign producers and that also provide major contributions to continued economic growth and rising standards of living.

Essentially Limited Role of Government

Although the potential contributions of government are important, and indeed necessary, they are limited to providing a helpful and supportive environment within which the direction and magnitude of achievements are determined by managerial vision, capabilities, and commitments. The world economy abounds with examples of governmentally dominated efforts to develop the capacity, efficiency, and international competitiveness of domestic industries. Most of these have achieved mediocre results at best. This may be due in part to the fact that governmental officials commonly lack the highly detailed knowledge of the distinctive problems, opportunities, competitive pressures, and needed responsive measures applicable to each industry that is the necessary foundation for successful developmental strategies. And it may also be due in part to the tendency of government-dominated policies to limit and even undermine the constructive potentials of entrepreneureal expedients.

Japan—the most recent successful instance of rapid and effective advances to world-class technological competitiveness of an array of industries—demonstrates the need for governmental efforts to be responsive to and supportive of privately formulated objectives and aggressively implementing efforts. Their experience offers an instructive contrast to the governmentally dominated efforts in Western Europe and the governmentally controlled efforts in most underdeveloped countries (Gold 1985b).

References

Gold, B. 1975. "Alternative Strategies for Advancing a Company's Technology." *Research Management* (July).

———. 1978. "Factors Stimulating Technological Progress in Japanese Industries: The Case of Computerization in Steel." *Quarterly Review of Economics and Business* (December).

———. 1980. "Evaluating the Technological Capabilities of Industries for Government Purposes." In B. Gold, G. Rosegger, and M.G. Boylan, Jr., *Evaluating Technological Innovations: Methods, Expectations, and Findings* (Lexington, Mass.: Lexington Books.

———. 1981. "Technological Diffusion in Industry: Research Needs and Shortcomings." *Journal of Industrial Economics* (March).

———. 1982a. *Productivity, Technology, and Capital: Economic Analysis, Managerial Strategies, and Governmental Policies.* Lexington, Mass.: Lexington Books.

———. 1982b. "Technological Challenges Confronting U.S. Industries." *Proceedings of a National Science Foundation Conference on Industrial Science and Technological Innovations.* Washington, D.C.: National Science Foundation.

———. 1983a. "On the Adoption of Technological Innovations in Industry: Superficial Models and Complex Decision Processes." In S. MacDonald, D.M. Lamberton, and T. Mandeville, eds., *The Trouble with Technology: Explorations in the Process of Technological Change.* London: Frances Pinter.

———. 1983b. "Technological and Other Determinants of the International Competitiveness of U.S. Industries." *Institute of Electrical and Electronic Engineers Transactions on Engineering Management* (May).

———. 1985a. "Approaches to Increasing the International Competitiveness of U.S. Manufacturing Industries." Prepared for U.S. National Research Council Manufacturing Studies Board, *The Race to the Year 2000: Strategies for Increasing U.S. Manufacturing Competitiveness* (Spring).

———. 1985b. "Some International Differences in Approaches to Industrial Policy." *Contemporary Policy Issues* (Spring).

Gold, B.; Peirce, W.S.; Rosegger, G.; and Perlman, M. 1985. *Technological Progress and Industrial Leadership: The Growth of the U.S. Steel Industry, 1900–1970.* Lexington, Mass.: Lexington Books.

"The Silent Crisis in R&D." 1976. *Business Week,* March 8.

9
Government Policies in Support of Automated Manufacturing: Japan, the United States, and Western Europe

Jack Baranson

T he introduction of automated manufacturing systems (AMS) on a timely and cost-effective basis is emerging as a key to international competitiveness in an ever-widening range of industries.[1] The rate and extent of introduction of these systems are a function of industrial management policies and practices and the national economic environment as it affects the demand for and supply of automated manufacturing equipment and systems. Both sets of determinant variables are in turn influenced by government policies as they affect private-sector risk propensities toward capital expenditures for new industrial plant and equipment and investments in industrial research, design, and engineering. Government measures in support of a rapid and extensive introduction of automated manufacturing include tax measures, joint funding, government procurement policies aimed at reducing private-sector costs and risks, and commercial and trade policies aimed at maintaining a competitive environment to reinforce demand for the new industrial systems. This chapter analyzes and compares the government policies and national environments of Japan, the United States, and selected Western European countries (France, Sweden, and West Germany) (table 9–1).

There are vast differences between market-driven and Soviet-style planned economies in both government policies and in their impact on innovation in general and the introduction of AMS in particular. In the Soviet economy, the risks and rewards of innovation (enterprise profits and individual earnings) are linked to government policies and organizational structures very different from the market-driven economies of the United States, Japan, and Western Europe. Policy and structural differences stem from differences in the autonomy of the enterprise in production management, supply procurement, industrial investment

This chapter is based in part on my *Robots in Manufacturing: Key to International Competitiveness* (Lomond Press, 1983).

Table 9–1
Comparison of Government Policies and Measures

Policies and Measures	Japan	Europe	United States
Industrial policy Trade policies Regulatory measures	Intervention to promote innovation visions Sunrise industries support long- term risk	France: Highly supportive of high-technology industries West Germany and Sweden: Rely more on market forces EEC trade barriers	Rely largely on market forces Adversarial government–industry relations
Economic measures Capital measures Tax incentives Interest rates Growth Employment	Funds to priority sectors Bank leveraging and tax-sheltered corporate reserves Promote export-lead growth Promote savings, low interest rates	France: Tax shelter capital funds in high-tech industries Germany and Sweden: mild limited intervention EEC: Declining growth rates, rising employment, rising interest rates	Tax incentives to promote capital investments RDE generally bud- getary deficits raise interest rates, appreciate currency, intensify foreign competition
R&D Procurement	Jointly fund R&D of next-generation technology Credits for AMS leasing	France highly supportive of AMS RD&E West Germany and Sweden: Limited support	Antitrust inhibits cooperative R&D efforts Strong support of defense-related R&D Tax policies neutral

decisions and R&D activities for new or improved products and processes, and the pricing mechanism governing both factors of production inputs and product output. Study of Soviet-type economies sharpens our perspectives of the forces that drive innovation in Western-type market economies and provide critical insights on how government policies can enhance (or inhibit) innovational dynamics.[2]

There are also dramatic contrasts between the market dynamics in the United States and Japan and prevailing conditions in the EEC, the result, once again, of respective government policies and their impact on national market structures. According to the *Economist* the EEC suffers from a balkanization of national markets.[3] This is, in part, the result of nontariff barriers, which in effect have raised national R&D and production costs and restricted access to one another's markets. Competition is the spur to innovation, but the ability to amortize the substantial funds needed for the new generation of products and production systems also requires access to sizable markets. The immobility of capital and people (relative to the U.S. economy) also has stifled the creation of new, particularly small enterprises, which, it is generally credited, are responsible for the introduction of new products and new or improved production systems. In contrast to conditions in the EEC, deregulation in the U.S. telecommunication and airline industries has given widespread inpetus to innovation from a flood of new small enterprises into these sectors. In Japan, the dependence on external markets and the intensification of international competition have been the innovative drives.

Impact of Government Policies on AMS Investments

AMS can produce a much wider range of product variations at relatively low volumes and still be cost-effective, maintain high technical standards, and most important, respond to the rapid and frequent changes in product design and production parameters now typical of world markets. The new industrial automation also has another competitive advantage over conventional high-volume manufacturing systems based on extended product life cycles and using expensive special-purpose equipment; it avoids the high risks of locking into capital amortization schedules and product designs that may be rendered obsolete by changes in market demand and shifts in competitive cost structures (as has been the case in the substantial decline of U.S. automotive manufacturers' shares, despite restrictive import quotas).

In market-driven economies, government policies affect the demand for and supply of automated manufacturing equipment and systems in a variety of ways. AMS investments mean substantial outlays and risks and require longer-term payback perspectives, and consequently, the risk propensities of industrial managers and corporate commitment to long-term growth and technological development are critical. Also important are the effects of government policies and regulations on capital markets, bank lending, and corporate risk management.

Government policies in support of innovation may include tax measures to reduce purchase costs of AMS products, cost sharing of high risks in the development of AMS products, government procurement to reinforce demand when AMS products are introduced into the marketplace, and education and training programs to increase the supply of needed technical and engineering personnel. Special programs to assist small- to medium-sized industry help to reinforce critical component supplier industries and innovative segments of the economy that have special difficulties obtaining required financial resources. Commercial and trade policies have an indirect effect on internal competition among AMS producers or on their competitiveness abroad. Protectionist measures depress domestic demand for the technological upgrading implicit in AMS products. Government-backed credits reinforce international sales of AMS products.

Government policies have an indirect effect on general economic conditions and market structures. For example, deflationary measures combined with high interest rates depress demand for capital goods in general and AMS products in particular. New capital investments in AMS also are influenced by AMS prices relative to the wages or replaced industrial labor. The size of the internal market influences the range and price of AMS products offered for sale. Competitive forces also influence effective demand for technological upgrading among user industries. Included under financial structures are the availability of industrial capital, credit terms, leasing arrangements, and the risk perspectives of suppliers of equity debt capital. Financial resources are also needed to fund research design and equipment expenditures and new or improved plant and equipment expenditures and new or improved plant and equipment, as well as to reinforce effective demand for AMS capital expenditures.

The introduction of AMS systems implies profound changes in industrial organization and management and high financial risk. Consequently government–industry relations, trade policies, and regulatory functions that affect risk management are critical. There are nonetheless wide differences in viewpoints on the proper role of government in managing technological change.

U.S. Government Policies and Measures

Under the Reagan administration, the prevailing philosophy has been that free market forces should allocate resources and make investment decisions in the private sector. Trade and industry policies are confined largely to maintaining domestic competition (supported by antitrust legislation) and promoting two-way international trade. U.S. national policies contrast dramatically with those of Japan. Aside from government support of R&D and tax and depreciation measures to encourage investment in general, U.S. government–industry relations continue to be adversarial rather than cooperative, consensual, and orchestrated as they are in Japan. Adversarial confrontation between government and industry, industry and labor, industry and consumers, and among industrial firms themselves drains vital human and financial resources that might otherwise be used to increase U.S. industrial competitiveness.

Tax Incentives and Regulatory Measures

Antitrust laws, originally intended to deter constraint of trade in the U.S. economy, in recent years have inhibited U.S. firms from mergers and/or joint action to share R&D costs or to utilize each others' corporate strengths to improve international market positions. As a consequence, antitrust laws have hampered the efforts of U.S. firms to meet international competition, since Japan and most Western European countries permit or encourage such joint action.

The Economic Recovery Act of 1981 permitted accelerated depreciation for the cost of new investments in plant and equipment and increased the size of investment tax credits for industry, but the Tax Equity and Fiscal Responsibility Act of 1982 effectively cancelled nearly half of the benefits business received in the 1981 bill.

Government Support for R&D and Government Procurement

The U.S. government has traditionally supported long-range, high-risk research and technological development (particularly in defense-related areas), leaving the private sector to fund R&D that has good potential for near-term return on investments. The U.S. government provides a market for the fruits of the R&D it sponsors through its defense procurement policies, thereby minimizing the costs and risks associated with both innovation and commercialization of new technology. The bias toward military and aerospace projects in government R&D funding and procurement, combined with the emphasis on basic research (with only long-term payoffs for industry), means that little government support is available that directly aids industrial competitiveness and commercialization. Funding of certain R&D projects is the only explicit way in which the government supports the expansion of AMS, but these expenditures are also generally limited to mission-oriented national defense needs.

The military focus of government R&D on manufacturing technology has two detrimental side effects from the commercial standpoint: (1) neglect of generic, systems approaches, limiting the applicability of results to civilian problems and settings, and (2) the emphasis on hardware and predominance of physical scientists and engineers on program staffs, which results in neglect of social and organizational factors in design of manufacturing systems, making user implementation of the technologies development more difficult. The Defense Department's Manufacturing Technology Program provides hundreds of millions of dollars annually for purchase of advanced manufacturing equipment.[4] But very little pressure is exerted on defense contractors to become cost-effective and internationally competitive through commercialization of technological innovations. In the past, military-funded R&D has led to the development of numerically controlled (NC) machine tools and automatic programmed tool (APT) language, both of which are now in commercial use worldwide, but the commercial spillover effects are not comparable to those realized in Japan.

AMS-Related Trade Policies

Persistent protectionist lobbying in the consumer electronics, steel, automotive, and machine tool industries has buffered certain industries against foreign competition and slowed the adoption of AMS.[5] The U.S. trade representative has argued that the potential threat of competition from automated factories abroad necessitates the short-term hardships resulting from reduced protection.

Japanese Government Policies and Measures

The government–industry relationship in Japan plays a major role in the process of formulation and implementation of Japan's economic and technological development policies. The Japanese government has strong confidence in competition and in market forces, but it also perceives a need to intervene from time to time in order to achieve and maintain a high level of economic performance. For example, there has been a sustained effort to encourage the movement of people and resources into sectors with high growth and high productivity. Areas of improving comparative advantage are encouraged to accelerate, and declining or poor-performance industries are encouraged to phase down.

The Japanese vision of the 1980s called for steadfast progress toward a "technology-based nation" and "knowledge-intensive" industries.[6] The strong commitment to movement in these directions can be traced back to the early 1970s, when government-sponsored studies, prepared in cooperation with Japanese industry, predicted the development of information-oriented societies and set out agendas to develop the complementary knowledge-intensive industries. Responsibilities for implementing these guidelines rests largely with the Ministry of Finance (MOF) and the Ministry of International Trade and Industry (MITI). The MOF is the ultimate source of financing, and it guides the industrial lending policies of commercial banks. In order to maintain and expand Japan's industrial growth while minimizing commercial risks, the banks and other investors tend to rely on the MOF–MITI perceptions of what are the most promising avenues of expansion and innovation.

A wide array of Japanese government policies and consultative procedures are designed to strengthen the country's already formidable industrial technology base. The Japanese government, in consultation with appropriate segments of Japanese industry, has established several guidelines and objectives in its efforts to stimulate further the country's technological development; emphasis is placed on the commercial application of current state-of-the-art capabilities and, increasingly, on the development and commercialization of next-generation technologies. The Japanese government has entered into cooperative contracts with large corporations leading to technological innovation, particularly in areas enhancing the international competitiveness of Japanese industry. This was the case in the automotive industry during the 1950s and early 1960s and again in the nascent computer industry during the

1970s. The 1978 Temporary Law for the Promotion of Specific Electronics and Machinery Industries promoted the aggregation of factories to internationally competitive scale by allowing cartel formation under government surveillance.

The Japanese government also encouraged and facilitated cooperation among firms in the same industry, thus avoiding the antitrust restrictions typical of the United States. Companies share information on new products under development in order to eliminate repetition of costly research and engineering. This acceptance of industrial cooperation strengthens Japan's competitiveness in the world markets.

Tax and Depreciation Measures

Japanese fiscal policy has a number of provisions designed to help the nation's technology positions. If a Japanese firm's R&D expenditures for a given year exceed the largest amount of annual R&D expenditures for any preceding year since 1966, 70 percent of the excess may be taken as a credit against the corporate income tax. Firms that are members of research associations can take an immediate 100 percent depreciation deduction on all fixed assets used in connection with research activities.

Government-Funded R&D

Although most R&D work in Japan is performed and financed by industry, government laboratories do conduct a limited, but significant, amount of R&D work in specific, well-targeted areas. These government laboratories are usually working on either basic research or new product conception. Targeted R&D activity by the government has played a substantial role in the dynamic growth of several Japanese industries, such as electronics and automotive in previous years, and currently in new, high-technology areas such as robotics and biogenetics. In performing these activities, the Japanese government has reduced the risk and cost to Japanese industry of developing new technologies.

The Japanese government also provides direct financial assistance to the private sector to develop its technological capabilities. The various types of government financial assistance represent a form of public subvention of private technology development efforts. Although the absolute amount of subsidization has not been large, it is well targeted to the promotion of specific industries and products that hold the potential for attaining world technological leadership.[7] Japan spends very little money on defense-related R&D, allowing it to concentrate its funding on projects with greater potential for private-sector commercialization. Japan's fierce competitiveness is based not only on its ability to research and develop new technology but also on its proved proficiency in accumulating and improving technology developed in other countries.

Government Measures Regarding AMS

The government uses a variety of financial and other incentives to encourage companies to enter growing industries, such as robotics. It is felt that domestic competition will lead to success in the international market, where much of Japan's rapid economic growth has come from. The government is offering support to AMS producers to facilitate the proliferation of companies in the market. Its promotional role has been aimed largely at intensifying competition and reinforcing demand for AMS. In fiscal year 1980, the following measures were implemented: a leasing scheme by the development bank of Japan, computer-controlled industrial robots were added to the list of equipment eligible for special corporate tax depreciation, and special financing for robots was provided by the National Finance and Small Business Finance Corporation for robots with industrial safety features and for the purchase of robotics to modernize small business operations.

European Government Policies and Measures

Because of the greater weight of exports in national income earnings and political pressures to maintain industrial employment, technological innovation (including automation) and increased productivity are major goals of West European governments. They have addressed this need by formulating national policies specifically directed toward robots and computerized manufacturing processes. But national policies vary greatly, ranging from France's designation of the robotic industry as a key sector for future public investment to Sweden's lack of specific measures aimed at AMS industries.

France

In France the Committee for Development of Strategic Industries (CODIS) has identified industrial robots and automated production systems as a key sector of the economy. Basically the government has two goals: to encourage the manufacturing enterprises to invest heavily in automatic equipment (so as to increase productivity and expand market share in France and abroad) and to facilitate the development of a strong French industry in the AMS sector. A key factor in implementing these measures has been the decline of the machine tool industry in France to eighth place worldwide.[8]

Robotics has been designated as a key industry, and approximately $400 million (2.4 billion francs) over a three-year period was budgeted in 1980.

The government set a goal for the manufacture of 5,000 robots and the establishment of 410 research positions by 1984 and for the creation of 2,000 qualified jobs over a ten-year period.[9] The Advanced Automation and Robotics Group, consisting of ten research institutes, has emphasized the development of robotics, advanced remote operations, and flexible production systems. The Mitterand government also planned an increase in procurement of robots, from 50 million francs to 1.2 billion francs over the three-year period. CODIS issued contracts to several French companies.

These restructuring measures reflect a policy change from stimulating demand to bringing together the user industries, the producers, and the government in a comprehensive program. An effort has been made to identify potential areas where robotics could be introduced, and consideration has been given to measures to facilitate acceptance of AMS systems. AMS production in France still has many deficiencies, particularly in the basic components sector. The government's goal has been to complete a robotics industrial chain, centering the robotics industry around a few of the largest enterprises, such as Renault's subsidiary ACMA. The supply end of the chain will be restructured to facilitate the regrouping of the marketing activities of small producers.

Sweden

Swedish government efforts in support of AMS development have been minimal until recently in accordance with traditional laissez-faire policy toward industry except to reinforce market adjustments to economic and technological change. In view of the latter, government financing of AMS research development and utilization has expanded since 1980. In the period 1972–1979, the Swedish Board for Technical Development (STU), which is under the Ministry of Industry, allocated about $800,000 for the development of the robotics industry. In 1980 STU's support of R&D in engineering industries increased significantly to about $40 million, with funds going for advanced R&D at universities, research laboratories, and industrial enterprises. Funding for computer-aided design and manufacturing (CAD-CAM) alone amounted to about $8 million during 1980–1985. The Swedish government has also proposed the establishment of three CAD-CAM centers as joint ventures between universities and government engineering development centers, and there is an agreement between STU and the Swedish Association of Mechanical and Electrical Industries to sponsor a five-year research program through 1985. The Computer and Electronic Commission recommended that the government promote wide diffusion of robotics and CAD-CAM through an information campaign among small and medium-sized firms, complementary software development loans with conditioned repayment, and the encouragement of related training programs.

West Germany

Government and industry support for manufacturing technology development (of which robotics is a significant part) has averaged about $100 million annually in recent years. The Federal Ministry for Research and Technology has sponsored a number of robotic manufacturing programs through several organizations. The Association for Fundamental Technology has managed programs in CAD and process control by computer, and the German Institute for Aerospace Research and Experimentation has coordinated and monitored advanced manufacturing technology programs, including the development of sensors and feedback systems for robots. The German Research Society receives about $30 million a year from the federal government and from state governments for research on computerized machine tools and robotics. Other sources of funding include the Frauenhofer Foundation, a cooperative organization of institutes for applied research; two of its members, the Institute for Production and Automation and the Institute for Data Processing in Technology and Biology, are involved in the development of industrial robots.

Concluding Observations

The key to innovational dynamics is the management of risk within an economy. The innovational thrust in a society depends heavily on a combination of public-sector policy, private-sector initiatives, and the participative role of financial institutions in risk management. The entrepreneurial function in seeking out innovational opportunities and in managing technological change is pivotal, but levels and quality of performance depend heavily on the policy and institutional environment. As part of risk management, public policy must also take on the task of economic and social adjustments to technological change. This may include subsidies to retain or relocate displaced labor force or adjustment assistance to business enterprises that require technological upgrading.

Notes

1. Automated manufacturing systems (AMS) refers to a broad range of equipment and systems, including computer-aided design and computer-aided manufacturing, robots, flexible manufacturing systems, and integrated machining centers.

2. I am currently directing a research project on the economic environment for introducing AMS into the Soviet Union and systemic differences between planned and market economics as they affect the rate of introduction of AMS.

3. See "How Europe Has Failed" and "Europe's Technology Gap," *Economist*, November 24, 1984, pp. 13–14, 93–98.

4. U.S. government support for R&D on robots was about $18 million in fiscal year 1982. In recent years, the National Science Foundation (NSF) has spent about $4.5 million annually on civilian robots and related research (distributed largely to universities and nonprofit laboratories in small grants of about $200,000 each). NSF primarily supports basic research centering on improved robot dexterity and sensory perception, higher-order robot programming languages, and computerized manufacturing and assembly. The National Bureau of Standards spends about $1.2 million per year on in-house robotics research, generally focused on robotic applications and interface standards. Each of the U.S. military services spends significant amounts ($1 million to 10 million annually) to support mission-oriented basic and applied R&D in robotics (Science and Technology Program). They also spend between $1 million and 5 million a year each on procurement to support adoption of AMS by defense industry suppliers (Manufacturing Technology Program). The air force particuarly has been active in promoting adoption of AMS by the aerospace industry (ICAM Program). For a detailed description of military involvement in AMS, see E. Martin, *Department of Defense Statement on Robotics Technology,* Subcommittee on Investigations and Oversight of the Committee on Science and Technology, U.S. House of Representatives, June 23, 1982.

5. The National Machine Tool Builders Association (which represents several AMS producers) has repeatedly lobbied against import penetrations, now near 40 percent, on grounds of national security.

6. See Jack Baranson and Harald B. Malmgren, *Technology and Trade Policy: Issues and Agenda for Action,* report prepared for the Office of the U.S. Trade Representative and the U.S. Department of Labor (October 1981), pp. 6–8, 64–66.

7. For example, Japanese industrial planning mechanisms set targeted dates for moving to next-generation technology in the very-large-scale integration (VSLI) area. This involved progressively moving from 4K to 1 million K random access memory. In the floppy disc field, used in office and home computers, the Japanese reduced the size of these discs from 8 inches to 3 1/2 inches. The line widths in VLSI devices are critical, and Japanese industry set goals to move from 6 micron to 1 micron tolerances.

8. The French government's first major industrial plan was developed for the machine tool industry. It provided for an expenditure of 4 billion francs for doubling machine tool production, reducing imports by half, and increasing exports over the next three years. The government's objective was to place 16,000 new computer-controlled machines in service by 1985 and thereby end the industry's seven-year crisis.

9. In 1980, France imported over 60 percent of the robots in use. The density of robots in use in France is relatively low: only 0.3 robot per 10,000 industrial workers as compared to 11.2 in Sweden, 4.4 in Japan, and 1.6 in the United States. See Jack Baranson, *Robots in Manufacturing: Key to International Competitiveness,* Lomond Press, 1983, p. 12.

10
Locational Perspectives on Policies for Innovation

John Britton
Meric Gertler

S ince their origin, urban agglomerations have served as centers for the discovery, development, and propagation of new ideas—both new products and better ways of making products already familiar. Historians have often remarked that the development and exchange of such ideas and the commodities they produce constitute the original and continuing raison d'étre of cities. It is our contention that this has never been more true than it is today in the developed Western countries. Yet Canadian policies for industrial and technological development have largely lost sight of this fact in recent years, failing to exploit fully the opportunities that currently exist in Canadian metropolitan areas. This is a serious weakness if it is recognized that Canada's limited industrial competitiveness—measured in terms of technology-intensive trade and trade in business—is at least partially due to less than superior performance in innovation by Canada's major centers.

Cities as Centers of Technological Renewal

Since Adam Smith, we have been aware of the economic benefits to be gained from the greater efficiency of specialization, based on a division of labor within the individual firm. Furthermore we have come to appreciate the economies resulting from the sheer size of production, as fixed costs imply lower unit costs at greater scales of output.

It has been pointed out more recently that both of these internal economies depend to a large extent on the external environment in which the firm functions. Specialization, for example, develops not only within but also among individual firms, with this interfirm division of labor introducing further efficiencies into production (Kaldor 1970). Over the years, location theorists, analysts, and urban economists have observed that these production advantages are, by definition, most prevalent in large, established metropolitan areas, where the consumer and producer markets are large enough to allow internal scale economies and to support greater specialization of firms.

Beyond these considerations are a host of other factors that lead to external economies in large urban areas. Briefly, inputs to production—both intermediate goods and specialized services—are readily available in a competitive environment that keeps prices low and ensures a variety of potential sources for key production ingredients (Alonso 1975). Inventories consequently can be kept lower due to the ease and speed of access to requisite inputs. Large pools of labor of all skill types and levels are close at hand. Information on markets and competitors propagates more rapidly, and the ease of achieving face-to-face contact with customers and suppliers facilitates dealmaking of all sorts (Oakey 1985).

Although these advantages are available to virtually all firms locating within large urban economies, they are particularly important for the innovating firm, which is frequently small, young, and attempting to enter a high-risk product market. For such firms, urban agglomerations offer an information-rich environment in which technological advances are monitored and propagated more readily. Indeed many such firms owe their existence to larger, more established firms nearby from which they have spun off, seizing the opportunity to exploit new technologies or to develop new products based on established technologies (Saxenian 1984; Rothwell 1984). Similarly, it is often the metropolitan centers that have provided the best growth conditions for technical university faculties to which some new technology-based firms owe their origins. Sources of venture capital, particularly equity and longer-term debt financing, are generally far more prevalent in large urban centers (Gertler 1984). Perhaps most important, a large, diversified local economy can provide the young, innovating firm with access to many forms of highly specialized professional and technical expertise that is too expensive for such firms to maintain in-house for themselves. This support base of producer services furnishes vital functions in the areas of product design, development and testing, marketing, and management consulting (Britton 1985).

The list of advantages we have just enumerated should be quite familiar. They represent the production and innovation-generating benefits that major cities have provided since their inception (Blumenfeld 1955). Although some have contended that the long-standing dominance of large metropolitan areas peaked in the early 1970s, embarking on a long-term downward spiral thereafter (Vining and Kontuly 1978; Lonsdale and Seyler 1979), such claims have proved to be inaccurate or premature (Garnick 1984). Indeed, we would argue that the agglomerative forces outlined here are becoming increasingly important as the nature and organization of production in Western economies continues to evolve. Three trends in particular merit attention.

Flexible Manufacturing

The recent development of so-called flexible technologies involves the use of reprogrammable, numerically controlled machines in association with broadly trained and experienced workers to produce relatively small batches of output (Piore and Sabel 1984). Under such new forms of production, failure to achieve long production runs is of reduced significance. These technologies derive greater efficiencies by enabling producers to implement new processes quickly, to respond to rapid changes in market demands, and to service segmented demand requiring differentiated products. Furthermore, these production techniques exploit the relatively low capital costs of the microprocessor. All of these changes imply that internal scale economies are becoming far less important for a wider range of firms than they once were. Logically external economies become all the more crucial within the process of innovation by small firms. Business behavior reflects not only the rapid perception of and response to qualitative shifts in the market but also increased interdependence of small firms with each other. This implies a proportionally greater impact of microprocessor technology in big cities.

Some confirmation of this locational logic comes from a recent study of spatial patterns of adoption of new production technologies (Rees, Briggs, and Oakey 1983). Among its more significant findings, the study concluded that older plants in the established manufacturing centers of the industrial Midwest and Northeast were adopting the most sophisticated technologies at the highest rates, while newer plants in the southern states were adopting more traditional and standardized technology. Furthermore, among single-plant firms alone, adoption rates for the newer technologies were greatest in or close to the sources of these technologies, suggesting a strong spatial contiguity effect. The overall picture that emerges is one of technological dominance and leadership in established centers of the Northeast and Midwest. These findings support our earlier depiction of large cities as the centers of technological development.

Clusters of Vertically Linked Firms

The emergence of complexes of interlinked specialist manufacturing and service firms—the second organizational trend—is illustrated most dramatically by the current industrial renaissance of northeastern and central Italy. Recent reports estimate that between 60 and 70 percent of employment in this region of 25 million people is in the manufacturing sector. Most of this employment is in firms of between five and fifty workers, with the average size near the lower end of this range, for a total of almost 500,000 registered manufacturing firms (Hatch 1985). Clusters of these small firms have formed in cities such as Modena, Prato, and Bologna as spatially interdependent, vertically linked production units bound together by the elaborate networking that close clustering permits. Frequently these clusters have been promoted by local governments, which provide the physical space and plans for manufacturing districts organized around collective producer services in accounting, engineering, management, and marketing assistance. These governments often generate a further stimulus to these clusters by favoring them with preferential procurement policies. Similar principles are apparently at work in other clusters of innovative firms elsewhere around the world (Miller and Côté 1985). In Ontario, the authors are currently investigating manufacturing–producer service linkages in the expectation of finding substantial interdependence, based on the increased proportion (14 to 23 percent, 1971–1981) of scientific and technological employment in the producer service sector, which is market dependent on the manufacturing sector.

Adoption of Telecommunications Technology within Firms

The third trend to reinforce the advantages of large urban centers is that the utilization of telecommunications technologies within large, multiplant firms has caused the higher-order headquarter functions, including research, product and process development, finance, and computer programming, to become even more centralized on a national scale than they were before (Hepworth forthcoming). In short, the advent of telecommunications technology has enabled large firms to restructure their internal division of labor spatially and to locate particular functions in their most appropriate or conducive location. For activities related to product and process innovation, as well as marketing, the best location continues to be large urban centers, despite the fact that telecommunications technologies have freed some of these R&D functions to locate on cheaper land in the suburban fringes of such centers. We present these conclusions knowing full well that they are at odds with the myth of the electronic cottage; both the evolving theory and emerging research findings attest to the continuing renewal of the attractive power of major cities.

Thus urban attractions remain even for the larger firm that is sensitive to the supply of highly skilled labor (which traditionally prefers an amenity-rich living environment) and values the ability to keep abreast of technological developments introduced by the competition or other sources such as universities. Indeed, given the propensity of large companies to seek to reinternalize the entrepreneurial spirit by swallowing small and technologically dynamic but cash-starved firms, there is a distinct advantage in locating close to the environs favored by such small ventures.

Regardless of their size, technology-intensive firms are dependent on both private- and public-sector contracts, and there is, therefore, an imperative for such producers to cluster in locations that afford them the best opportunities for face-to-face contact with actual and potential customers. Recent evidence for Canada (Steed and de Genova 1983; Ontario Ministry of Treasury and Economics 1982), England (McQuaid 1985), and the United States (Saxenian 1984) confirms the importance of this consideration in the rise of high-tech clusters in Canada's Ottawa Valley, England's M4 corridor and West London Crescent, and California's Silicon Valley. It is against this background of recent trends that the locational evaluation of Canada's industrial policies should be undertaken.

Canadian Industrial Policies

Inherent in the Canadian policy structure are biases that mean that incentives for industrial innovation do not enhance the developmental advantages of the major industrial centers. Canada operates three styles of innovation-related policies: federal tax concessions for R&D, grants or loans of various types by federal and provincial governments for firms undertaking industrial innovation but particularly R&D, and public procurement at three levels of government that can act as a stimulus for industrial innovation. Tax concessions notoriously favor large firms and focus on narrowly defined R&D activity. By their nature, therefore, they do not assist the large number of small firms locationally concentrated in major industrial centers. By comparison with tax concessions, Canada's direct grant policies are of greater importance because of the financial capital that is mobilized to encourage industrial innovation within small- and medium-sized enterprises (SMEs). Government procurement is potentially a major source of stimulus, but the consensus of opinion would seem to be that cooperative local procurement is as yet poorly organized, provincial balkanization has been developed to a high degree, and federal procurement, including offsets from defense contracts, is an area of conscious, but not effective, managerial activity. This chapter focuses on grant and loan programs while acknowledging that more explicit research is required on the strengths and omissions in procurement policy as a stimulus for innovation.

In addition to the National Research Council (NRC), which has a well-articulated but financially limited function to increase technology transfer, innovation, and R&D, two major federal actors have developed programs to assist Canadian industry: the Departments of Regional Economic Expansion (DREE) and Industry Trade and Commerce (IT&C). Broadly, DREE's mandate was to compensate economically depressed or lagging regions for their apparent lack of industrial opportunity by encouraging the job creation potential of these regions so that stabilization, if not growth, might result. By contrast, IT&C's functions were focused on innovation, technological change, R&D assistance, and the development of Canadian firms, primarily through its Enterprise Development Program (EDP). Rather than pursuing a spatial equity approach that excluded southern Ontario from DREE's assistance, IT&C assisted technology-intensive sectors and firms and favored Ontario in pursuing this mission—over 53 percent of EDP grants of $119 million in 1981–1982 (Economic Council of Canada, 1983). EDP was devised as a program that assisted small- and medium-sized firms, but it was also given a mandate to ease the process of adjustment to structural economic change for long-established firms. Hence, in 1981–1982 about 35 percent of its total allocations went to just under thirty firms with sales greater than $25 million (and grants of Canadian $1.5 million each), while about five hundred enterprises shared the remainder with grants averaging less than $150,000 each. Within the Toronto region, however, 70 percent of assistance (1981–1982) was allocated to the metropolitan fringe, and within this area impetus was given to new ventures, especially in electrical products (39 percent) (Gardner 1983).

The Industrial and Regional Development Act of 1983, which created the Department of Regional Industrial Expansion, amalgamated most of the activities of DREE and IT&C and combined most of the program funding from the two departments into its Industrial and Regional Development Program (IRDP). While, on the surface, the focus of DRIE's activity is concerned with innovation, restructuring, modernization, and international competition, in fact the pattern of assistance raises questions about the meaning of DRIE's program guides (table 10–1). For example, it is difficult to explain why many traditional manufacturing industries have received the largest shares of assistance (low rankings) when aiding innovation is a major element in the DRIE program.

Although our intention is to explore options for innovation policies in Canada, it is first necessary to understand the shortcomings of current policies when evaluated from a locational perspective.

Program Biases against Metropolitan Areas

There are strongly negative biases against metropolitan areas in the four-tier classification system used to apportion IRDP disbursements; the most-developed areas of Canada containing 50 percent of the population are in the lowest-priority tier and receive a proportionally lower rate of assistance than less-developed areas. This IRDP weighting against metropolitan areas exemplifies the need for federal policy to compromise between two quite different sets of goals. Canada has a long-standing involvement in redressing regional disparities in economic development, but in IRDP this goal has been combined with federal attempts to provide assistance to innovative and

Table 10–1
DRIE Assistance to Industrial Sectors, July 1983–March 1984
(sectoral rank order)

Number of Firms Assisted		*Assistance (millions of dollars)*	
1. Food	61	1. Machinery	15.5
2. Wood	42	2. Construction and heavy construction	11.0
3. Machinery	39		
4 Electrical	37	3. Other industries	8.8
5. Metal fabricating	30	4. Paper products	8.7
6. Other industries	24	5. Wood	6.6
7. Chemical	23	6. Metal fabricating	5.9
8. Furniture	19	7. Food	5.2
9. Plastic products	17	8. Electrical	4.4
10. Other manufacturing	16	9. Primary metal	4.3
		10. Chemical	3.0
			73.4
Total	381		82.6

Source: Canada DRIE (1983–84).

research-intensive firms. It is becoming increasingly clear, however, that this sort of goal mixing is counterproductive as a basis for assisting national economic development. This is illustrated by DRIE's mandate in managing IRDP, which amounts to maintaining and modestly redistributing the location of employment. The record of the first two years shows little attempt to realize or stimulate the latent advantages of Canada's major industrial centers.

The evidence to justify a negative assessment of IRDP lies within its own annual reports on the tier system of grants. Essentially, the system of tiers formalizes the Canadian geography of unemployment and regional disparities in income by classifying locations into one of four tiers according to level of need. The four tiers allow progressively greater levels of assistance to areas exhibiting the greatest economic hardship. The metropolitan areas, because of their higher income levels, are designated as tier I areas and thus receive a less than proportionate amount of assistance.

In 1983–1984, for example, tier I centers received 47 percent of assistance; in 1984–1985 this dropped to 42 percent. Examination of 1984–1985 records, however, shows that very large grants (to lever substantial corporate investments) exercise a disturbing influence on the tier allocation of funds. Only ten grants of $5 million or more were made in 1984–1985, but these took 34 percent of the total financing made available under IRDP. These were dominated by two major grants: $60.5 million to American Motors (Canada) in Brampton, Ontario, and $22 million to General Motors of Canada in Oshawa, Ontario. These exceedingly large grants are out of place in a program that allocated a balance of $272 million to 1,454 other firms. When an adjusted set of totals is produced, eliminating these large grants, tier I centers received only 34 percent of total IRDP disbursements.

This pattern of allocation is particularly disturbing because the forces of agglomeration have been shown to be central to technology-based development elsewhere in the industrial world. There are, of course, only a limited number of such locations in any country that possess structural advantages that merit expenditures designed to stimulate a critical mass of innovative firms. But placing nearly two-thirds of the assistance funds for industrial renewal outside those regions with demonstrated ability to generate and nurture firms makes a mockery of Canada's professed policies for technological change. It appears to be a political rather than an economic model that underlies the operation of IRDP. This interpretation is reinforced by the way federal and provincial policies are linked through economic and regional development agreements (ERDAs) that do not involve direct regional representation. Thus, metropolitan centers are not involved in economic goal setting with the provinces or in determining patterns of delivery of financial stimulus. This too is a questionable practice given the size of metropolitan centers, their past attraction for firms, and their possibilities for generating new business.

Usually the theory invoked to rationalize government assistance for innovation is one that emphasizes the need, at the level of the firm, to offset problems of risk and appropriability associated with R&D and new product development. In addition, it is recognized that the public interest is served by governments addressing a low level of innovation. In particular, there are locational imperatives that should be allowed to direct assistance into those regions where superior infrastructural conditions prevail and where greater indirect benefits are likely to result. Criticism for failure to implement this principle effectively should not be leveled solely at IRDP. The government of Ontario, for example, has invested in a set of technology centers responsible for certain forms of technology transfer, and all are located outside the industrial heart of the province. Secondary industrial nodes have been favored in a few instances, but only political explanations satisfy basic criteria of locational credibility. The consequence of this eccentric location pattern is a penalty of reduced accessibility to these technological services for firms in Ontario's industrial core, an area responsible for generating more than half of Ontario's net increase in manufacturing establishments. Many of these are small and are the very firms that would benefit most from improvements in their technological infrastructure.

New Technology

In spite of the services supplied by Ontario's technology centers and the Technology Information Service of the National Research Council, Canadian governments have not recognized adequately that many SMEs identify and serve market niches within traditional and modern industries and depend on a variety of input linkages for scientific testing, design, and marketing as the way of exploiting their growth potential. Taken as a whole, Canadian technology policies are dedicated inordinately to offsetting R&D expenses of industry and to funding government R&D. This focuses attention on innovation through the generation of new technology rather than on innovation through the use of existing technology in which design, ease of manufacture, and marketing inputs may depend on inputs from specialist firms. There is, of course, a limited group of firms that makes technological breakthroughs and whose intellectual resources mean that external production linkages are more likely and more important. But this dependence of manufacturing on producer services is true for a wide range of SMEs that characteristically have underdeveloped internal functions related to design, engineering, and marketing.

Metropolitan regions with their localization of producer services provide superior access to such services and offer optimal opportunities for small, innovative manufacturers to interact with each other. Therefore it is in these regions that linkage networks can best be fostered. There are, however, limited policy initiatives in Canada that address the need to nurture and develop these networks, and thus there are no significant experiments underway that may guide the encouragement of small manufacturers to innovate in an incremental fashion, using ongoing consulting arrangements with producer service specialists.

Large Firms

Since the majority of small firms are clustered in metropolitan regions, the fact that programs pay limited attention to the needs of small firms amounts to a further bias against metropolitan areas. Taxation concessions for R&D are a prime example of a policy with a very limited client base. It is mainly large firms that are successful in exploiting the tax credits, small firms being in a fragile tax position and thus essentially bypassed by the program. Similarly, DRIE's mandate is to assist regional development, but considerations relevant to the development of small businesses or networks of SMEs either are ignored or misunderstood.

Toronto Case

The constraints on Toronto's ability to generate locationally determined agglomeration economies are not addressed by IRDP's provisions. Despite Toronto's nationally dominant economic size and its centralization of the highest order of service functions and labor skills, its agglomeration advantages, as they affect industrial innovation, are strongly limited by the small scale of the Canadian industrial economy. There are therefore pertinent limitations to the quality of the Toronto agglomeration when international competition is the standard of judgment.

Toronto has two additional disadvantages. First, within Canada and within southern Ontario in particular, foreign ownership is concentrated in the Toronto region. An effect of foreign ownership in Canada, as has been established in previous research, is to create substantial international leakages of development impulses from the economy (Britton and Gilmour 1978; Britton 1985). It is inescapable that Toronto is the national concentration of the effect of these leakages so that the flow of goods and services from manufacturing results in reduced effective demand for producer services and manufactured components.

Second, Toronto has a highly diversified industrial economy, and while this has acted traditionally as a buffer to the impact of cyclical economic processes, it also dampens the possibility of regional gains from specialization, which would be some compensation for the effects of the small national economy and foreign ownership.

Toronto leads Canada in the size and growth rate of the office sector (Semple and Smith 1981) and in producer services (Britton 1985), and it is very strong in cultural industries and in terms of university quality. Therefore it has most of the advantages normally associated with those industrial regions whose success derives from high levels of innovation and growth of technology-based industry. Yet Toronto's industrial economy is little different in structure from that of the nation in that it contains a high percentage of manufacturing activity in medium-technology sectors and a very modest proportion of activity based on new technology. It would appear, therefore, that the Toronto region is not the industrial leader of the nation, despite its industrial scale. Rather, in microcosm, it is a reflection of the structure of Canada.

It is worrying to consider the policy implications of the level of assistance to firms in the Toronto region. In 1981–1982 EDP allocated nearly one-third of its resources to assisting and stimulating firms in the region. With the advent of IRDP, however, Toronto's share dropped to 5.1 percent of disbursements in 1983–1984 though it contains 12 percent of Canada's population and employs nearly 18 percent of Canada's work force in the natural sciences, engineering, and mathematics, an indicator of its technological capability and potential for industrial innovation. This bias against Toronto is again evident in 1984–1985; it received only 7.8 percent of the adjusted total of IRDP disbursements.

Lines of Innovation Policy Action

Although this analysis has identified a policy problem, there is still a need to specify how a solution can be defined. The intent and structure of policies therefore should be examined against the set of possibilities. Two dimensions to technological policy are used in the following discussion: (1) the dichotomy between policies that are concerned with the conditions of survival and growth of existing firms and those that are concerned with the generation of new businesses and (2) the distinction between policies that improve the management of the existing industrial system and those that seek to modify its components and therefore restructure that system. Together these two dimensions define four policy domains in which innovation-enhancing policies may exist (table 10–2). Innovation policy in Canada is distinctive in that most activity has occurred in cells I–III where new public expenditures can be taken without the adverse political reactions that might be imputed as reactions by a conservative business community to policies that could be taken in cell IV.

Cell I: Managing the Existing System with a View to Enhancing the Generation of New Firms

International experience suggests that new firms are generated predominantly from the base of existing corporations and from universities in the case of technology-based small firms (Braden 1977; Rothwell and Zegveld 1982; Utterback and Reitberger 1982). The rate of new firm formation from corporations seems related to the degree of enlightenment of existing management, while it is thought that the fertility of universities can be assisted through industry–university research contracting. Although there is little literature that reports on the success of policies to increase the importance of university origins of firms, most federal and provincial ventures are at an early stage of application. The Economic Council of Canada, however, has reported convincingly on healthy rates of new firm formation. Improvement in the availability of venture financing for new, technology-based firms has been the most dramatic source of assistance for new firms, and this is a product primarily of provincial legislation.

Cell II: Modifying the Structure of the System to Generate More Firms

In the belief that conventional sources of firms are inadequate, Canada and most other industrial countries have adopted a variety of policies to increase the rate of formation, and/or survival, of new technology-based firms. Incubation schemes, science parks, and combinations of these two are designed to advance the emergence of firms from universities in particular.

Since most of these schemes are property based, they tend to be expensive, and overseas experience emphasizes that success depends on the managerial quality of the incubation scheme or park. Nevertheless, these ventures

Table 10–2
Industrial Policy Domains

	Survivors	New Firms
Manage existing industrial system	IV	I
Modify industrial system structure	III	II

tend to house firms that likely would have been created in less attractive facilities, and they do not increase the rate of new firm generation (Goddard and Thwaites 1983; Monck and Segal 1983).

Cell III: Modifying the Structure of the Industrial System to Promote Survival of Existing Firms

The set of policy options in this cell has been the focus of public expenditures, particularly by the government of Ontario, and is less speculative. Projects are usually quite visible, and they frequently feature construction activity. The Ontario Research Foundation and Ontario's technology centers are prime examples; they are both supply-side responses to lags in industrial innovation. They are technology-transfer schemes that do little directly to increase industrial demand for research, services, or production-related technology. Nevertheless, the arguments about international leakages of intermediate demand from the Ontario economy, leading to failure to meet thresholds for various producer services, justify this type of supply-side intervention. At the same time, the limited level of innovation among Canadian firms clearly indicates that stimulation of demand for the services supplied by public agencies and private firms is necessary. Without such measures technology-transfer centers will be incapable of stimulating complex networks of linkages that are necessary as a technology support structure for a significant proportion of firms.

Cell IV: Managing the System to Augment the Performance of Survivors

Policies for stabilization and for longer-term assistance for development are found in cell IV. In this category are included programs that purport to increase the growth of productivity and the level of R&D. Much assistance for development is delivered through the tax system, and this means that there is no explicit direction of assistance to sectors, regions, or firms because fiscal policies are intended to affect supply and demand in a passive manner. Therefore it is not surprising that these types of policy do not depend for their conception and application on an understanding of the functioning of the production system and thus on the linkages among firms both within and between sectors.

Other countries, however, have gone further with experiments concerned with policies, at national and regional levels, directed toward improving the survival and development of firms within the existing production system. Policies in the United Kingdom, for example, depend on the properly applied knowledge of linkage systems and on a mode of application that is activist rather than passive in orientation. Direct approaches are made in order to reach those firms whose contacts and linkages fail to make maximum use of inputs from the producer service sector. This type of policy targets small- and medium-sized manufacturing firms regardless of location and obviates the antimetropolitan bias inherent in the policies currently in force in Canada. The British experiments, by indicating how much more could be done in Canada, confirm the impression that Canadian policies fitting cell IV studiously avoid intervention by direct approaches to firms. Furthermore, the implications from British experience are that apprehension about the political risks of direct approaches is unfounded, that qualified program staff can be found, and that the benefit-cost ratio for this approach can be impressively high (Rothwell 1984).

Activist Policies for Innovation

In recent years activist policies concerned with technology transfer have been developed in Britain—centrally devised programs of the Department of Trade and Industry (DTI) and regional schemes relying on local initiatives—that are innovations worth considering in Canada. In both cases intermediaries facilitate the input of technical knowledge to manufacturing firms.

Design Advisory Service

Although the DTI operates four schemes to transfer current technical knowledge to existing small- and medium-sized firms, the Design Advisory Service (DAS), begun in 1982, is singled out as the clearest policy innovation relative to current Canadian practice. The goal of this program is to improve the products and/or processes of small firms by means of inputs from technical consultants. A producer service intermediary organizes the subsidized first use of these consultants. The rationale for DAS is that few small firms have in-house technical services to supply and implement improved product design, engineering, production, and marketing ideas, yet inferior industrial performance indicates inadequate use of these inputs. The theory that is central to the scheme is that a one-time subsidized experience in the use of consultants will lead to similar linkages in the future.

The firms that are targeted are found in traditional and modern manufacturing industries in which it is possible for a small firm to identify and continue to serve a market niche, provided it retains its competitive edge. Thus 55 percent of the client firms have been in mechanical and electrical engineering, metal goods, and clothing and footwear, and two types of services have dominated demand—industrial design and styling and mechanical engineering. From the standpoint of Canadian policy development, however, the significance of the DAS is that 60 percent of applications have been stimulated by direct approaches to firms made by field officers with substantial industrial experience. Furthermore, the DAS draws much of its inspiration from research that demonstrates the importance of continuous incremental product improvement made in recognition of production, technological, and market factors.

Regional Schemes of Technology Transfer

Although it is delivered through regional contact offices, the DAS is liable to the criticism of most other central programs: that it has no regional affinity and that local offices are only referral points. Perhaps for this reason and in order to intensify technology transfer to existing small firms, regionally based schemes have emerged recently. To some extent, too, these schemes have their origin in the qualified success of research parks as regional initiatives and the realization that care and nurturing of small firms is both a necessary condition for the survival of most and that the expensive property-based research parks have neither housed many firms nor assisted significantly those that they have attracted.

Regional technology transfer schemes in Britain are concerned with the formation of networks that link universities, manufacturing firms, and consulting companies. The Welsh Development Agency, for example, has developed Wintech as a mobile science park to improve the technology used by existing firms. Staff advisers assist in establishing technology transfer mechanisms by informing the region's firms about new opportunities to increase their competitiveness.

Flexible network formation is also the guiding principle underpinning the scheme now beginning operation in Newcastle. Its goal is to upgrade the competence of industry so that innovation is more likely. The demand for enriched inputs is to be met by moving technology from universities into firms, by commercial work undertaken in the universities, and by manufacturing firms' using appropriate consultants and relevant databases made accessible by the scheme. Demand for these inputs, currently at low ebb, is to be stimulated by the proactive assistance of all plants, including branch operations that lack identification with the economic health of the northeast. Newcastle is producing a centralized network dependent on staff as intermediaries and on one-stop field officers who operate throughout a contact sequence, thus implementing the results of an experimental inquiry that used paired comparisons of firms to evaluate the effectiveness of the proactive advisory methodology at the regional level (Thwaites 1983).

Conclusion

Metropolitan regions have a powerful and increasingly important potential to support the generation, development, and successful marketing of industrial innovations. It follows that public policies to promote technological development would operate more effectively and efficiently by exploiting these metropolitan advantages. Yet current Canadian policies ignore this potential and indeed contain several systematic though largely unintended antimetropolitan biases. Reviewing a number of possible technology development strategies, we have chosen to emphasize policies that actively seek to link small-sized manufacturers with producer service firms whose inputs they require in order to be successful innovators. Implicit in this discussion and in our review of some recent British initiatives is the realization that the forging of such links is most easily and effectively done inside the metropolitan environment. This is particularly true for Canada, where producer services are even more highly localized in metropolitan centers than is true for manufacturing.

Having taken that position, we must address the inadequacies of current innovation policy in Canada. A substantial part of Canada's current efforts to promote industrial innovation is being exerted through the program activity of DRIE; embodied in DRIE's mandate are the twin goals of technological development and the amelioration of regional economic disparities. By trying to achieve both of these objectives, it in fact can do neither well. By failing to exploit the innovation-supporting environment of large cities, DRIE promotes the inefficient and counterproductive application of scarce federal resources, an act we liken to watering infertile ground. These objectives must be uncoupled and pursued through separate program initiatives. Certainly the existing political realities and the chronic interregional immobility of labor suggest that regional development should be maintained as an important federal objective. At the same time, however, it is imperative that Canada recognizes, through its policy structures, how small in number are the urban agglomerations capable of accommodating and nurturing Canada's technological renewal.

Although some previous policy arrangements—for example, those administered by IT&C until 1983—may have exhibited fewer of the antimetropolitan biases reviewed earlier, the overwhelmingly sectoral organization of its programs effectively sacrificed the efficiencies to be gained by pursuing a more spatially integrated, linkage-sensitive approach. We are therefore not advocating a return to the old order. Rather, the extension to the argument developed here suggests that it is predominantly within metropolitan areas that activist policy instruments can best be implemented in order to augment the specialization and innovation of small manufacturing and service firms. Furthermore, the policy stance we recommend could ultimately work to the advantage of both established metropolitan centers and the more economically depressed regions of Canada if firms in large cities are encouraged to grow to a size where a spatial decentralization of some of their production activities to lower-skilled, cheaper-wage labor markets is a logical outcome.

References

Alonso, W. 1975. "Industrial Location and Regional Policy in Economic Development." In J. Friedmann and W. Alonso, eds., *Regional Policy*. Cambridge: MIT Press.

Blumenfeld, Hans. 1955. "The Economic Base of the Metropolis: Critical Remarks on the 'Basis-Nonbasic' Concept." *Journal of the American Institute of Planners* 21:114:132.

Braden, Patricia L. 1977. *Technological Entrepreneurship*. Michigan Business Reports 62. Ann Arbor: University of Michigan, Graduate School of Business Administration.

Britton, John N.H. 1985. "Research and Development in the Canadian Economy: Sectoral, Ownership, Locational, and Policy Issues." In R. Oakey and A. Thwaites, eds. *Technological Change and Regional Economic Development*. London: Frances Pinter.

Britton, John N.H., and Gilmour, James M. 1978. *The Weakest Link: A Technological Perspective on Canadian Industrial Underdevelopment*. Background Study 43. Ottawa: Science Council of Canada.

Canada. Regional Industrial Expansion. 1983–1984. *Industrial and Regional Development Program Annual Report*.

Economic Council of Canada. 1983. *The Bottom Line: Technology, Trade, and Income Growth*. Ottawa: Economic Council of Canada.

Gardner, Robert L. 1983. *Industrial Development in Metropolitan Toronto: Issues, Propsects and Strategy*. Toronto: Municipality of Metropolitan Toronto, Economic Development Office of the Metropolitan Chairman.

Garnick, Daniel H. 1984. "Shifting Balances in U.S. Metropolitan and Nonmetropoli-Area Growth." *International Regional Science Review* 9:257–273.

Gertler, Meric S. 1984. "Regional Capital Theory." *Progress in Human Geography* 8:50–81.

Goddard, John B., and Thwaites, Alfred T. 1983. "Science Parks in the Context of National, Regional and Local Technology Policy." *Planner* 69, no. 1:36–37.

Hatch, C. Richard. 1985. "Italy's Industrial Renaissance: Are America's Cities Ready to Learn?" *Urban Land* (January):20–23.

Hepworth, Mark E. Forthcoming. "Information Technology and Regional Development," *Regional Studies*.

Kaldor, Nicholas. 1970. "The Case for Regional Policies." *Scottish Journal of Political Economy* 17:337–348.

Lonsdale, Richard E., and Seyler, H.C., eds. 1979. *Nonmetropolitan Industrialization.* Washington, D.C.: V.H. Winston and Sons.

McQuaid, Ronald. 1985. "The Role of Defence Procurement in Regional Development in the U.K." M4 Working Note 14. Department of Georgraphy, Reading University.

Miller, Roger, and Côté, Marcel. 1985. "Growing the Next Silicon Valley." *Harvard Business Review* 63:114–123.

Monck, C.S.P., and Segal, N.S. 1983. "University Science Parks and Small Firms." Paper presented at National Small Business Conference, Durham University, September.

Oakey, Ray. 1985. "High-Technology Industires and Agglomeration Economies." In P. Hall and A.R. Markusen, eds., *Silicon Landscapes*. London: Allen & Unwin.

Ontario Ministry of Treasury and Economics. 1982. "High-Tech Industry in Ontario: Performance and Government Support." Toronto: Economic Research Branch, Office of Economic Policy.

Piore, Michael J., and Sabel, Charles. 1984. *The Second Industrial Divide.* New York: Basic Books.

Rees, John; Briggs, Ron; and Oakey, Ray. 1983. "The Adoption of New Technology in the American Machinery Industry." Occasional Paper 71. Syracuse: Metropolitan Studies Program, Maxwell School of Citizenship and Public Affairs, Syracuse University.

Rothwell, Roy. 1984. "The Role of Small Firms in the Emergence of New Technologies." *OMEGA* 12:19–29.

Rothwell, Roy, and Zegveld, W. 1982. *Innovation and the Small and Medium Sized Firm.* London: Frances Pinter.

Saxenian, Anna Lee. 1984. "The Urban Contradictions of Silicon Valley: Regional Growth and the Restructuring of the Semiconductor Industry." In L. Sawers and W.K. Tabb, eds., *Sunbelt/Snowbelt: Urban Development and Regional Restructuring.* New York: Oxford University Press.

Semple, R. Keith, and Smith, W. Randy. 1981. "Metropolitan Dominance and Foreign Ownership in the Canadian Urban System." *Canadian Geographer* 25:4–26.

Steed, Guy P.F., and de Genova, Don. 1983. "Ottawa's Technology-Oriented Complex. *Canadian Geographer* 27:263–278.

Thwaites, Alfred T. 1983. "Regional Technological Change Centres." Discussion Paper 47. Centre for Urban and Regional Development Studies, University of Newcastle upon Tyne.

Utterback, J.M., and Reitberger, G. 1982. *Technology and Industrial Innovation in Sweden: A Study of New Technology Based Firms.* Cambridge, Mass.: MIT, Center for Policy Alternatives.

Vining, Daniel R., and Kontuly, Thomas. 1978. "Population Dispersal from Major Metropolitan Regions: An International Comparison." *International Regional Science Review* 3:49–73.

11

Cooperative Research and Development Centers: Government, University, and Industry Roles, Responsibilities, and Results

William A. Hetzner
J.D. Eveland

There has been increasing interest and activity in recent years in developing research collaborations between university scientists and industry. A variety of institutional modes are being used to structure these collaborations, often with the financial assistance of government agencies (Brodsky, Kaufman, and Tooker 1980). One such program is University/Industry Cooperative Research Centers, which has been sponsored for more than ten years by the National Science Foundation (NSF). Since 1981 the NSF's Productivity Improvement Research Section has coordinated an evaluation of more than twenty centers funded by this program.

Progress of the evaluation has been discussed in a variety of documents (Tornatzky et al. 1982; Eveland and Hetzner 1982; Eveland, Hetzner, and Tornatzky 1984; Hetzner and Eveland 1983; Eveland 1985). This chapter differs from its predecessors on two important dimensions. First, we are beginning to receive and analyze data from a relatively large number of centers, some of them longitudinal in nature. Second, with the maturity of a number of centers, there seems to be a growing concern about the dimensions of industrial participation in the program. Earlier reports deal primarily with the roles and responsibilities of universities and government funding agencies. We will also discuss data concerning the existing roles and responsibilities of industry participants.

University/Industry Cooperative Research Centers

A University/Industry Cooperative Research Center is a "university-based, typically interdisciplinary program of research supported jointly by a number

Any opinions, findings, and conclusions or recommendations expressed in this chapter are those of the authors and do not represent the views of the National Science Foundation.

of companies" (Tornatsky et al. 1982). NSF support partially funds initial planning and development of a center, with sustaining support provided most often by a group of industrial firms. In some cases state government has augmented center funding. There are, of course, many other models of collaborative research mechanisms that involve intensive interaction between universities and firms (Brodsky, Kaufman, and Tooker 1980) but few that involve both an interdisciplinary *program* of research and multiclient support.

Both university and industry sponsors must agree to a research agenda. This agenda functions for the firm much like a research mutual fund, with each firm typically interested in more than one but not all of the research projects.

The emphasis on a program of research also has implications for the organization and management of centers. In developing its research agenda, the university generally allows participation of client firms in both recommending research projects and evaluating their results, a significant departure from more traditional collaborative arrangements. Centers therefore are both programmatic and administrative innovations for the university and the participating firms.

The NSF centers program is an elaboration of a major applied research initiative, the Experimental R&D Incentives Program (ERDIP). In 1972, at the request of President Richard Nixon, NSF established ERDIP, while the Department of Commerce established a companion program, the Experimental Technology Incentives. The specific objectives of these programs were to increase nonfederal investment in R&D and to promote increased utilization of new technology by all sectors. These programs also encouraged cooperative efforts among government agencies, universities, and private-sector organizations.

There were a number of initiatives, in addition to the University/Industry Cooperative Centers Experiment, started as part of ERDIP, including the Innovation Centers Experiment, Federal Laboratory Validation Assistance Program, Experiment on Federal Actions to Accelerate the Utilization of Civilian Oriented R&D, and the Medical Instrumentation Experiment (Colton 1982). All of these were intended as experiments and not as long-term government programs.

There are a number of problems with conducting experimental p ograms in government, not the least of which is bureaucratic inertia, or the tendency to maintain programs no matter what their effects in order to preserve one's job or organizational status. Within NSF, this bureaucratic inertia is counterbalanced by the lack of support for, if not open hostility to, applied research. The net result of these countervailing forces is that while bits and pieces of all of these experiments survived for a while, the centers program is the only one still in existence. For the first seven years (1972–1979) survival can be attributed to the tenacity of the program manager. The last six years (1979–1985) are the result of the success of the program itself.

The program has not only survived, it has managed under great duress to remain faithful to the objectives and requirements of ERDIP. The program managers have systematically reduced funding levels (with some success) and duration of funding (with less success). They have assisted in the establishment of management and social science–based centers and are currently attempting to put together multiuniversity centers. In short, it is still an experimental attempt to overcome identified barriers to the flow of information and technology between organizations while requiring a "convincing commitment of non-Federal resources" (NSF 1972).

During the first five years of the program, three cooperative university–industry centers were funded from fourteen experimental development projects, which were planning grants to study the feasibility of various university–industry linking mechanisms. The objectives of these grants were to define the cooperative effort, to obtain initial financial commitments from industry, to establish data collection agreements, and to determine how patents would be allocated among the participants. Only three of the fourteen met the requirement to the satisfaction of external reviewers. The resulting centers were both organizational and technologically different. North Carolina State University established the Furniture R&D Applications Institute, MIT the Polymer Processing Center, and Mitre Corporation acted as intermediary in the university–industry interface as part of the New England Energy Development Systems Center. After five years, only the Polymer Processing Center was able to attract sustaining industrial support, which it maintains today. The lack of an R&D tradition seemed to be the major problem with the Furniture R&D Applications Institute, while the use of an intermediary proved cumbersome for the NEEDS center (Colton 1982). As a result, the MIT Polymer Processing Center became the prototype for the Centers program (Tornatsky et al. 1982). This model is a university research group consisting of an administrative core that supports and coordinates a series of interrelated research projects, each of which involves several faculty, staff, and students. While NSF funding partially supports the initial development of the center, generally for five years, sustaining support is provided by a group of industrial firms.

In addition to the Polymer Processing Center, NSF has committed planning grants for twenty more centers, with another ten in the planning stage. In spite of modest funding, most planning grants resulted in establishing operational centers. For the first few centers, NSF provided about one-half of first-year funds for center operations. This proportion has been substantially reduced for centers since 1983. NSF funds decrease each year, requiring firms or other government agencies to increase their level of support, to increase the number of center members, or both. In addition to the MIT center, two centers became free-standing in 1984, and two others are in their last year of funding and will continue under industry and state government sponsorship.

The twenty current centers leverage NSF funds with industry and state government funds at about seven to one. NSF will contribute $3 million in 1985, industry support is estimated at $14 million, and state and local governments another $13 million.[1] Nearly 250 firms currently participate in the program, with over 600 employees of these firms participating in the research and administration of these centers. The total cost of participation (fees, travel costs, and time) per firm is estimated by NSF program managers to be between $20,000 and $100,000 annually. Clearly centers constitute a convincing commitment of nonfederal resources. What remains to be documented is if they in fact increase utilization of new technologies or anything else of tangible of benefit to their participants.

In fact, centers no longer have to result in utilization of new technologies since ERDIP and its offshoots are no longer programs of the NSF. Indeed, technologies, embodied in new products or processes, are not the expected outcomes for a firm participating in the center. Firms expect centers to expand general knowledge and improve graduate education rather than to result in new products or processes. This, of course, could change over time, and therefore we still consider utilization of new technologies as a potential outcome of cooperative centers in the evaluation effort.

Evaluation Effort

The Centers program has supported the need for systematic evaluation of individual centers, as well as the overall program itself from the earliest days. For the initial three centers, a two-tiered program of evaluation was established. The center itself was responsible for an internal evaluation, while a third party conducted a primarily quantitative external evaluation. Grad (1979) provides a thorough description of this external evaluation: "Program evaluation has been fully implemented only in the MIT Polymer Processing Program. In this instance, the data have been used to develop a model for generalizing the Cooperative R&D concept and, thus, have been useful" (p. 27).

With the completion of the external evaluation contract, NSF program staff continued to maintain an evaluator at each new center. Evaluators were (and are) typically faculty from the unviersity with some background in social science research and usually evaluation research experience. They were not part of the same school as members of the center and were funded under a separate (and modest) subcontract as part of the center grant. With the lapse of the external contract, however, NSF program staff were somewhat uncertain as to what the internal center evaluators ought to do, and they asked for the assistance of the Productivity Improvement Research Section in defining these responsibilities.

The result has been an integration of internal and external evaluation activities. Evaluators, with the assistance of NSF program and evaluation staff, have developed a fixed set of evaluation activities, protocols, and instruments to gather data about center operations and outcomes.[2] Internal formal reports are the responsibility of the center evaluator and are done according to an agreed upon schedule, typically twice a year. External reporting of aggregate program data is the responsibility of the Productivity Improvement Research Section and does not occur on any fixed schedule.

The evaluation has been divided into four components. The first component is the documentation effort, an attempt to maintain an ongoing description of the center. The purpose of this effort is to record events and identify individuals critical to the development of a center. The product of this portion of the evaluation program is a series of historical profiles (Eveland and Hetzner 1982; Eveland, Hetzner, and Tornatzky 1984) of centers, which is edited by NSF. NSF staff and evaluators have established a set of needed data elements and protocols for the documentation effort and are moving toward a standard instrument for updating a center's profile. Documentation information also establishes the context of the more quantitative data gathered in the other phases of the evaluation.

The second major component of the evaluation is a network analysis conducted at the end of the first and last years of NSF funding of a center. The network analysis is a picture of who says what to whom and how often. The properties of communications structures are presumed to be a significant measure of their operations and effects. Eveland (1985) describes the theoretical basis for the network analysis, the standardized data collection methodology, and analytical procedures developed for the network analysis and the results of first-year data from nine centers.

The third component of the evaluation is a description of the organization structure, procedures and policies of the center, and its relationship to the larger university. If the network analysis is a map of the actual communications structure of a center, this component is a description of how the university thinks communications and other systems are structured. It describes control and reward systems: who reports to whom, how much money and other resources university participants can commit without someone else's signature, what behaviors are rewarded (or not rewarded) by the university, and the roles played all center participants. Data are collected from all participants in the center: university faculty, staff and students, industry scientists and R&D managers, and even government funding agency representatives when appropriate. Organization structure is determined by a combination of standardized interviews and questionnaires, observtion of meetings, and analysis of written documents generated by center personnel. Center structure questionnaires are collected at the end of the first year of operation and yearly thereafter. In general reporting of the results of the center structure component to the center itself tends to be informal.

The final component of the evaluation is the measurement of a critical dependent variable: identification of expected benefits for the participants in the center and evaluation of the extent to which these expectations are being met. Expected and realized outcomes vary not only between the university and industry but also among the individual firms. Expectations and outcomes will also vary over time. Information about outcomes is collected yearly from firm and university participants using a common structured interview or questionnaire format. A report describing the profile of expectations and outcomes for a center is reported yearly in an internal document developed by the evaluator and sent to all participants.

For the latter two evaluation components, we have first-year data from six centers, second-year data from one, and third-year data from another. The total respondents were 65 faculty and 133 industry participants from all of these centers (Gray and Gidley 1985).

All instruments used in the evaluation program are the product of cooperation between NSF and the evaluators. There is a rather large standardized set of questions used by all centers. Each evaluator has the option of adding questions to tailor these instruments to the needs and pecularities of each center. Each new evaluator is given the opportunity to work out the pattern of instrumentation best suited to his or her situation.

All evaluators meet every six months to discuss the instruments, data collection methods, and individual and aggregate analyses. These meetings have also proved quite valuable in assisting the evaluators in defining their roles and responsibilities. Since 1983 annual meetings for center directors also have been held. Fruther, one meeting of industry representatives for nine centers was held in 1984. As in the case of the evaluators, these meetings have been helpful in defining roles and responsibilities. This is especially true to industry representatives. There has been a general tendency to view industry as having a more or less passive role and only financial responsibility for center development. This meeting seemed to demonstrate that firms are concerned with the survival of the centers and may be willing to do more than simply vote with their feet.

Some Findings from the Documentation Effort

The documentation effort has been reported on in some detail elsewhere (Tornatzky et al. 1982; Eveland and Hetzner 1982; Eveland, Hetzner, and Tornatzky 1984; and Hetzner and Eveland 1983). The focus of these reports, however, has been on the initial development of a center. Some of the preliminary findings reported here related to later stages of center growth.

Industry and university participants must agree on basic purposes. From the earliest stages, the core of the model is the accomplishment of basic research of relevance to industry. The comparative advantage of universities is their basic research capability. Firms are generally better able and equipped to conduct applied R&D. Conflicting goals seem to occur when university scientists stress industrial relevance and/or industry sponsors expect to solve specific problems from their participation in a center. This early finding of the documentation effort is borne out in later data from empirical data on center structure and outcomes.

Risk sharing is an essential characteristic. Centers do in fact function as a research mutual fund. For each project, risks are shared across sponsors; for any given sponsor, risks are shared across projects. This aspect of a center has been especially useful in marketing to potential sponsors.

Slow, steady growth through predictable stages must be maintained. These stages are not easily foreshortened or skipped. Centers are not normal activities for a university; there is a great deal of managerial learning that must take place. Centers that have tried to skip the planning grant stage or have tried to grow too rapidly have faced a great deal of instability. Reaching agreement on basic purposes, establishing a realistic and industrially relevant research agenda, and building an organization all take time—about three to four years from idea to steady state for a center. There also seems to be an upper bound on the size of a center, both in terms of funding levels and number of sponsors. Centers that have successfully grown significantly in size have done it with some combination of state government funding and cooperation with an existing organizational entity. These mergers have required some change in the centers' missions to accommodate their new sponsors.

Government involvement is important in early development. In the initial stages of center evolution, a large component of risk results from the unfamiliarity of the cooperating parties with each others' goals. Third-party financial and managerial assistance by government has proved useful thus far. Further, NSF approval given through peer review seems beneficial in marketing the center to industry and to state government. Even after five years, many of the centers maintain some level of an NSF presence, typically in the form of managerial assistance.

Industrial input to the center design is crucial. The initial research agenda must reflect industrial concerns. In general, universities are not fully aware of industrial research interests or how to identify these areas. There is always a tendency to develop a quick fix, to offer a long list of projects the faculty think ought to be of interest to industry. Centers, however, cannot be easily grafted onto an already existing university operation. Industry must be involved in center operations from the beginning. Existing industry contacts are often used to develop the initial research agenda; however, these contacts are generally not widespread enough to support a center. The center must develop a systematic and ongoing means of involving firms in, at a minimum, setting the research agenda.

A diversified, flexible research agenda is essential. Unlike unrestricted grants to a university, centers involve a formal diversified portfolio of projects, which should be well defined before the center initiates formal contact with potential industrial sponsors. Among the array of projects, there must be some that appeal to each potential sponsor firm, but it is unlikely that any firm will find the entire portfolio equally attractive. NSF program managers spend a large percentage of their time advising centers about the specification of the research agenda, with systematic input from industry. University researchers are not accustomed to specifying what they will do in the level of detail required by potential industry sponsors.

There seems to be some evidence that it is possible to have too much diversity in a program of research. While diversity certainly helps market a center, it may create difficulties in operating it. Centers with firms in vastly different lines of business have had difficulty developing consensus about project selection and evaluation. Factions of sponsor firms develop and are often at odds over how resources should be allocated. As a result, membership tends to be highly volatile.

Research of interest to industry is almost always interdisciplinary, while research in universities is most often not. It is important that a center avoid excessive dependence on a single department or discipline for its technical and administrative base. It is in the bringing together of different disciplines that basic research begins to achieve some industrial relevance. In order to conduct interdisciplinary research, a strong center director, respected by all participants, seems required. Universities are not accustomed to interdisciplinary research and reward, and control systems tend to act against faculty who do such research. Thus far, only strong leadership has been able to overcome these barriers to interdisciplinary research.

Some Preliminary Findings from the Network Analysis

Centers differ greatly in their communications networks. For example, the communications stars vary across centers among center director, faculty, postdoctoral fellows, and graduate students. Although the dimensions of diversity are easy to recognize, the origins and meaning of this diversity are less clear. We do not know to what extent these variations are the result of the scientific–technical areas involved in center research, differing university or firm cultures, simple geographic distance or propinquity, or the individual personalities represented at each center. Perhaps more important, we do not know which variations are planned and to what degree they can be altered by center participants.

University–industry ties are weak. There is far less communication between the university and industry groups than there is within these groups.

University–industry ties tend to be less frequent, to relate to narrower ranges of topics, and to use fewer channels of communication than do intragroup connections. This finding is based on communication that takes place monthly or more frequently. If we consider communication that takes place once or twice a year as meaningful, then the centers are reasonably effective linking agencies. There is regular interaction among all center participants at this frequency. There is also evidence that in their first years, centers do not radically change established communication patterns, either within the university or between the university and industrial participants. But it is not at all clear that these established interaction patterns are frequent enough to be working research relationships.

Communications channels matter. Centers currently tend to rely on formal channels (meetings) to convey information to industrial sponsors. The informal interactions—face-to-face meetings and telephone calls—normally associated with working scientists are not a major factor in the present centers. This observation does have direct implications for center planning and management. If formal meetings continue to carry the bulk of communications with industrial sponsors, it is essential that those meetings be carried out carefully. In general, universities do not expend much effort in putting together their presentation for either technical or operational meetings with sponsors. They may need to pay closer attention to these presentations in the future. Further, it is not clear to what degree center administrative practices and arrangements deliberately facilitate or retard the development of multiple working research relationships. Certainly anecdotal evidence indicates that some centers, if not actively discouraging access to university personnel on the part of industrial participants, do not go out of their way to encourage it. It will be interesting to watch whether there is a greater tendency toward informal interaction as centers age and participants gain more working experience with each other. Older centers tend to have slightly more informal contacts than the newer ones, although not dramatically so. If practice makes perfect, the centers may get better at using multiple channels of communication.

It is premature to prescribe. With only first-year data in hand—and data limited in critical dimensions—we have no basis for concluding that some centers have better communication patterns than others or that certain administrative arrangements result in better communication. We know that patterns and arrangements differ, but we do not know what the long-term effects of these differences might be or how they are likely to change as more experience is gained.

In general, it is safe to say that centers would be advised to pay more direct attention to their communications. Increasing communication is, after all, one of the major explicit purposes of the centers program, and frequently cited as a reason for participation.[3]

Preliminary Findings about Structure

The analysis of center structure does indicate that centers change the way research is managed and conducted in universities, and this is true in ways that even we did not expect (Gray and Gidley 1985).

Center participants tend to be senior-level people. Industry representatives tend to have extensive experience in industry and in R&D but little prior contact with the university. Thus, while industry representatives are generally both relatively old and male, they are not necessarily part of an established old-boy network. Thus centers must be considered as important in their own right and are not just social clubs.

Faculty researchers also tend to be relatively senior, with about two-thirds being tenured associate or full professors, but this is more reflective of the composition of participating faculties than any implicit or explicit selection process. We felt that junior faculty would be less likely to participate in center research because of publication delays, but we were wrong. In general, junior faculty are no more or less likely to participate. While center researchers are relatively senior, they are no more senior than the general population of faculty (Walton, Eveland, and Tornatzky 1985). Apparently the advantages of getting started early on an established research project outweigh any potential disadvantages.

A firm's participation in a center is limited to a very few people, while university researchers tend to be heavily involved in the centers. As the network analysis indicates, centers do not cast a large net in any one sponsoring firm. Participation in a center is often facilitated by a senior-level champion, but higher-level management does not take an active interest in the operations of the center. Further, even individuals working with the center tend to remain at arms length, reporting little or no involvement in day-to-day center administration or operation. Others in the firm are kept abreast of center activities primarily through written reports.

In general, industry usually interacts most directly with the center through central or divisonal R&D and engineering groups. Other groups such as marketing or strategic planning have little or no contact with center personnel.

In contrast, faculty researchers and center administrators tend to be heavily involved in center activities. On average, faculty report that 25 percent of their total time is spent in center projects, which means that for many of the faculty researchers, the center is their only active research. Further, high-level university administrators maintain relatively frequent contacts with center personnel. There is also frequent interpersonal interaction between faculty and staff on both technical and managerial issues.

Centers do change the management of academic research, with faculty and staff recognizing that there is significant industry influence on project selection and evaluation. Faculty see themselves as retaining control over how the research is conducted. The universities that participate do not appear to be threatened or overly concerned about loss of academic freedom. Rather, industry influence is not seen as dominating a center but as equitably shared with faculty and center management.

On the other hand, centers are not seen as greatly affecting the R&D activities with participating firms. Again, given the patterns of communications within sponsoring firms, this is not a surprising finding.

Preliminary Findings about Outcomes

Faculty and industry participants show remarkable goal congruence. Both groups feel that the most important goal for these centers is expansion of general knowledge, while the least important are products that can be patented and commercialized. There are differences between the two groups on the middle goals (improvement of graduate students' understanding of industry, improvement of graduate students' training, and redirection of university research toward industrial problems), but this is more reflective of the differing missions of these groups. The level of agreement achieved certainly suggests that centers span the boundary between what have been quite divergent groups and that they have reached agreement on the basic purposes of a center.[4]

Industry does not expect tangible outcomes from centers but rather increased ability to interact with outside scientists, better personnel recruitment, and other less tangible outcomes related to increasing their knowledge base. The most tangible benefit resulting from centers is in new projects that are stimulated by participation in the centers. The number and amount of resources devoted to new projects is significant across centers. This finding seems at odds with perceptual data on the lack of influence of the center on industry R&D, and we have not yet resolved these differences.

For faculty the most tangible reported outcome is the importance of center participation in consideration for promotion, tenure, or salary increases. University administrators seem to be sending out a message that faculty should be explicitly rewarded for center participation, at the same time maintaining the more traditional criteria of research and publications. Apparently, industrially relevant basic research can be considered good research by the scientific and engineering community at large.

In general, both industry and academia are satisfied with the results of center activities. If one takes the data at face value, participants are ecstatic about centers. All participants in all centers report high satisfaction with all aspects of center operations. While faculty are relatively less satisfied with the technical quality of the research, communications between the center and industry, and center administrative practices than the industry participants, overall satisfaction levels of both groups are quite high. These data, however, do not square with behavioral measures of satisfaction. In one center with high turnover, participants still reported they were satisfied as they dropped out of the center. Another relatively rapidly growing center with no dropouts reported the lowest levels of satisfaction. The one factor that seems to account for relative satisfaction levels is reliance on NSF funds. The more reliance, the more industry representatives and faculty are satisfied. There may be a presumption that if they do not profess satisfaction, NSF funding will be cut off. As more centers become free standing, we anticipate more discrimination on this measure.

Summary and Conclusions

In our first look at the evaluation of centers as a whole, one factor that stands out is the passive role and limited responsibility assumed by industrial sponsors. On the other hand, the federal government—or more accurately certain government program managers—and universities have committed considerable time and resources to making centers work.

In general, firm participation is limited to one or two relatively senior people, who meet with center administrators at least twice a year and make suggestions about what projects seem to be progressing satisfactorily and what new projects the center ought to consider. There is little, if any, contact between university faculty and industrial scientists. In addition, communication within a firm concerning the center tends to be limited to written reports. Clearly the concerns about the passive role and limited responsibilities assumed by industry expressed in the meeting of industrial sponsor representatives seem to be very real, but their dimensions are even greater than these representatives seem to realize.

Industry sponsors are not just passive actors in the management and operation of a center. They do little to ensure that information concerning the center and its outputs are disseminated within their own firms. To some extent the NSF program, including the authors, can be considered as responsible for this state of affairs. We assumed that university management policies and practices would require most of our efforts, while industry could take care of itself. As a result, most of NSF's and the center evaluators' time has been spent on providing advice and assistance to the universities. On the whole, we can be very pleased with the ability of universities to adopt and adapt to the center's concept.

Industry, on the other hand, may see the centers as having potentially significant importance, but they are not structuring their interactions with the center in ways that will take advantage of center outputs. The lack of internal communication within industrial sponsors has critical implications for both the effective utilization of research results and developing an adequate constituency within the firm dedicated to the long-term survival of the center. If industrial sponsors are concerned with effective information transfer and for the survival of the center, they must begin to cast a larger net of interpersonal communications within their firms. NSF and the evaluators should encourage firms to become more involved in center activities.

Notes

1. New Jersey recently passed a referendum providing $90 million in support for the development of NSF-type centers. A similar referendum was defeated in Rhode Island.

2. These activities are described in "Evaluation Notebook for Center Directors and Evaluators," available from the University/Industry Cooperative Research Centers program of NSF.

3. See the Centers *Historical Profiles* (Eveland, Hetzner, and Tornatzky 1984) for illustration.

4. The ordering of goals is precisely opposite for research collaborations in the University/Industry Cooperative Research Projects program, which typically invovles one-on-one interaction between a university scientist and an industrial researcher on a single research project. For specific projects, products that can be patented and commercialized are the most important outcome and expansion of general knowledge the least (Johnson and Tornatzky 1984).

References

Brodsky, N.; Kaufman, H.G.; and Tooker, J.R. 1980. *University-Industry Cooperation: A Preliminary Analysis of Existing Mechanisms and Their Relationship to the Innovation Process.* New York: NYU Center for Science and Technology Policy.

Colton, R.M. 1982. *Analysis of Five National Science Foundation Experiments to Stimulate Increased Technological Innovation in Industry.* Washington, D.C.: National Science Foundation.

Eveland, J.D. 1985. *Communications Networks in University/Industry Cooperative Research Centers.* Washington, D.C.: National Science Foundation.

Eveland, J.D., and Hetzner, W.A. 1982. *Development of University/Industry Cooperative Research Centers: Historical Profiles.* 1st ed. Washington, D.C.: National Science Foundation.

Eveland, J.D.; Hetzner, W.A.; and Tornatzky, L.G. 1984. *Development of University/Industry Cooperative Research Centers: Historical Profiles.* 2d ed. Washington, D.C.: National Science Foundation.

Grad, M.L. 1979. *Evaluation Status and Planning Report III: Cooperative Research and Development Experiment.* Denver: Denver Research Institute, October.

190 • *Competitiveness through Technology*

Gray, D., and Gidley, T. 1985. "Draft Final Report of the Output/Structure Questionnaire." Raleigh, N.C.: North Carolina State University, January.

Hetzner, W.A., and Eveland, J.D. 1983. "Assessment of University/Industry Cooperative Research Centers." Paper presented at Evaluation 83, Annual Meeting of the Evaluation Research Society, Chicago, October 20–22.

Johnson, E.C., and Tornatzky, L.G. 1984. *Cooperative Science: National Study of University/Industry Researchers.* 2 vols. Washington, D.C.: National Science Foundation, November.

National Science Foundation. 1972. "Program Announcement: Experimental R&D Incentives Program." Washington, D.C., November.

Tornatzky, L.G.; Hetzner, W.A.; Eveland, J.D.; Schwarzkopf, A.; and Colton, R.M. 1982. *University/Industry Cooperative Research Centers: A Practice Manual.* Washington, D.C.: National Science Foundation.

Walton, A.E.; Eveland, J.D.; and Tornatzky, L.G. 1985. *The Organization and Management of Academic Research.* Washington, D.C.: National Science Foundation.

12
State-Level Manufacturing Technology Initiatives: Design Issues

Louis G. Tornatzky

Revising the Terms of the Industrial Policy Debate

It is generally conceded that technology, particularly process or production technology, is a major ingredient in international economic competitiveness. Thus far however, at least at a national level, debate among various analysts has been regarding the appropriate mixture of federal government fiscal, tax, and regulatory policies that might influence technological growth. Two features of this debate are worth noting: this has largely been a discussion among macroeconomists and their fellow travelers, and the terms of the debate have been increasingly ideological in nature.

On one side of the issue (Magaziner and Reich 1983) there has been a call for a massive public investment in targeted industries so as to encourage technological growth and ultimately internaitonal competitiveness. Contrasting views, usually from a more conservative political segment (U.S. Congress, Office of Technology Assistance 1984; Nelson 1984), have questioned many of the premises of the public investment proponents. Their basic counterargument is that government does not do well in identifying investment opportunities in technology, particularly when compared against unfettered market forces. Common to both these arguments is the notion that if somehow money is spent—whether that money is public or private is largely immaterial—then industrial revitalization and international competitiveness will result.

One way out of this apparent deadlock is to understand that technology development and deployment is something other or more than merely a problem of investment. In order to arrive at a pragmatic approach for government, we must first understand in a more detailed manner the process of technological innovation as it exists rather than as some assume that it should be. Technological innovation is a function of both exogenous and endogenous factors. Our public debate and policy actions have focused more on the former than the latter. A good case can be made that the process of technological innovation is decentralized, industry specific, geographically idiosyncratic, and occurs primarily within organizations.

Process of Technological Innovation: The Case of Manufacturing

Although largely unknown by the principals in the industrial policy debate, there is a relatively large—albeit piecemeal—literature on the process of technological innovation (Tornatzky et al. 1982). At a fairly general level we understand that it involves a number of different actors, organizations, and institutions, operating over an extended period of time. We also understand that technological innovation unfolds over a set of stages or phases, with somewhat different stages or phases involved in the creation of new technology, as opposed to those involved in the dissemination, implementation, and use of that new technology.

Technology can be conceived of as knowledge but knowledge that is embedded or expressed in physical artifacts, processes, tools, and machines. Correspondingly, the creation of new technologies is generally conceived as an evolutionary process that begins with fundamental science (presumably developed at universities), that leads to applied R&D in industrial settings, and then is transformed into marketable or usable products and processes. Several important phenomena are involved here, such as the management of the R&D process, the necessary linkages between universities and industry, and the dissemination–marketing approaches that need to be used by the creators of the new technologies. For example, a great deal is known about the ingredients of quality research teams (Allen 1977), the relationships involved in university–industry research collaboration (Johnson and Tornatzky 1981, 1984), and the importance of interactive and interpersonal media in the dissemination of innovation (Fairweather, Sanders, and Tornatzky 1974; Stevens and Tornatzky 1979).

There is also some consensus on the various stages that users of new technology go through. Generally this is conceived as proceeding from initial awareness of an innovation, through decision making and adopting, implementation, and ultimately routinization, whereby the new becomes the not new. To demonstrate more specifically, we know that the perceived characteristics of technologies (Tornatzky and Klein 1982) to a significant degree determine their ease of adoption and implementation. Thus, the more complex or incompatible that new technologies are, the more likely they are to result in significant resistance from users. Not surprisingly, the extent to which adopters can work through these uncertainties, the more expeditious the process becomes. We know that participative decision making on the part of potential users generally tends to increase the ease of adoption and implementation

(Tornatzky et al. 1980). We also know that as technologies increase in complexity, the implementation stage of the total process becomes protracted and increases in importance. To the extent that technologies cannot be plugged in the more difficult their deployment is, and the process may extend for years. So much for simple investment decisions.

Clearly the process of innovation and technological change is much more than a simple capital investment problem. Money is a necessary but not sufficient ingredient in technological change. Accordingly, government should pattern its activities on the nature of the phenomenon rather than according to some notion of what an appropriate policy action is.

Regarding government programs in the area of manufacturing technology, not only should the general nature of the innovation process guide the design of government initiatives but so should the peculiarities of advanced manufacturing technology and the manufacturing sector.

Considering the former, we need to realize that advanced manufacturing technology exacerbates problems associated with innovating. The new technologies are complex and radical and arouse uncertainty. For example, the decision to invest in advanced manufacturing technology cannot be justified on simple economic relative advantage, at least with traditional accounting procedures. Issues of market strategy, product flexibility, and future product quality—all difficult to quantify—must be used in justification decisions.

The radical nature of the technologies also places great strain on human resources. A recent survey of the National Electrical Manufacturers Association (1984) identified lack of staff knowledge as a major obstacle to automation. It is also clear that new production technologies often necessitate major changes in the design of jobs and work organizations (Gustavson and Taylor 1982).

Finally, the implementation of advanced manufacturing systems is such that the process is longitudinal to the extreme. Cases of systems taking years to come up to speed are not uncommon. This exacerbates technical assistance needs, such as those with equipment vendors (Ettlie 1985) or other third-party information sources.

It is not surprising that the deployment of advanced manufacturing in U.S. industry leaves much to be desired. A national survey of 303 manufacturing companies (Majchrzak, Nieva, and Newman 1985) reported that 56 percent of the respondents had no automated equipment in place. In a survey of 887 Iowa manufacturers (Swanson 1984), 66 percent of the respondents indicated that the level of their process technology was low or medium.

There are significant differences between larger and smaller firms. Considering firms in the Iowa study with 500 or more employees, only 16 percent placed themselves in the low to medium level of their process technology. Interestingly, virtually all (97 percent) of these same larger manufacturers in the Iowa sample felt a need for more information about process equipment, as opposed to roughly 70 percent for firms with 50 employees or fewer. Similarly,

41 percent of the larger Iowa firms felt a need for scientific information, as opposed to approximately 13 percent for firms of fewer than 500 employees. These size-specific findings are echoed elsewhere (U.S. Congress, Joint Economic Committee 1983; American Machinist 1983).

It is important to realize that manufacturing is comprised of a heterogeneous set of economic units. While some of the major world corporations are manufacturing concerns, an overwhelming percentage of manufacturing establishments are smaller firms of fewer than 500 employees. Similarly, although manufacturing in general has been lagging in the deployment of new technology, there are not only differences between larger and smaller performers but differences between different industrial sectors within manufacturing (for example, autos versus electronics).

Of particular interest is the extent to which manufacturing companies rely on equipment vendors for information and assistance regarding new manufacturing technologies. In the Majchrzak, Nieva, and Newman (1985) report, 87 percent of respondents noted that vendors or manufacturers of computer-aided equipment were a source for delivering education and training on the new technologies. The Swanson study (1984) also reports that manufacturing representatives and sales representatives were the most commonly used sources of information about new technology. Moreover, it appears from the Iowa data that equipment manufacturers were a highly desired source of information; way down on the list as a credible source of information was government. Trade associations were a used and apparently credible source. Interestingly, although universities and colleges were only moderately used for information in the Iowa sample (31 percent), there was a considerable desire on the part of respondents to make greater use of this source (57.1 percent).

It is also worth noting the content and format of the information desired by manufacturers in the Iowa sample. For the most part, these companies wanted technology information about technology already in use or technology about ready for use as opposed to the latest in science. Although there was no breakdown by firm size, one might expect differences. Similarly, the preferred format for information was generally summary briefings or bulletins, with conferences and workshops also being judged to be desirable ways to accelerate technology transfer.

Current Practice in Government Programs

Evidence from Foreign Competitors

In confronting this diversity of problems, government agencies have a number of options. Before examining the ones that have been chosen by state governments in the United States, let us first consider the experiences of nations that are competitors of the United States.

Japan and other Western European competitors are not standing still in terms of government assistance in the deployment of new manufacturing technology. These efforts have been reviewed by the U.S. Congress, Office of Technology Assessment (1984) but can be briefly summarized here. In Japan, for example, special implementation assistance is provided to small- and medium-sized firms. In the machine tool industry, government-sponsored technical centers provide cost-benefit estimates, customized software, and training to firms interested in numerically controlled (NC) machines. The Japanese government has also provided low interest or interest-free loans to small- and medium-sized firms, particularly for the installation of industrial robots. Other activities include a major flexible manufacturing systems demonstration project, targeted incentives in the form of a generous depreciation allowance for equivalent acquisition, wide-scale dissemination programs, and government laboratories engaged in R&D of future robotic applications and advances.

The concern for small- and medium-sized firms is also shared in West Germany, where the activities of the federal government are also supplemented by the activities of the states. One program helps defray the costs of technical personnel and smaller companies; another program provides technical assistance to small- and medium-sized firms. Sweden has a consulting program designed to assist firms in implementation and various educational programs focused on technology-relevant training.

In Great Britain, activities include a 50 percent subsidization of consulting services for up to fifteen man-days, one-third funding for both application development and equipment purchases, short courses for managers, and regional demonstration centers. The program has been most helpful to small- and medium-sized companies, which comprise 90 percent of the beneficiaries of the robotic procurement and deployment activities.

It is possible to extract some common approaches from these efforts. One is that they all seem to be predominantly focused on small- to medium-sized firms. Also, they seem oriented toward specific applications and implementations assistance rather than R&D. In that spirit, whatever direct financial assistance is provided is directed toward acquisition of new equipment or supportive training and consultation to help implementation of that equipment.

This contrasts significantly from U.S. federal government efforts in support of manufacturing technology (Hetzner, Tornatzky, and Klein 1982), which are heavily weighted in support of R&D, as opposed to dissemination and assistance. Moreover, the vast majority of U.S. federal funds in support of manufacturing technology are tied to Department of Defense objectives.

Lessons from Existing State-Level Programs

The U.S. government is not the only actor in technology development and deployment. As noted by the Office of Technology Assessment (1983), a variety of state-level programs have been initiated since 1980, with a major focus on innovation and industrial revitalization. These programs include commissions to study the problem, university–industry cooperative research programs, and new enterprise development efforts.

To the extent that these programs have focused on new manufacturing technology, they have tended to cluster around two types of activities. Not surprisingly, these different foci roughly parallel the previous discussion of the innovation process. On the one hand there have been R&D initiatives, which are generally oriented to the creation of new technologies. Let us call these manufacturing R&D centers. On the other hand, there have been efforts concentrated on the dissemination, transfer, and use of already-existing manufacturing technology. These programs are the equivalent of manufacturing extension services.

Manufacturing R&D Centers. Since 1982 several state-funded research and development organizations with some focus on advanced manufacturing have been established. I will confine my remarks to the efforts in Pennsylvania, Ohio, and Michigan.

The Pennsylvania Ben Franklin Partnership is perhaps the most widely known and firmly established (Plosila 1984). The focus of the program is on advanced technology (rather than high technology), which is to suggest that the program is not preoccupied with creating entirely new industries but in spinning off applied research to existing companies. The organizational locus of the program is in Advanced Technology Centers, located on university campuses. Each center conducts applied research, engages in education and training activities, and assists in entrepreneurial support. A key feature of the program has been the matching arrangement, whereby state funds are forthcoming only if industrial contributions are secured. In fiscal year 1985, state funding of $18 million was matched by $33 million in private-sector contributions.

In Ohio the Thomas Alva Edison program was started in 1984 as part of that state's overall economic development strategy. The program has many similarities to the Pennsylvania effort in that it features university-based research centers oriented around specific technology areas. Also similar to the Franklin program, the Edison effort calls for industrial matching of funds, although the program operations have been less stringent and have permitted fairly soft matches.

In the initial wave of Ohio grants, two awards were made to manufacturing technology centers (Ohio Governor's Office 1984). An award of $4.1 million was made to the Cleveland Advanced Manufacturing Program, which consists of a consortium of Case Western Reserve, Cleveland State, and Cuyahoga Community College. To some extent the different functions have been assigned different organizational homes: CCC is heavily involved in operator shop floor training; Case Western Reserve is addressing the more theoretical portions of the agenda; Cleveland State's piece is probably more of an applied research problem solving role. A grant of similar size was made to the Institute of Advanced Manufacturing Sciences, located at the University of Cincinnati.

Michigan's centerpiece effort is the Industrial Technology Institute (ITI), founded in 1982 with an initial $17 million in funds from the state. Current foundation support or earmarked support constitutes another $50 million. At the present time ITI has one hundred employees organized into four laboratories or centers: the Flexible Manfuacturing Laboratory, the Flexible Inspection and Assembly Laboratory, the Communications Network Laboratory, and the Center for Social and Economic Issues. Each center has a charge to conduct applied R&D addressed to a variety of clients: manufacturing companies, large and small; government; and the academic community. Thus far, the clients have primarily been large manufacturing concerns, particularly in the automobile industry. A few government grants have been obtained, as well as some exploratory work with industrial associations. Although there is a center dedicated to data base development and public affairs, there have been limited attempts to foster broad-based dissemination and knowledge transfer, particularly to smaller companies.

In attempting to gain some perspective on these three states' R&D initiatives, several features stand out. They are clearly oriented toward the technology creation side of the technological innovation process. Moreover, there is an emphasis on collaborative work with industry, with an obvious tilt toward larger firms. The University/Industry Cooperative Research Centers program (Tornatzky et al. 1982) operated by NSF was an explicit or implicit model for both the Edison and Franklin programs. That program was designed to link academia and industry research through a multiproject program of applied research, funded primarily by company membership fees. It has been supported by Fortune 500 companies almost exclusively. Finally, it should be realized that all of these R&D centers have tended to place less emphasis on the problems of transferring technology.

Manufacturing Extension Services. In contrast, several of the state industrial initiatives identified by OTA were more directly engaged in knowledge transfer and dissemination and some in manufacturing. In a study being conducted jointly by the Industrial Technology Institute and the Kennedy School of Harvard University, a sample of those programs has been identified that are explicitly charged in fostering the adoption and implementation of manufacturing technology. The study included a national telephone survey of programs akin

198 • *Competitiveness through Technology*

to manufacturing extension efforts. The sample was drawn from a variety of sources, including the previous OTA (1983) survey and through a snowballing process using knowledgeable informants. The sample is neither complete nor representative in any statistical sense. It does, however, capture most of the significant state programs providing direct technical assistance to manufacturing companies. The results are based on preliminary analyses (Wyckoff 1985), with data available from fourteen programs.

Data were gathered in six areas: program history and goals, program size and budget, staffing, organization design, technical focus, and client characteristics. In each area, information was obtained about current program practice, problems experienced, and suggestions for future changes.

Half of the programs have been created since 1980, reflecting recent concern with manufacturing technology. Most of the programs were university based, with approximately 40 percent of them having deans of engineering as founders. Several programs identified problems of trying to mesh the technical assistance and outreach objectives of program with the university incentive structure that rewards more scholarly activity.

The budgets for the programs range form $27,000 to $1.2 million per year. Half of this budget was from state government sources, with other sources being university funds, client fees, and various grants and contracts. There are some significant problems reported in the instability of the funding base of the programs.

Average staff size is sixteen, with a predominant representation from the engineering sciences. There have been major problems with finding and retaining qualified personnel. The low salary structure of the university and the professional demands of academia apparently make it difficult to identify and hold people who have industrial experience and who can also retain some respectability in the university. In addition, personnel are often hired away by the firms being helped or by other state programs. To the extent that faculty members were used as technical staff, there are significant problems in meshing the interests of these programs with the culture of the university. As one program director put it, "The concept of making faculty accessible to the outside world is heresy to academia."

Generally the programs tend to divide themselves into three types of operations. One might be called a full service or active program, in which the program conducts a problem identification and analysis and then provides assistance to a client company. Another group of programs function as brokers, doing some preliminary needs assessment, and then referring clients to other programs or resources. The third type of program is essentially passive, merely providing the client with access to technical reports or data bases. Interestingly the programs that are the most active were experiencing excess demand for their services; the broker and passive programs were having difficulty in finding clients.

One major operational problem identified by program administrators was that of maintaining a level of expertise across the variety of problems presented by the client base. In other words, the requests for technical assistance were so diverse that they stretched the capabilities of necessarily small staffs.

The technical foci of these programs tended to rest on three areas: microcomputers, robotics, and CAD-CAM, broadly construed. To some extent, the programs reported difficulty in keeping up with the technological developments in these fields and being quite dependent on industry for their information sharing, which in turn will be shared with other clients. Again, the diversity of the user or client group is so extensive as often to overwhelm the technical capacities of the programs.

To summarize some of the experiences of these existing state programs, a few lessons seem relatively clear. One is the difficulty in dealing with a highly diverse clientele, across a fairly diverse set of technologies and idiosyncratic applications. This raises the issue of whether a single program staff, without technological resources, can meet the needs of a clientele group. It is also relatively clear that such programs have some difficulty in combining the worlds of action and the worlds of academia. While the university seems a logical, neutral site for such programs, the evidence raises doubts as to whether they can survive and flourish in such settings. At the same time, it appears that the active, full service programs are exactly what industry clients want; this creates an interesting dilemma.

Principles for Program Design

What follows is a set of design principles, or discussion issues, that might be used to guide the design and implementation of government programs to assist manufacturing technology deployment. Some of these principles are based on empirical data; others are best guess approximations to what we know about this field.

Empirically Guided Program Development

The process of technological development, adoption, and implementation is imperfectly understood. In that spirit, the design of any pragmatic program to assist industry ought to be guided by empiricism and real-time data rather than inflexible guidelines. To the extent that design options can be built into the program as alternatives, then real-time social experiments ought to be built into program operations. At the very least, systematic outcome evaluation ought to be gathered on program effects and to sort out the relative impact of various program features. It should be realized that a large and respectable literature (Cook and Campbell 1979) exists for designing retrospective and real-time evaluation of programs. This fact is usually lost to engineering and technical specialists who usually run such programs and are largely ignorant of social science techniques. To my knowledge, none of the various state industrial initiatives has been systematically evaluated for effects on client firms. Ironically the only federal money available (from NSF) for evaluating such efforts was eliminated in recent budget and programmatic cuts.

Technology Development versus Technology Deployment

The process of technological innovation encompasses both technology development and dissemination and implementation. For the most part, U.S. federal policy has emphasized the development of basic research and basic science and the capitalization of technology development rather than the subsidization of deployment. The assumption has been made—in my view wrongly—that the market will handle the spread of technology once developed. In contrast, we have the experience of foreign competitors in focusing on technology deployment and the simple fact that manufacturing technologies developed over twenty years ago have not been widely adopted by U.S. companies.

Even if one chooses to use public monies to support technology development, such as in the funding of basic and applied research in universities, there are design options and how best to do that. For the most part, university research has not been respondent to industrial needs; in fact, only a small part of it is directly supported by industry funds.

Two design principles emerge from this brief overview:

1. State initiatives to foster manufacturing technology ought to focus more on transfer, dissemination, and implementation assistance rather than the development of basic or applied knowledge.

2. To the extent that support is given to R&D, the structure ought to be built into the program such that R&D is clearly responsive to industrial needs, such as in already existing university-industry cooperative research programs.

Small versus Large Firms

This is largely a question of where are the most significant market failings in the technology deployment process. A good case can be made that the most significant needs and targets of opportunity are among small- to medium-sized firms. Evidence suggests that these companies are less advanced in their state of technology, more dependent on equipment suppliers, less tied to university knowledge sources, and more vulnerable when incorrect equipment purchases or programs are initiated.

On the other hand, it is clear that many large firms are also in trouble in terms of their technology deployment efforts; however, they are not unaware of the existence of new technologies, nor do they usually lack the resources for adoption and implementation. For larger firms, the problem may be more in terms of how to organize the introduction of new manufacturing technology into a fairly ponderous corporation, alter the strategic planning process, and plan for change. These are less technical considerations than organizational design and intervention issues, but the following design principles might be argued:

3. Direct technical assistance ought to be given to small- to medium-sized firms in building awareness of new technology and assisting in the adoption and implementation process.

4. Assistance that is subsidized by public expenditures might be given to larger firms, but this assistance ought to be other than research, development, and implementation assistance. The focus here should be on organizational design considerations and strategic planning.

Mixture of Technical versus Social Organizational Assistance

A mistake can be made by construing the technological change process pertaining to manufacturing as purely technical in an engineering and computer science sense. The more we are learning about the process of implementing advanced manufacturing technology, the clearer it becomes that major issues are involved in the functioning of the firm and human resource considerations. For example, it is relatively clear that the major unhidden cost of implementing advanced manufacturing technology is that of training. For the most part, purchasers of new technology are relying on vendors for training services, despite the demonstrated failings by vendor companies. Similarly it is clear that major changes will be made, and are being made, in the area of job design and organizational structure as the new technologies come on line. These include changes in compensation systems, job descriptions, and the relationships among various functions of the company such as marketing and engineering, and the integration of manufacturing and the strategic planning function. Rarely do equipment vendors provide meaningful assistance in these sociotechnical design areas. While perhaps self-serving, an additional design principle might be as follows:

5. A significant market failure is in the provision by equipment vendors of social, organizational, cost justification, and training pertaining to the implementation of advanced manufacturing technology. Assistance in these areas is a legitimate and needed area for government intervention.

Locus of Assistance Programs

On the basis of current experience, it is still unclear where government assistance programs ought to be situated organizationally. It is clear that government is not a highly credible source of technical information for manufacturing companies; however, it is also clear that the current major sources of assistance and information, such as vendors, are less than fully reliable.

What may need to occur is a political or credibility laundering of government assistance programs. Thus, government may serve as the initiator and funder of assistance programs, but those programs, rather than situated in government departments, might better be contracted out to third parties such as universities, nonprofit institutes, and/or trade or professional organizations. There are obvious opportunities for collaborative programs or the creation of various third-party assistance centers. An additional design principle ought to be as follows:

6. Government assistance programs, even if funded by government, ought to be situated in nongovernment institutional settings.

Active Approaches

It has been a repetitive finding in the literature on innovation diffusion that active, participative, interactive, and aggressive efforts work better. Our analysis reinforces this. Market pull of advanced manufacturing technology has not worked; technology push is needed. Whether a principle or not, we might recommend:

7. Technology transfer programs need to market their services actively, help clients identify their problems, and work to find technology solutions.

Leverage

While difficult to quantify or put into operation, an implicit design feature of the more successful programs already in operation seems to be the notion that one should get the most bang for the buck in terms of assistance offered. This means that one should perhaps not provide assistance in a full array of technologies or for all potential clients or indiscriminately throw money at problems. It does mean that assistance ought to be targeted on technologies where the most potential benefit and productivity for the largest clientele can be realized in the shortest period of time. It also means that some sort of client triage ought to be initiated: companies that are hopelessly noncompetitive ought not to benefit from scarce public resources, nor should companies with extensive resources be subsidized by public expenditures. If a publicly supported assistance organization becomes nothing more than an additional consulting pool for a Fortune 500 company, it remains to be seen how those public monies have been wisely spent. Perhaps stating the obvious, the following principle ought to be added:

8. Leverage in the selection of clients, technologies, and specific services ought to be an explicit guideline in program design and operation.

Summary

The several principles outlined in this chapter can be used to structure what we see as an essential public need: government assistance for the deployment of advanced technology. Echoing our initial argument, however, we also believe that such programs can be initiated without straying into the uncharted depths of industrial policy, as currently construed.

References

Allen, Thomas J. 1977. *Managing the Flow of Technology.* Cambridge: MIT Press.
American Machinist. 1983. "The 13th American Machinist Inventory of Metalworking Equipment 1983: Measuring the Effect of NC." *American Machinist* (November).
Cook, Thomas D., and Campbell, Donald T. 1979. *Quasi-Experimentation: Design and Analysis for Field Setting.* Chicago: Rand McNally.
Ettlie, John. 1985. "The Implementation of Programmable Manufacturing Innovations." Unpublished paper. Ann Arbor: Industrial Technology Institute.
Fairweather, George W.; Sanders, David H.; and Tornatzky, Louis G. 1974. *Creating Change in Mental Health Organizations.* New York: Pergamon Press.
Gustavson, Paul, and Taylor, James. 1982. "Socio-Technical Design and New Forms of Work Organization: Integrated Circuit Fabrication." Unpublished paper, January 6, 1982.
Hetzner, William A.; Tornatzky, Louis G.; and Klein, Katherine. 1983. "Manufacturing Technology in the 1980's: A Survey of Federal Programs and Practices." *Management Science* 29 (August):951–961.
Johnson, Elmima C., and Tornatzky, Louis G. 1981. "Academia and Industrial Innovations." In *New Directions for Experimental Learning: Business and Higher Education—Toward New Alliances,* edited by G. Gold. San Francisco: Jossey—Bass.
——— . 1984. *Cooperative Science: A National Study of University and Industry Researchers.* Vol. 1. Washington, D.C.: National Science Foundation.
Magaziner, Ira C., and Reich, Robert B. 1983. *Minding America's Business.* New York: Vintage Books.

Majchrzak, Ann; Nieva, Veronica; and Newman, Paul. 1985. "CAD/CAM Adoption and Training in Three Manufacturing Industries." Unpublished final report submitted to the National Science Foundation, Productivity Improvement Research Section.

National Electrical Manufacturers Association. 1984. *Summary Report for the Automated Systems User Survey of NEMA Membership.* Washington, D.C.: National Electrical Manufacturers Association.

Nelson, Richard B. 1984. "The State and Private Enterprise in High Technology Industries." Unpublished working paper. Cambridge: Kennedy School of Government, Harvard University.

Ohio. Governor's Office. 1984. Press release. July 11.

Plosila, Walter. 1984. "Pennsylvania's Ben Franklin Partnership: The State as Catalyst." *Bell Atlantic Quarterly* 1 (Winter).

Stevens, William F., and Tornatzky, Louis G. 1979. "The Dissemination of Evaluation: An Experiment." *Evaluation Review* 4:339–354.

Swanson, David H. 1984. "Research Needs of Industry." *Journal of Technology Transfer* 9:39–55.

Tornatzky, Louis G.; Hetzner, William A.; Eveland, J.D.; Schwarzkopf, Alex; and Colton, Robert. 1982. *University-Industry Cooperative Research Centers: A Practice Manual.* Washington, D.C.: National Science Foundation.

Tornatzky, Louis G. and Klein, Katherine J. 1982. "Innovation Characteristics and Innovation Adoption-Implementation: A Meta-Analysis of Findings." *IEEE Transactions on Engineering Management* EM-29:28–45.

Tornatzky, Louis G.; Fergus, E.; Avellar, J.; and Fairweather, G.W. 1980. *Innovation and Social Process.* New York: Pergamon.

Tornatzky, Louis G. et al. 1982. *The Process of Innovation: Analyzing the Literature.* Washington, D.C.: National Science Foundation.

———. 1984. *Industrial Policy Movement in the United States: Is It the Answer? A Staff Study.* Washington, D.C.: GPO.

U.S. Congress. Joint Economic Committee. 1983. *New Technology in the American Machinery Industry: Trends and Implications,* by J. Rees, R. Briggs, and D. Hicks. Report to the Joint Economic Committee, U.S. Congress, September.

U.S. Congress Office of Technology Assessment. 1983. *Technology, Innovation, and Regional Economic Development.* Washington, D.C.: GPO.

———. 1984. *Computerized Manufacturing Automation: Employment, Education and the Workplace.* Washington, D.C.: GPO.

Wyckoff, Andrew. 1985. "State-Level Efforts to Transfer Technology to the Manufacturing Sector." Unpublished paper. Ann Arbor: Industrial Technology Institute.

Index

Government: (*Continued*)
and broad perspective in, 142–143;
in state-level programs, 196–199;
support of industrial growth by,
87–88. *See also specific countries*
Great Britain. *See* Britain

IBM: equity investment in Intel, 52–53;
manner of structuring to enter per-
sonal computer industry, 53
IMF. *See* International Monetary Fund
Import. *See also* Trade of products and
technologies, 71, 117
Incentives. *See* Depreciation incentives;
Financial incentives; Tax incentives
Industrial and Regional Development
Program (IRDP), of Canada, 164;
bias against metropolitan areas,
164–168
Industrial policies: Canadian, 163–164;
Japanese, 27–28
Industrial sector, structure and dynamics of, innovation policy and,
110–112
Industrial Technology Institute (ITI),
197
Industry(ies): concentration on some or
all of, 139; government efforts to
strengthen technological capabilities
of, 125–134; government support
of growth of, 87–88; involvement
in cooperative R&D centers, 183;
organizational structure and, 186;
selected for investment, 140;
synergies among, 34–36; traditional, preserving, 94. *See also*
specific industries
Industry dematurity: example of, 4–5;
innovation and, 5–6; managing, 8–9
Industry maturity, 3–4: economic crisis
created by, 97; in foresight nations,
27; migration to, 7–8; reversing
migration, 8–9
Industry-specific policies, Canadian, 85
Information: government role in developing base of, 126–127; government's passive stance toward dissemination of, 105; necessity of
sharing, 91; on new manufacturing
technologies, sources of, 194; role
in Japanese industrial policy, 28; for
technology development programs,
201. *See also* Data bases

Information processing: manufacturing
as, 20; product complexity and,
21–22
Innovation. *See* Technological innovation
Innovation policy: activist, in Canada,
171–173; approaches to, 107–114;
Canadian, 169–171; controversy
over, 191; framework for, 119–
120; issues in, 115–119; Japanese,
100; need for, 97–99; in 1970s and
1980s, 99–104; past problems of,
104–106; tools of, 99–100
Innovativeness, organizational flexibility
and, 14–15
Intel, IBM's equity investment in, 52–53
International Monetary Fund (IMF), 69
Investment: in AMS: government policies on, 149–150; in Japan, 154;
incentives for. *See* Depreciation incentives; Financial incentives; Tax
incentives. public versus private,
191; selection of industries for, 140
IRDP. *See* Industrial and Regional Development Program
IT&C. *See* Department of Industry
Trade and Commerce
Italy, firm linkages in, 161–162
ITI. *See* Industrial Technology Institute

Japan: automotive industry in, 29; evolution of trade frameworks in,
70–73; government policies and
measures affecting AMS in, 152–
154; government support of innovation in, 195; innovation policy in,
100; model for government role
provided by, 144; national strategy
in, 88; policy focus of, 27–28;
R&D in, 117: government support
of, 153–154; U.S. knowledge of,
33–34; semiconductor industry in,
111; trade with Canada, 74–75;
trade potential of, 75; worker support of technological improvement
in, 135–136

Kyocera, linkages of, 53

Labor costs, competitiveness of U.S.
industry and, 22
Labor management relations: achieving
consensus and, 91; reducing risks of
innovation and, 129–130

About the Contributors

Robert U. Ayres is professor in the Department of Engineering and Public Policy at Carnegie-Mellon University, where his research interests include the economic implications of robotics, computers, and new developments in manufacturing technology. Since receiving his Ph.D. in physics, he has worked at the Hudson Institute, Resources for the Future, and the International Research and Technology Corp., of which he was cofounder. He is author of *Technological Forecasting and Long Range Planning* (1969).

Jack Baranson is a leading consultant to foreign governments and transnational corporations on technology in world business, trade, and development. He received his master's degree from the Johns Hopkins School of Advanced International Studies and a doctoral degree in economics from Indiana University. Dr. Baranson's publications include *Technology and the Multinationals* (1978), *The Japanese Challenge to U.S. Industry* (1981), and *Robots in Manufacturing: Key to International Competitiveness* (1983).

John Britton is a professor of geography at the University of Toronto. He took his B.A. and M.A. degrees in geography from the Universities of Sydney and Melbourne. As a Commonwealth Scholar, he gained his Ph.D. in economic geography from the London School of Economics and Political Science. Dr. Britton's research interests in industrial location and development have led to several articles in professional journals, two books, and contributions to several other books.

Mike Cassidy is a New Democratic Member of Parliament for Ottawa Center. He studied political economy at the University of Toronto and the London School of Economics and recently completed his M.B.A. at York University.

J.D. Eveland, director of technology applications research for Cognos Associates, Palo Alto, California, has a B.A. in history from Reed College, an M.P.I.A. from the University of Pittsburgh, and a Ph.D. in administration and organization behavior from the University of Michigan.

Meric Gertler is an assistant professor in planning and geography at the University of Toronto. He holds a master's degree from the University of California, Berkeley, and a doctorate in planning and development from Harvard University. Dr. Gertler has worked in both provincial and federal economic development agencies, including the Ontario Ministry of Industry and Tourism and the Department of Regional Economic Expansion, Ottawa.

Bela Gold is Fletcher Jones Professor of Technology and Management, the Claremont Graduate School. He has had extensive experience as an economic adviser on domestic and international problems in the U.S. government and as an industrial consultant. Dr. Gold has served on many advisory boards and committees, including the Advisory Committee on Federal Policy on Industrial Innovation, the National Research Council Assembly of Engineering Committee on Computer-Aided Manufacturing, and the National Science Foundation Ad Hoc Committee on National Issues on Robotics.

Dr. Gold is author of *Productivity, Technology, and Capital* (1979), and coauthor of *Technological Progress and Industrial Leadership* (1984), and *Evaluating Technological Innovations* (1980).

William A. Hetzner received his B.S. in industrial engineering from the University of California and his Ph.D. in industrial engineering from Northwestern University. He is currently at the Center for Social and Economic Issues, Industrial Technology Institute, Ann Arbor, Michigan.

Mel Horwitch is a member of the corporate planning, policy, and strategy group at the Alfred P. Sloan School of Management, MIT. He received his A.B. from Princeton University and his M.B.A. and doctorate from the Harvard Business School. He has worked in both government and private industry and has been a consultant to numerous private firms and public institutions. Professor Horwitch has written extensively on management, technology, and energy affairs. He is a contributor to *Energy Future: Report of the Energy Project* at the Harvard Business School. His most recent book i *Clipped Wings: The American SST Conflict* (1982).

Alan M. Kantrow is associate editor of the *Harvard Business Review* and a senior research associate at the Harvard Business School. He is also an adviser to the Cambridge Research and Development Group, a principal of the Winthrop Group (business consultants), and serves on the Research-on-Research Committee of the Industrial Research Institute and on the Advisory Board of the Global Competitiveness Council. Dr. Kantrow received his A.B. degree from Harvard College and his Ph.D. from Harvard University.

Roy Rothwell is senior fellow, Science Policy Research Unit, University of Sussex, England. He received a B.Sc. in applied physics from Brighton Polytechnic in 1964 and completed a Ph.D. thesis entitled "Some Electrical Properties of Variously Doped Lead Zirconate Titanate Ceramic" at Brighton Polytechnic/Admiralty Materials Laboratory. In addition to numerous articles, he has coauthored four books with Walter Zegveld: *Technical Change and Employment* (1979), *Industrial Innovation and Public Policy* (1981), *Innovation and the Small and Medium-Sized Firm* (1982), and *Reindustrialization and Technology* (1985). He also coauthored *Design and the Economy* (1983) with P. Gardiner and K. Schott.

Bruce Rubinger is the director of studies with the Global Competitiveness Council, an independent think tank that specializes in international technical issues. He holds degrees in electrical engineering and control systems and a doctorate in systems science from the Polytechnic Institute of New York. He has pursued studies in economics and system dynamics at MIT.

W.H.C. Simmonds is a consultant, Integrative Studies, Ottawa, Canada. He has undertaken a variety of projects since his retirement in 1982 from the Industrial Development Office of the National Research Council of Canada. He published a book, with Harold Linstone, entitled *Futures Research: New Directions* in 1978. His background includes degrees in chemistry from Oxford University, membership in the Institution of Chemical Engineers since 1945, and a degree in sociology from Sir George Williams University.

Louis G. Tornatzky is director of the Center for Social and Economic Issues, Industrial Technology Institute, Ann Arbor, Michigan. He received a B.A. in psychology from The Ohio State University and completed his Ph.D. in psychology at Stanford University in 1969.

About the Editor

Jerry Dermer, at the time this book was prepared, was coordinator of the Policy Area at the Faculty of Administrative Studies, York University. He has also taught at the University of Toronto, the University of Illinois, and the Sloan School of Management at MIT. Dr. Dermer's specialty areas are strategic management, public policy formulation and implementation, and the design and implementation of planning and control systems. He has written two books and numerous articles on these areas as applied to private, public, and voluntary sectors. Over the last decade he has consulted to governments, corporations, voluntary organizations, and cooperatives in Canada and the United States. Dr. Dermer is a professional engineer (Ontario) and holds an M.B.A. and a Ph.D. in accountancy.